So You Want
to Direct TV?

So You Want to Direct TV?

Sixteen Professionals Share
Their Paths to Success

JACOB PINGER

Foreword by Samba Schutte

McFarland & Company, Inc., Publishers
Jefferson, North Carolina

LIBRARY OF CONGRESS CATALOGUING-IN-PUBLICATION DATA

Names: Pinger, Jacob, 1970– author.
Title: So you want to direct TV? : sixteen professionals share their paths
to success / Jacob Pinger.
Description: Jefferson : McFarland & Company, Inc., Publishers, 2020. |
Includes index.
Identifiers: LCCN 2020023459 | ISBN 9781476679587 (paperback) ∞
ISBN 9781476640235 (ebook)
Subjects: LCSH: Television—Production and direction—Vocational guidance.
Classification: LCC PN1992.75 .P56 2020 | DDC 791.4502/33023—dc23
LC record available at https://lccn.loc.gov/2020023459

BRITISH LIBRARY CATALOGUING DATA ARE AVAILABLE

ISBN (print) 978-1-4766-7958-7
ISBN (ebook) 978-1-4766-4023-5

Front cover image © 2020 Shutterstock

Printed in the United States of America

*McFarland & Company, Inc., Publishers
Box 611, Jefferson, North Carolina 28640
www.mcfarlandpub.com*

Acknowledgments

I want to express my deepest gratitude to all the directors who took part in this project. They are special individuals who gave of themselves bravely with the goal of fostering openness and transparency in Hollywood. I say "bravely" because too often the business of television is dominated by fear of expressing the truth.

In particular I want to thank the following directors for the inspiration and guidance they provided: Bethany Rooney, Jay Karas, Hanelle Culpepper and Jude Weng.

Bethany Rooney embodies the notion of demystifying Hollywood. Her book *Directors Tell the Story*, which she co-wrote with her fellow director Mary Lou Belli, has deservedly become the standard how-to manual on directing television. I have read it twice (so far) and it showed me the path forward in pursuing this book.

Jay Karas provided constant support and encouragement from the moment I had the good fortune to shadow him on an episode of a show he directed. His unflappable positivity on set showed me that true confidence means you are not afraid to share of yourself with others.

Hanelle Culpepper was my knight in shining armor, swooping in to save the day when I needed one last director to interview. She shared her belief in me with her colleagues and I was inundated with interested responses. Thanks also to the worthy directors that I was not able to include in this book simply due to page limits!

My guiding light and mentor during this process, Jude Weng, is a remarkably generous human being, fully invested in the concept of paying it forward. Without her encouragement, contacts and early support, this project would not have happened. It was probably my fear of disappointing Jude that gave me the grit to see it through.

I also want to thank my good friend, author James C. Udel. When things seemed stalled, James' vitally timed nudging helped me keep moving forward. His wonderful book *The Film Crew of Hollywood*, also published by McFarland, provided me an excellent role model. I owe James a round of drinks.

Thanks also to Adam Leipzig for his professional insights and my father and fellow author Robert Pinger for his unconditional encouragement.

Lastly, I cannot forget the original inspiration provided by my mother, author Susan Philips. Her interview-based books *In the Heart of Another: Immigrant Women Tell Their Stories* and *An Intricate Dance: Stepparents Tell Us How They Found Their Rhythm* show us that our work is made more powerful when it is accompanied by the intention of making the world a better place.

Table of Contents

Foreword

BY SAMBA SCHUTTE

We were on the last day of shooting Season One of our NBC sitcom *Sunnyside* when Jacob, one of three camera operators squeezed into a bar booth to get an awesome two-shot, approached me and told me about his book. As soon as he mentioned the words "diversity behind the camera," I was stoked to have the pleasure of writing this foreword.

If "diversity" was a word that could only be described in a picture, it would most probably be my goofy face: My father is a white, Dutch, Catholic man and my mother is a black, Mauritanian, Muslim woman. I was born in the Sahara Desert, grew up in Ethiopia until I was 18, then moved to Holland to get my B.A. in Theater and kick off my entertainment career. Nine years ago, I moved to Los Angeles to pursue my career at a higher level and ended up marrying a Californian woman who happens to be a Baha'i. Diversity—of cultures, backgrounds, careers and personalities—has been at the forefront of everything I am, everything I do and everything I represent.

That's why I love that Jacob interviewed such a wide range of talented directors for this book. I've had the pleasure of working with a few of them—Anya Adams, Payman Benz, Jay Karas and Linda Mendoza. It is important to highlight the role of diversity behind the camera, and I hope this book will also inspire any aspiring storytellers out there. Everyone can have a unique point of view, and there is a place for that voice in the entertainment industry.

I've been lucky to work on all levels of content creation on multiple continents: live theater, student films, web series, indie movies, commercials, video games, studio films and network TV shows. At the end of the day, the most important topic on everyone's mind is always "How do we make this content better?" My quick answer: the diversity of the people you're working with.

Yes, some fine TV shows were made half a century ago when the people behind the camera were all from the same race, background and beliefs. But there's a reason that, over the past 10 or 15 years especially, there has been a major outcry for more diversity. I believe this is due to the fact that the types of stories people are craving have very noticeably started to change. More than ever before, people want to feel seen, heard, represented and appreciated. The old "norms" are being questioned because they don't truly reflect the types of stories, faces and "real world" issues that audiences are dealing with. In a media landscape where consumers are becoming all-powerful with their choices of what to stream and when, studio executives are confronted with the simple fact that television *must* be made in a way that entertains, yet also inspires, enlightens and educates us on the day-to-day issues we *all* face in this ever-changing world.

If authentic stories are to be told, then both the performers and people involved in production have to understand the experiences of the people whose stories they are portraying. In the case of *Sunnyside*, a show about a disgraced city councilman helping a group of immigrants on their path to becoming U.S. citizens, most of the cast members and writers were immigrants or descendants of immigrants. This kept the episodes as true to the immigrant experience as possible, while also successfully dealing with the constraints of network television. Such diversity is what people are demanding and, when done right, it has proven to be immensely profitable. So it's ethical and you make money; you can't go wrong!

Idealistic rants aside, my experience shows me that the energy one feels on a set, the quality of the performances brought out of the actors, and even the motivation of the crew, are all enriched when there is more diversity behind the camera. For example, when your crew is not just a group of men but also has an equal number of women doing the heavy lifting, there is a greater sense of mutual respect and camaraderie. I have noticed it create a greater sense of ease for any female directors, performers and crew members. Through the sense of balance, the environment feels less intimidating. It calls for people to develop better communication and social skills and, if there are additional people of diverse ethnic backgrounds on board, even cross-cultural learning.

On *Sunnyside*, I played an immigrant from Ethiopia, and I had great conversations with the crew about growing up there. We even discussed cultural differences that they would have otherwise probably never heard of. Something about knowing there are people around with different backgrounds—be it cultural, career-related or orientation—invokes a desire to learn and grow. It motivates people to showcase the best version of themselves. It inspires us to make better content.

One of the things I enjoy about being a regular on a network series is getting to work with a new director every episode. As an actor, I have had the invaluable experience of working with a range of visions, voices, personalities, approaches and communication styles. No two journeys to becoming a TV director are the same; each person brings their unique story with them—a different upbringing, background, skill set and motivation. When a show's roster of directors comes from diverse backgrounds, you immediately get more interesting material.

Even within the confines of a showrunner's vision, a TV director can still make an episode their own. The way that Payman Benz directed was very different from how Jay Karas got a specific performance out of me. Both are wonderful directors with rich backgrounds in comedy—Payman more with improv and sketch comedy, and Jay more with comedy specials. Yet both had effective approaches. Payman let us go loose with improv and kept rolling to capture any unscripted magic long after we were done with the scene. This gave the actors a sense of freedom and excitement with each take and made us feel like our choices were trusted. Jay allowed for some improv too but wanted us to play more within the range of what was scripted. Not only did that give Jay an abundance of choices in the editing room, it also allowed the cast to discover new layers to our characters. Their styles are different, yet both super fun, and the end results equally satisfying. That fluidity of different voices is what makes for more exciting content and dynamics on a set, rather than having the same monotonous voice and vision.

In Holland, I was a correspondent and writer for the Dutch version of *The Daily Show*, called *De Nieuwste Show*. I was one of just two diverse people on a crew of 50. I think there were maybe five women. For two seasons, it was the same jokes, same dynamics and same point of view. And then it stalled; the show had no way to grow, excite, entice or innovate.

It could not connect with an audience that was growing more globally minded and evolving faster than the TV content it was being provided. The show inevitably got canceled. This was 12 years ago. The statistics are starting to improve.

A 2018 study by the Directors Guild of America (DGA) showed that in the 2017–2018 season, of the first-time episodic television directors hired, 31 percent were ethnic minorities and 41 percent were female. In 2009, those numbers were just 12 percent and 11 percent, respectively. Today's audiences refuse to be fooled. They can detect authenticity immediately. And if there is one thing I know will keep them engaged, it is having proper representation not only in front of, but also behind the camera. That means giving opportunities to the diversity of voices and visions that reflect the world we live in today.

Again, I love that Jacob put this book together. I love that it will inspire diverse storytellers to be proud of their heritage, for that is what makes them unique. My hope is that this book motivates them to pursue their passions, and to make TV content that is richer, fresher, more authentic and more representative than ever before.

Samba Schutte (Facebook.com)

Be open to diversity. Surround yourself with diversity. Feel empowered by diversity. Don't be threatened by it. I promise it will help you be the best you can be, and I, for one, have definitely got your back. So go for it, and learn from this wonderful book. Godspeed on your adventure!

Samba Schutte is a Dutch-Mauritanian comedian, actor and writer who was raised in Ethiopia. He starred as Hakim on the NBC sitcom Sunnyside *along with Kal Penn, won the top national comedy award in Holland, and was a correspondent and writer on the Dutch version of* The Daily Show.

Preface

So you want to be a television director? What's your plan? Does your uncle run a network? Is your mom a famous actor? Are you a trust-fund baby who can afford to live in L.A. making expensive short films and writing scripts until you get a big break? No?

Well, I've got some good news for you. Not one of the television directors that I interviewed had any of those advantages either. And here is some more good news: The moment you opened this book, you had access to 16 director mentors who are going to share their personal stories of triumph and setbacks. They will give you advice about how to avoid pitfalls and stay motivated. Most importantly, they will show you exactly how they got there in order to help you figure out your own path to becoming a TV director.

Hollywood is a mystifying place. The most mystifying part is how to break into it. It's not hard to find good sources of information about the craft of filmmaking. There are dozens of film schools, books, websites and even YouTube videos dedicated to teaching you the nuts of bolts of making a movie. But where can you learn how to navigate the opaque world of television and actually get your big break? Until now, the answer was that, unless you personally knew a working TV director, there was nowhere you could go to learn what it takes to land your first job.

In addition, these 16 generous mentors will teach you what it's actually like to be a working TV director. Directing for television is a unique and difficult job. The pressure and politics can be enormous. This book will give you valuable insider information about the day-to-day grind, such as what to expect in meetings with showrunners, how to behave on set and what kind of industry terminology you need to know.

So what makes me the best person to write this book? In short, I'm an insider. I have been working in television for almost 20 years. I began as a production assistant at the age of 19, and gradually worked my way up to be an IATSE Local 600 director of photography and camera operator. I have worked on movies, music videos, reality shows, industrials, commercials and of course television series. I have probably worked with close to 100 directors, and yet, even after all my years in the business, I realized that it was a mystery to me how these individuals came to land the job. Who were they? Where did they come from? What were their unique skill sets? What did they have in common? What did they do to prove themselves, and to whom? In short, how did they get to this set, on this show, on this day? It all seemed like a secret club with no visible front door. And that's what prompted me to write this book: to figure out how to open that door, and de-mystify Hollywood.

My quest started as a personal journey: I wanted to know how this strange system worked. Also, I have my own ambitions to direct, just like you. As I scratched the surface, I quickly realized that there was a much bigger story to tell: Hollywood has a long and unfortunate tradition of putting up walls to keep people out. In fact, one of the directors describes it as a "white-walled country club" that you must be invited into. That needs to change. Our world is not served by keeping people out for whatever reason, whether it's their gender, their skin color, their family's nation of origin, their orientation or their inherited wealth. And the only way to do that is to pull back the curtain.

To my great fortune, I had access to 16 fascinating directors. Half of them are women and half are men. They represent a tremendous range of diversity, both ethnically and in terms of their personal backgrounds. No one in this book comes from Hollywood royalty— no nepotistic family connections here. These are all individuals whose incredible stories of overcoming challenges and setbacks will make you cheer. Not one of them takes their success for granted because they all earned it.

This book has another purpose. In fact, it is the deeper inspiration behind why I chose to undertake the project. I want these interviews to inspire you. I want this book to convince you that no matter who you are, no matter what you are, and no matter where you come from, you *should* become a television director. Look in the mirror. What do you see? You know what? It doesn't matter what you see. This book proves that the only thing you should see looking back in the mirror is a director. So go for it! That doesn't mean it will be easy. In truth, everyone must forge her or his own path. So ask yourself this question: "Is directing something that I *must* do?" If the answer is yes, then you better read this book.

INTERVIEWS

Linda Mendoza

Linda Mendoza speaks with her entire body like an orchestra conductor—leaning forward at the waist, her long black hair waving and her arms reaching out as if they might grab you and shake her vision into your head. She is a powerful force on set. When I visited her in the hills above the San Fernando Valley, I discovered that she is also a powerful force in her own home. As I entered the kitchen, I was confronted by a pair of extremely friendly German Shepherds, the size of small horses. With a wave, Linda sent them away.

Linda's life and work are steeped in history. She is one of those individuals who has personally experienced more than her share. But she also carries the weight of many broader narratives—that of the Latino experience in America, that of the tragedy and rebirth of Rock City, USA, and that of the evolving legacy of the original Americans. Linda was forged in Detroit steel.

· · · · · · · · · · · · · · · · · · · ·

LINDA MENDOZA: I am as American as apple pie. I was born and raised in Detroit, Michigan, in the '60s. The home of Motown and the Big Three. I am a multi-cultural face in a very American mentality. The world was not as diverse when I was growing up. My school was literally white kids and black kids. And then there was me, this little brown girl in the middle of these black and white faces. I didn't fit in anywhere. I was the poster child for being bullied. It was really hard for me to have any kind of confidence. I was very shy. My dad died when I was 12 and I was raised primarily by my mother. We were typical working-class Detroiters. I went to public school and then to Wayne State University downtown. I did not go to school to be a director. I never really thought of that possibility growing up. I was going to school to be a sociologist.

Linda Mendoza originally came to Hollywood from Detroit with dreams of making it in the music business (Tim Kahle).

My single mom was always wary of people because she experienced racism firsthand. My father, who was Spanish and half Native American, was very dark. And my mom who is Spanish, German and

9

Irish was very fair. But she identified as Mexican. She saw racism when she was allowed into a restaurant but my father was not.

I had two brothers and a sister. Unfortunately, my mother, my father and both my brothers all died tragically. My mom was in a car accident in the snow. She hit a wall and was in a coma for ten years. My little brother was a witness to a murder when he was 17 years old. He was the only witness because the other kid who was with him was the shooter's brother. We believe that my brother was killed so that he wouldn't be able to testify. And then my older brother just disappeared off the face of the earth. These things don't ever go away. They're part of your fabric.

JACOB PINGER: I'm sorry. I didn't realize I was jumping right into that without any warning.

LM: Well, my one-woman show is called, *Cursed! My Road to Hollywood*, for a reason.

JP: What was the area of Detroit like where you grew up?

LM: I was in the heart of Detroit by the city airport on Connor. I went to Laura F. Osborne High School. It was just a straight-ahead, working class neighborhood.

JP: What did your parents do?

LM: My mom worked as a buyer at J.L. Hudson's department store downtown. When the factories started exploding in the '70s, she got a job working at Chrysler's. And that's where she worked until her accident. She was on the assembly line.

I also worked on the line at Chrysler's Lynch Road Plant one summer. I was 19 years old and I was in my second year of college. I was the floater, meaning I covered the breaks on the line. I could catch on really fast how to do anything. I would put the glue around the trunks to install the rubber weather stripping. I screwed on the silver trim that went along the back window of the station wagons. I would put in antennas. I would install glove boxes. We were building Dodges. I was a summer hire. So after 89 days, I was gone.

I went back to school in the fall and I took a lot of Latino studies in college as well. I wanted to know more about my ancestors. My mother was all about assimilation so I don't even speak Spanish. I'm like the worst Latina ever.

JP: What did your dad do?

LM: My dad was a cement mason. He worked putting in roads, driveways, backyards and whatever else the company did. My dad died when he was 37 because he had a heart defect. The work that he was doing was very hard. It took a big toll on his body.

JP: When you were growing up, how did you identify racially?

LM: I guess I identified as Mexican. But everybody thought I was Chinese. I would often stare in the mirror looking at myself wondering why God made me like this.

JP: Like what?

LM: This brown girl of Mexican descent, born to be tortured. You know what I mean?

JP: I don't. I can't say that I do.

LM: [*laughs*] Shit, that's funny. Of course you can't, you're a white dude!

JP: Other directors I interviewed have also grown up in situations where their race was not the majority. They tended to identify with one race or the other at different points in their lives.

LM: I think I always identified more with just being American. But when I was about 15, my boyfriend took me to an all-black church that I ended up joining for several years.

JP: Was your boyfriend black?

LM: No, he was Italian.

JP: Wow…. Detroit!

LM: Yeah, Detroit. I have a cousin who's fricking Syrian and Mexican. That is not a combo you see often. Dearborn, Michigan, has a huge Middle Eastern influx.

JP: How did the '60s play a role in your development?

LM: The '60s was such a liberating time. I grew up with a very forward-thinking mother who always said that you could do anything you want in the world as long as you are educated. She was all about me doing something with my life. Detroit was a very working-class city, and everybody worked their butts off all the time. That naturally became my work ethic in everything that I've done. I don't take anything for granted.

JP: Were you the first person in your family to go to college?

LM: Definitely. My mom didn't even graduate high school. But she was a very deep thinker. And it's helped me have critical thought, which is important in life.

JP: Were any of your family members actually from Mexico?

LM: My grandmother was. She came over when she was about one year old during the Mexican Civil War … 1912. Truly amazing. My great-great grandpa owned a huarache factory in Mexico. That got burned down in the Civil War. All hell was breaking loose there. My grandmother was the original wetback. She literally came across the Rio Grande River.

JP: Were you raised Catholic?

LM: No. Everybody automatically assumes that I'm Catholic because I'm Latin. However, my grandmother was a Pentecostal minister, and I was raised Southern Baptist in the northern city of Detroit. So there are some issues there.

JP: Was the black church that you went to a Baptist church?

LM: It was nondenominational. It was called The Temple of I AM. And the minister was a black homosexual man who dressed like a Catholic priest when he did the service. That is where I started to find my voice as an individual. It was all about *I am who I am*. Meaning, you have it in you. It really is how I still live my life today. It's in the Bible. Exodus 3:14. "Tell them I Am has sent me unto you." His name is in the Bible. I'm not a typical Christian who believes in Jesus as my savior. But I am Christian in that I believe Jesus was a true son of God. We are all children of God. Jesus is the way. He was the one who kind of figured it out a lot quicker than any of us.

JP: How long were you part of that church?

LM: I was about 15 when I started going. I was 20 when I moved to L.A. So about five years.

JP: How did your family end up in Detroit?

LM: My grandmother worked for Alcoa Steel in Texas. They offered her a supervisor position in Detroit, so she moved the whole family. My grandfather was a mechanic, and he could work anywhere. He worked on Army Jeeps during World War II. He was amazing. When he moved to Michigan, he became the head mechanic at the Stroh's Beer brewery. Then he opened his own garage and had two gas stations.

JP: Nothing about your early life indicates that you would end up in Hollywood. What was your relationship to TV and movies as a kid?

LM: It's funny that you say that because I always loved television and movies. My mom loved old movies. We would watch [the TV series] *Rita Bell's Prize Movie*, and I learned about all those old movie stars. In high school, I took early morning classes so I was home by one every day. I would turn on the television and watch *Bill Kennedy at the Movies*. I would also wake up in the middle of the night to watch movies. This was well before they had VCRs, and I would set my clock to get up at two in the morning to watch *The Bishop's Wife*, or *Ghosts on the Loose* with the East Side Kids. Whatever was on.

I've always been passionate about TV and movies, and I've always loved music. All we did in Detroit was dance and play music every single day. Literally, that's no lie. I would put on an album and clean my house. Music defines me. I grew up to be a rock'n'roll girl, I loved the Who, Led Zeppelin and the Beatles. When I first came into the business, I wanted to do music videos. I ended up doing live music for several years. I've probably shot over 300 bands.

JP: At what point did you have an inkling that there was a career path in entertainment?

LM: First of all, I'm one of the very few people who ever came to Hollywood not to work in the movie or TV industry. I came to L.A. for a record company, Peaches Records and Tapes. I was working in their Dearborn store and they wanted somebody from the store level to help them transition to computer. My job was to figure out how to go online, so to speak, which is ironic because today I know absolutely nothing about computers. They flew me out here, got me a car for a month and paid my first month's rent. This was a serious job for a 20-year-old in her third year of college.

JP: Peaches was a national chain?

LM: Yeah. And that's how I came to California. My dream was to own my own music store and be a sociologist.

JP: In L.A.?

LM: That's where I ended up, so why not? But when Peaches went under, I needed a job and I got hired as a page at a TV station. Somebody I knew from Detroit said, "Hey, they're looking right now. They want women and they want people of color." So I got hired in a pair of shorts and a tank top. Is that not insane?

JP: That was the moment you swapped over from music to TV?

LM: Yeah. And I didn't even know what a boom mike was. I knew nothing. At that point, I had been in L.A. for nine months. I went to L.A. City College and started taking TV classes. I ended up with five years of college and no degree. But I had a job. You can't do that today. Now you need a degree. But in 1978, I got away with it.

JP: What television company hired you?

LM: KTTV, Metromedia Channel 11, which is now Fox. I was only a page for three weeks. Sometimes they would have me fill in when the executive assistants didn't come to work. One day I got assigned to the production department answering phones for Nancy Hamilton, the V.P. of production. There was another woman who worked there, Gerry. She scheduled all the production teams, like stagehands, grips, set builders, etc. I was in the office the day that she got a call saying her mom had died. So Gerry had to take time off and the studio was like, "Oh my God, what are we going to do?" I said, "I can fill in." I told you, I'm a quick learner! So I spent the afternoon with Gerry before she left and I ended up scheduling the crews for three weeks until she got back. Then I got offered the engineering scheduling job. So I started scheduling all the engineers for the Dodgers games. That meant the technical director, the camera operators, the utility, the sound and the playback guys. And I was scheduling all the sound stages. They were shooting *The Jeffersons, One Day at a Time, Diff'rent Strokes, Facts of Life* and also big specials. I was scheduling all the camera operators, video recorders, boom operators … you name it. I was learning about what it took to put on a show.

I decided I wanted to get into production. I wanted to do something creative. I wanted to be the unit production manager on a show. But because I was so good at being the engineering scheduler, nobody wanted to let me move over. That's how corporations work. If you are already working for them in one area, they don't want to upset the apple cart. I knew

I would have to quit my scheduling job in order to get into production. I took a big chance and went to Norman Lear's company, which was there at KTTV. I went and tried to get in as a writer's assistant, but I failed the typing test so I didn't get it.

I was on vacation and had gone in to get my check at KTTV and one of the unit production managers said that a friend needed someone to take over her production assistant job immediately. She said, "You have to go over to Dick Darley's office at Sunset Gower Studios right now." So I walked over the six blocks, went up to meet Dick and I got hired to be his new assistant. He just liked me. I went back to my engineering scheduling job and gave them one week's notice.

I worked with Dick Darley for a couple of years as his assistant doing big commercials for Toys "R" Us and Corning Ware. I was meeting people, and beginning to understand what the camera really does, learning about editing, graphics. It was an amazing growth period for me. Then I found out that a big producer-director named Bruce Gowers needed a new assistant. Bruce did a lot of work in music. He is the godfather of rock'n'roll music videos. He shot *Bohemian Rhapsody*. He worked with the Stones, Rod Stewart, John Mellencamp … the list goes on. I met Bruce at Martoni's Restaurant on Cahuenga, which is not there anymore, and he was a big supporter of diversity before that was popular, and Bruce saw this kind of odd-looking Mexican girl. I had the worst perm and really bad pink glasses. I don't know what I was thinking with that look, but he hired me anyway. He was amazing. I worked for Bruce for 13 years. I was his assistant, then his production supervisor, and then his assistant director.

JP: So that was a great marriage of your love of music and TV.

LM: Absolutely. It was everything I wanted in one. And what was interesting about Bruce was that he did both single-camera and multi-camera. He showed me early on how you could go between the two, because we would do single-camera elements and then we would do the live, multi-camera show. My mom always told me, "Don't let anybody tell you that you can't do something." Everyone was saying that you had to choose to be either a multi-cam or single-cam director, and I just never understood why. They are both about character. They are both about story. The only thing I don't like is drama. I don't want to worry about six act breaks.

I completely missed talking about *Saturday Night Live* and *In Living Color*. Those shows were a big step for me when I went from being a production supervisor to an AD [assistant director]. I was the production supervisor on the first 13 episodes of *In Living Color*. And then they offered me the post AD job, which was to take the sketches and go cut them. Then I got an offer to AD *America's Funniest Home Videos* with Dave Coulier. So I went and did that for about two or three weeks. And I was like, "Is this what I want to do for the rest of my life?"

At that point, I got a phone call from a friend in New York. They needed somebody to come and work on *Saturday Night Live*. They flew me out for an interview. I got offered the job immediately. I came back and replaced myself on *America's Funniest Home Videos*. I took about an $8000 per month pay cut to go to New York and become the booth P.A. (production assistant) for *Saturday Night Live*. I knew that ultimately it was going to mean a lot more for my future in terms of knowledge and understanding. I had bigger goals and I wanted to do comedy. So I went and worked on *Saturday Night Live* as a booth P.A. from 1990 to 1991.

JP: Up to that point in your career, how do you think race and gender played a role?

LM: Oh, it totally played a role. For me, it played a role in a really positive way, because

I was at the forefront of hiring women, and diverse women in particular. I got a lot of opportunities because I was a Latin female. Those opportunities were given to me, but I had to work extra hard to make them pay off. Not to male-bash, because I've never been about that, but I will say that white males often get second chances. That's not so much the case for Latin females or maybe any person of color in this business.

JP: I've seen that the issue of diversity in the film industry has two strains. On the one hand, there is the experience of an individual, and on the other hand there are the systemic issues.

LM: I think I experienced more discrimination getting single-camera work because of my work in variety television than I ever did because of being a Latin female.

JP: Even though you didn't personally feel racism, why do you think the industry as a whole is so behind on the issue?

LM: I think it's just the age-old problem that people in positions of power are primarily white. And so their contemporaries and friends are probably the same. People want to hire somebody they know and trust. On several shows I worked on, I was the only female and the only person of color who got an episode to direct. My thought has been, "Well, these are still baby steps to success." I think they are starting to realize the scope of the problem now, with all these directing programs that are mainly going to people of color and women.

A lot of those programs came along well after I started to direct. I feel like the people who hire me do so because they know I'm prepared and I put the money on the screen. But I also feel that I am replaceable when they fill those directing slots because I'm the Latin female. Now they have other women and other people of color that they have to put in those slots. So ironically, I feel like this whole big diversity push is actually affecting me negatively because I'm the one that is replaceable. Not that I don't have work, but I do feel that is happening.

JP: Perhaps in the minds of studio and network executives, it can become more of a quota system than a true dedication to diversity.

LM: Correct. It's just a way to cover their asses. That's truly the bottom line.

JP: Going back a bit: You worked for Bruce Gowers for 13 years. You must have absorbed a tremendous amount.

LM: I thank him every day because I would not be half the director I am without Bruce's genius. I fricking hit the jackpot when I got to work with him. It's fascinating to look back at the way my life has unfolded and the connections that somehow created this weird jigsaw puzzle of my experiences. I have been kissed by Jimmy Page. Paul McCartney once said to me, "Linda [McCartney] and I were in bed the other night wondering where we first met you." A Beatle pondering me! I was on tour with Genesis for six months. I've been all over the world. This does not happen to Mexican girls from Detroit!

JP: When you worked with Gowers, did you have any opportunities to direct?

LM: Yeah, he actually gave me a couple of opportunities to direct. We were doing a show called *Roundhouse* for Nickelodeon and I got an opportunity to direct that when I came back from the Genesis tour.

JP: Was that your first directing gig?

LM: No. My first real directing gig was when I was co-producing the Montreal Comedy Festival. I directed a little show at one in the morning called *Comedy from the Danger Zone*. My cast was Dom Irrera, as the host, with Bobby Slayton, Louis C.K., David Cross, Andy Kindler and Nick DiPaolo. It was their very first TV show, before they were famous.

JP: That was directing a live event?

LM: Live with five cameras capturing the moments.

JP: And *Roundhouse* was a scripted show?

LM: It was scripted sketches, four cameras, multi-cam, fast-paced, and a lot of music. It was pretty cool.

JP: When did you know you wanted to be a director?

LM: Well, for me it was always baby steps. When I was still working for Bruce and trying to be the best production supervisor I could be, his regular AD left to go direct something, and I got an opportunity to be Bruce's AD for *The MTV Video Music Awards*. After that, I started to AD for him regularly, and we went everywhere. We did *The MTV Video Music Awards* for eight years. We did *The Billboard Music Awards*. We went to Europe to do the *MTV Europe Music Awards*. We were all over.

JP: Did you make a decision at some point that you wanted to be a director?

LM: Honestly, I did not make the full transition to directing for a couple of years after that opportunity on *Roundhouse* and in Montreal. The reason was that I liked the security of Bruce's work and also I felt like he was going to give me more opportunities. And he did. The following summer, he was the main director at the 25th anniversary of Woodstock, and he gave me the secondary stage to direct. After that, I ended up directing a Showtime special. I think it was at that point that I decided, "Okay, I'm going to become a full-time director."

JP: Can you tell me about the leap you took when you decided you were going to stop being an AD and said, "I'm going to be a director now"?

LM: It was scary because nobody knew me from Adam as a director. Once I made that decision, I did not work for five months. But during that time, I took classes. I took a writing class, a scene study class, and an acting class to help me understand how to talk to actors and how to break down a script. I also wanted to put myself out there with the acting stuff and get up in front of people, because if I have to tell an actor how they're supposed to feel when they're coming through a door, I need to know how to do that without giving them bad line readings. You have to set the actor up emotionally with direction. I actually kept going to those classes throughout my first couple of years of directing.

After five months, I got a little comedy show. And after that, I got a little music show. Then I did a series called *Hard Rock Live* for VH1. I started getting more little shows here and there as a director. I got offered *The Rosie O'Donnell Show* in New York. They'd come to me two other times offering me a directing job but I didn't want to work on a daytime talk show. I wanted to stay in music and comedy. But when they came back a third time, I thought, "Okay, I must be meant to go to New York." So I went to New York and three weeks later I met my husband on a blind date. That same year, I got offered *The Chris Rock Show* on HBO and I became the house director. I directed 51 out of 56 episodes. I did that for four years. In the meantime, I was picking up comedy specials and doing a lot of *MADtv*.

Then during my last year on *The Chris Rock Show*, we had Bernie Mac on as a guest. I knew him because I had directed a short series with him for HBO, *Midnight Mac*. Bernie was so happy to see me directing *The Chris Rock Show*. He was like, "Hey, I might be getting a sitcom. If it goes, you're going to be on it as a director." And Bernie was true to his word. When I got back from New York, I met Larry Wilmore and Ken Kwapis. After the meeting, I called my agent all excited and my agent was like, "Yeah, yeah, yeah. If you get an episode, it'll probably be on the back nine." Well, I ended up getting the second episode of the first season. I got to shadow Ken Kwapis, who directed the pilot and first episode. That's when I directed my first episode of narrative network television. And my episode of *Bernie Mac* was the one that was played on the screens through the entire World Series that year. It's kind of crazy. I ended up being a house director.

JP: *The Chris Rock Show* led to *Bernie Mac*. What happened at that point? Did you ever feel the need to choose between directing single-cam or multi-cam?

LM: Well, yeah. It was interesting because after I did *Bernie Mac*, I was only getting single-camera offers. I couldn't get arrested in multi-camera. All of a sudden, I got put in that pigeonhole of being a single-camera director. So it actually took quite some time to get back into the multi-camera world. I love it. The show I'm doing now, *Reverend Run*, is a multi-camera show. I did *Fuller House*, did a ton of stuff for Disney. *Girlfriends* for UPN. I loved both formats. I like multi-cam because you're staging a play. It's just a whole different way of looking at a story when you present it for a live audience. Single-camera allows you to be a little more creative with the camera, and you're telling a story in a much more intimate way. In multi-cam, you're at the proscenium. It's long lens so you feel the distance. In single-camera, you're right in there with the camera, and so emotionally it's different. But in either case, as long as the laughs come when they're supposed to, you're doing your job.

JP: What's the difference in directing the actors between multi-cam and single-cam?

LM: I don't approach it any differently because story is story no matter how you slice it. Where they're coming from, and where they're going to, and what's happening in the moment, none of that changes for an actor. The scene is still the scene whether you shoot it with four cameras or you shoot it with one. The toughest part for the actors in single-cam is redoing the scene multiple times when you change angles. In multi-cam, you're catching the moments for all the actors at the same time.

JP: So from the standpoint of directing the actors, you're focusing on the same things?

LM: Kind of. The big difference is the staging, because in multi-cam, you have to stage it like a play. You have to stage it for the proscenium. And you have to stage it for four cameras, whereas in single-camera, you don't do that.

JP: I've never worked in multi-cam, but I would guess you would have to block it so that you never have somebody deliver a line with their back to the audience.

LM: Correct. You wouldn't do that. But honestly, in most single-camera shows, they don't like jokes on the back either because jokes don't play on the back. They play on the face, unless it's for a specific beat. But really the simplest difference between multi-cam and single-cam is staging.

JP: You're probably the best person I've talked to about pigeonholing in the business because you are successfully going back and forth between single-cam and multi-cam shows. For somebody who doesn't know anything about the business, how would you describe what pigeonholing is?

LM: Pigeonholing is when people assume you're only good at one thing. When you do drama, they assume you can't do comedy. That's a pigeonhole. When you mainly work in single-camera comedy, that means they don't think you can do multi-cam comedy. If you work in variety television, you get pigeonholed because they feel that you don't understand story or character. So it's very difficult to cross over into a narrative format. That was probably my biggest obstacle.

JP: Why is pigeonholing so prevalent?

LM: Because people have no vision. They want to believe that if you only do one thing, then you're only going to be good at that one thing. There are a lot of multi-cam directors that cannot get hired on single-camera shows because the producers feel that they don't know how to transition. The only thing I will say about *that* is, unless you really understand it, it is hard to do both. They have two completely different mindsets in terms of how you shoot, break down the script and plan your workweek. The workweek in single-cam and multi-cam is completely different. In multi-cam, you go in on day one and you have a table read and the production meeting. Day two, you put it up on its feet. You get the rewrites from the table read and then early in the afternoon, you do a producer's run-through. Day three, you get the rewrites from the producers' run-through, and you put it back up on its feet. You make the adjustments from the rewrites. They've added a scene. They've changed a scene. They've added somebody into a scene. A scene is no longer in the living room, now it's going to take place in the bedroom. You have to adjust to all those things. And then you do a network-producer-studio run-through. Then you get their notes: "Make sure she hits this a little bit harder," or "I think that we've got to ground this and maybe lay it in a little bit earlier" … whatever it is. So you take all those notes, and you get your script for the next day and then you start blocking, because you need to go in with a plan whether it's multi-camera or single-camera. You should have a plan. Then you shoot Thursday and shoot Friday, and basically your week is done.

In single-camera, you have a week of prep and a week of shooting. You go in on day one of prep and have a concept meeting and maybe some location scouts. Then you're going deeper. "Okay, how big is the party going to be? Are we going to do it in a fancy restaurant or are we going to do it in a diner?" You start to make those decisions based on your concept meeting, and you go find those locations. By Thursday of your prep week, you're really getting ready. You're starting to define where those sets are going to be. You're walking through them, you're figuring out how you're going to shoot it. Friday you do the tone meeting. Monday you start shooting. And you have five days to shoot the same amount of material that you shoot in two days on a multi-cam.

JP: Which would you say is harder?

LM: It really depends. For me, they are both equal. But for some people who do single-camera, it might be harder for them to stage flat for multi-cam. And for people who do multi-cam, it might be harder to understand how to build the story with camera cuts and set-ups. I'm just lucky that I've been able to learn both. Knocking on wood, and thanking God at the same time.

JP: What have been your biggest setbacks?

LM: I can give you three examples of where I fucked up. The first one was when I was directing a cable show called *Good Girls Don't*. This was one of my very first jobs, and the very first time I was doing a hybrid show, meaning that it had both multi-cam and single-camera elements. The actors were really having story and script issues. What I didn't realize was that the writers always want you to put up what they wrote and let them see that it doesn't work. So when the actors had issues with the script, I made the mistake of asking for the producers to come to the stage to deal with it. The producers got really mad at me because I didn't say to the actors, "Let's just put it up and try to make it work." I was booked to do two episodes and they ended up replacing me on the second one. That was a huge lesson.

JP: So that was a fire-able offense?

LM: Yes. And it was rough. I thought, "Oh, my God. I'm an idiot." These are life lessons that they don't teach you in film school. There is no Executive 101 class to tell you to make sure you put the scene up first before addressing the script issues. And also, do it to the best of your ability. It was a huge lesson.

My second biggest lesson was when I came back from directing *The Chris Rock Show* and was directing on *MADtv*. From my booth P.A. experience at *SNL*, I was used to the writers being in charge of their pieces, and basically armchair-directing the actors over the director's shoulder. So when I was on *MADtv*, it was like I had gotten so used to the writers giving notes on the material that I had become more concerned with camera positions as opposed to character notes for the actors. And Nicole Sullivan, who was on the show at the time, said out loud, "We need somebody who's concerned about the material. She's just worried about her cameras." And that's when I realized that this wasn't just about covering closeups and head-to-toe shots. This was about story. I still ended up doing the show because I was able to hear her, and I upped my game. It forced me to really understand something a little deeper about directing than just the technical parts. Even though I had taken all those acting and story classes, it's not the same as being there. Being on the set in the reality of that moment is nothing like school.

My one and only movie was *Chasing Papi* for Fox. I felt that we did not get any support in marketing. I really took that to heart and it kind of ruined me for about six months. I was so depressed. It was like everybody telling you that your baby is ugly. It was really hard to get past that. It was a big life lesson for me.

JP: The reception to the film was not what you hoped it would be?

LM: Right. People would say horrible things. Like, there was an *L.A. Weekly* review that said, "She must have learned her comedy from Cantinflas." It was such an insult. Cantinflas was one of the most brilliant comics ever. The reviewer was basically saying that because I liked a Mexican comic, I didn't know anything about comedy. That's how I looked at that.

JP: What was the film's connection to Cantinflas? Just a racial connection?

LM: Just a racial connection.

JP: That's racist.

LM: It was totally racist. We had all these great reviews in *People* and *Us Weekly* and *The L.A. Times* and a really decent review in *The Hollywood Reporter* and *Variety*. And the one piece of reporting that the studio put out for the movie was a little thing in *The Fresno Bee*. That was on the one-sheet, *The Fresno Bee*. It was just a little black and white blurb in a corner of the paper. And I realized they really didn't care about the movie because there were no ads on television, like during *MADtv*, which had a huge Latin audience. They didn't run any commercials during *George Lopez*, which was on ABC at the time and also had a huge Latin audience. And there was even a WB show that the studio could have advertised on, *Greetings from Tucson*, about a Mexican family in Arizona. And so the movie kind of failed. And it hurt my career. I went into director jail for almost a year.

JP: What is director jail?

LM: Director jail is when you can't get a meeting. You can't get hired. I never got another movie after that, and it took me about a year to get back into the good graces of TV because some of the people that I had worked for were like, "Oh, she's a movie director now." And it took a while to get back in because people are dumb. But you know what? I've had more ups than downs, and that just goes to show the longevity in my career.

JP: Would you say that was your biggest dip?

LM: Probably. It's been pretty steadily uphill since then.

JP: What do you think about the value of film school these days?

LM: Well, it's great that there are so many film schools that kids can go to and really get their hands dirty in a way that's safe. I don't think it translates to real life, though. It's never the same when you're working with a little group of 20 kids each doing five different jobs. And then you go onto a real set where you can't touch this because that's electric, you can't touch that because that's script, you can't touch that because that's craft service. You know what I mean? Even the little schooling that I had didn't translate to reality. I think the most annoying thing about those schools is that they produce some kids who think they can come out and just start directing. I find that insulting because it's a very hard job with a lot of pieces and a lot of elements. And you don't learn that in school, no matter how you slice it. You just won't. Those kids drive me a little crazy.

JP: One of the things I noticed in your credits is a lot of projects that combined different cultures coexisting together, and fish-out-of-water stories. For instance, on *Superior Donuts*, your *Iceman Cometh* episode and also in the episode of *Kimmy Schmidt* where Titus sings his one-man show. The *Kimmy Schmidt* episode in particular got into some very tricky cultural territory. Really brave.

LM: That episode was very controversial. And I think maybe Tina Fey gave it to me because I had actually done a one-woman show.

JP: It seems to me like you've gotten a lot of projects that have tread on some potentially scary cultural territory.

LM: Yeah. *Ugly Betty* too. I've also done quite a few African-American shows. So I would say that there's a weird theme there. I think it's because I handled a lot of that material in early *Bernie Mac*. And I really handled it with care and thoughtfulness, but also a lot of funny. I think a lot of it has to do with some of that earlier work I did because that's what I would send out as my calling card reel.

JP: Would you say that was something you pursued or did it just sort of happen?

LM: It was happenstance. Those were the shows that were coming after me.

JP: It surprises me that you would say it was happenstance that you found those kind of storylines to direct because it's such a hard thing to pull off well. In my mind, this is an argument for diversity in Hollywood, because how would you be able to handle those kinds of storylines without having a director who understands diversity?

LM: I guess I say it's happenstance because they sought me out to do their programs for whatever reason. Maybe it was because I was a minority, or maybe it was because I was a woman that they thought I would have a different understanding of their particular program. But it wasn't like I looked for that material. They found me. It's always been about getting my reel out there. Let me go and meet people and whomever I connected with has hired me. It's that not everybody is going to be right for everything. And you just have to find where you fit in. I went and did a *Suburgatory* and I could not relate to the people on that show. It was a very difficult show for me. I love the actors and most of the actors loved me. But it was so specific in its style and tone. And the executive producer would never give me any time. So it was very hard to navigate that show. And subsequently I didn't get asked back. And that's okay. Like I said, not everything is for everybody.

JP: I think that, in terms of the people that I've sought out to interview, a big part of my thinking on what is diversity comes not just from the race and gender of the director, but the actual life experience and background of the person. So for me, I would posit that your approach to those programs had more to do with being Linda Mendoza growing up in Detroit in the '60s and the life experiences you've had as being key to the real depth of the diversity you brought to those stories.

LM: I would say that's probably very true because I understand it in a very intimate way. Like I said before, in Detroit there were white kids, black kids and me. And so I was the diversity poster child, because if you were white or black, that wasn't necessarily considered diverse. As long as you weren't brown. And I was pretty brown. I am 31 percent Iberian

Peninsula, which is Spain, 29 percent Native American and ten percent Irish. And then a mixture of everything else for the other percentages.

JP: Do you know your Native American heritage?

LM: My great grandmother was full-blooded Apache. I have a really rich background.

JP: Texas to Motown. It really is very American.

LM: It's so American. You can't get more American than me, even though to some people, the color of my skin is not American. But I'm actually American as apple pie … just with a tan underneath.

Eric Dean Seaton

Calm, cool and collected. Amongst the fiery chaos of a television production, Eric Dean Seaton exudes the confidence of a Buddhist monk walking on a little pillow of air. You just can't ruffle the man. When he speaks with you, he gives you his full attention, and whatever you say will elicit that trademark gentle smile. No yelling, no freaking out, no belittling of people. Ever the collaborator.

When I sat down with Eric in his home study I realized that his long fascination with comics is not just a childhood obsession. Rather, it reflects a profound interest in the capacity of people to achieve things beyond their expectations in the service of making the world a better place. Eric's work and life journey seem deeply connected to the concept of the Hero's Journey. Perhaps this is the source of his calmness in the face of disorder—a connection to something deeper.

· · · · · · · · · · · · · · · · · · · ·

ERIC DEAN SEATON: I grew up in Cleveland, Ohio, and from a very early age I loved storytelling. I was a latchkey kid. Both my parents worked. My mom was an educator, and my dad worked out of town for the government. He would come home on weekends. I grew up in front of the television. I watched all the old comedies, and I would always watch the credits. When I finally got into the business, I knew everyone's job from watching the credits.

I grew up in an Orthodox Jewish neighborhood in Cleveland Heights. We were one of the first black families to live there. Everyone who lived north of us in the neighborhood was a concentration camp survivor. I had a job delivering newspapers and I had a giant German shepherd that I would bring with me. About a month into the job, my dad was home for a week and went on my route with me. We came home and he goes, "You can't take your dog anymore." And I said, "Why?" He explained World War II to me—the concentration camps and the Holocaust, graphic

Eric Dean Seaton fought hard to make the leap from directing on kids' shows to network half-hour comedies (Jacob Pinger).

21

details and all. That's one thing I'll say about my dad. He did not hold back. He wanted me to know how humans can be to one another.

The people in the neighborhood were super-nice, though. They would give me Christmas gifts, and really educate me on the world and how people are judged by their race, color and religion. I think because it was an Orthodox Jewish neighborhood, my dad probably thought it was going to be safe to live there. Kind of like *The Jeffersons*, we were moving on up. But at three years old, I learned about the N-word. When we first moved to the neighborhood, someone spray-painted the N-word all over the car of some friends who came to visit us. So I learned the N-word at age three, and about the Holocaust at age eight, and that comedy can come from pain.

JACOB PINGER: What were your childhood friendships like?

EDS: Until I went to high school, most of my friends were white. That changed in my freshman year in high school. One time I was walking down the hall with some of my white friends from grade school, and I'll always remember this: One of my friends went up to a senior Italian guy, and my friend said, "I want you to meet Eric." And the senior said, "I don't like niggers." I was standing ten feet away. And my friend said, "No. He's not like that. He's different." And I remember going home thinking, "I'm not different."

JP: That was your friend who said that?

EDS: That was my friend, somebody I went to grade school with. And from that moment on, I was like, "Holy crap. I don't think these people are really my friends." All the other black kids in the high school were bussed in. So they had known each other since the second grade. Most of my friends were white, because I grew up from second grade with the white kids. Then halfway through my freshman year, I started hanging out with the black kids. They accepted me for me. But I hated high school. I hated everything about it. It wasn't until I went to college that everything changed for me. I went to Ohio State, and that was the greatest experience of my life.

JP: Did your parents have feelings about whom you should be friends with?

EDS: Yes. My dad used to say, "White people are only good to compete against." And what he meant by that was, "You need to be as good as them to get ahead." It was good advice, but it was a horrible way to say it. I think because he did not elaborate on it, I just thought he was a racist nutcase. We would battle over that all the time.

And by the way, when I played football in eighth grade, my dad was an assistant coach, and he would take all my white friends out to get ice cream. They would think he was the sweetest man in the world. They had no idea that he would ever say something like that, or their mouths would drop. But that is what he would say when we were at home. Out in public, he was always a charmer. But his message was that you need to be better than to be equal. Kind of wish he had just said that, though [*laughs*]

JP: What TV shows did you like as a kid?

EDS: *The Jeffersons* and *Happy Days* were my two favorite comedies. They were polar opposites, which is why I think I do pretty well in comedy. I connected to *Happy Days*, because the Fonz was so cool. I wanted to be the Fonz. I watched *The Jeffersons* with my dad, and *All in the Family* too. Do you know how racy those shows were? I loved how everyone was always cracking on each other, and how they would fight, and all the racial stuff. I can quote lines from *The Jeffersons*. That show paralleled my life because most of my friends were white. We all watched *The Jeffersons*, but my dad could give a rat's ass about *Happy Days*.

To spend time with my dad, you had to watch what he wanted to watch. On Friday nights at ten p.m. I would go downstairs to watch *Dallas* with him. Saturday night we watched *The Love Boat, Fantasy Island,* and cop shows like *Hawaii Five-O* on Sundays. That's why I love shooting action.

When I came home from school in the afternoon, I watched all the reruns: *Gilligan's Island, The Munsters* and *I Love Lucy.* But I hated *My Three Sons,* and I hated *The Brady Bunch*—just too cookie cutter for me. Their reality was not mine. Not even close. On *My Three Sons,* they would go out and do sports in dress shoes, and I would think, "This is ridiculous." I didn't realize it then, but I was literally studying television.

JP: Were you connecting with comic books simultaneously?

EDS: Yeah. It was in the late '70s and early '80s. My dad would come home on the weekends and he had a routine. He'd drive home Friday night from Chicago, and on Saturday morning I would wake up and he would take me to a coffee shop where they sold comics. He'd buy me comic books and I would sit in the car and read comics all day. I just loved it.

JP: Who were your favorite superheroes?

EDS: Teen Titans and Iron Man. And by the way, people don't realize that Iron Man was a drunk. That comic taught me all about alcoholism.

JP: A big theme that runs through your work is people with special powers, many of who are trying to save the world or at least make it a better place.

EDS: That's been a resounding theme in my whole life. I always had that thing of wanting to see myself represented, and to save the world. The first movie I saw was a James Bond film. I remember asking my dad, "Are there any black secret agents out there?" And he goes, "Yeah. We just haven't seen 'em yet."

JP: Are your parents proud that you became a director?

EDS: I took my mom to the NAACP Image Awards and we went down the red carpet. She had never been on the red carpet, and I remember her saying, "This is good. When are you gonna get an Oscar?" That's how my parents were. My dad too. He never said "Good job" to me. It was always, "What can you do next?" Before I got my first directing job, he wanted me to become a teacher. And I was like, "How can I teach kids to follow their dreams if I give up on mine?" And we had this huge fight. We didn't talk for two years. And when I got my first directing episode on *That's So Raven,* I took the whole check and bought my parents tickets to Hawaii. When they came out west, they stopped on a layover to see me. One morning I took my dad to get *The New York Times,* which he loved to read. I got back in the car and I gave him the paper, and he goes, "You did good." That was his way. He never said, "I'm sorry." He never said, "I'm wrong." Now he lives in assisted living and I hear that he brags about me to the nurses. But he never says anything to me. I think that's the way he was raised.

JP: That's a very old-school way of parenting.

EDS: Completely old-school method. To be honest, my dad and I did not have a great connection.

JP: How did you gravitate towards film and TV as a career?

EDS: When I was a senior in high school, I didn't know what I wanted to do. So I wrote Bill Cosby a letter about directing. I just wanted to know how I could meet some directors. I actually didn't want anything from him but some advice. It was probably the saddest letter ever. It was basically saying that I grew up in Ohio, didn't know anybody and didn't know anything. But since he worked with directors, maybe he could tell me how to meet some of them.

JP: How did you know where to send the letter?

EDS: I didn't even know that they did the last *Cosby Show* in New York. I had gone to the library and got an address. It was basically the William Morris Agency. I mailed the letter to Bill Cosby and his agent read it and gave it to him. I ended up doing an internship on the last season of his last series. I saw all these amazing directors who had been in the game for a really long time. I learned all these comedy rules. And a lot of the rules still stand today.

I did the internship for six months, and then went to college. When I graduated, Bill Cosby wrote me a recommendation letter, but by then his influence was gone. Eventually, I realized why Bill Cosby had responded to my letter. When I was interning, I saw that he got a thousand letters a day and that everybody was asking for money. In the six months I was there, I can honestly say I don't think I ever saw another letter like mine that was just asking for advice.

JP: What did you study at Ohio State?

EDS: Even in college I wondered, "Can I really do film and TV?" So I had architecture as a minor, even though I didn't want that. Then one day I saw a black friend of mine, Derek, walking through campus with film equipment. I said to him, "What are you doing with all this gear?" and he went, "Oh, I'm in the film school." I asked, "They have a film school here?" So I followed him and sat in the back of his film class. The next day, I changed all my classes to be in film. And this is the point of representation: It's about what kids are able to see. I saw a person who looked like me doing film. And because I saw somebody who looked like me doing it, that made me go sit in the back of his film class. It changed my life.

JP: Then you moved to L.A. after college.

EDS: I moved out here and I didn't know anybody. I had no connections. My uncle lived in Anaheim and he used to play for the Harlem Globetrotters. He had emphysema, bronchitis and asthma. So to cover the rent, I would take care of him during the day, and then I had a night job delivering scripts. The crazy thing is, I'm lucky I survived. I would drive on the highway all night. I would almost fall asleep driving to Anaheim to deliver a script, and I would have to pull over at a gas station. But I learned L.A. inside and out. I started working my way up from night P.A. to regular P.A., to stage P.A. to second AD [assistant director] to first AD and then I got to be director. Every step was in two and a half years. Two and a half years as a P.A., two and a half years as a second AD. Two and a half years as a first AD.

The advice I always give people is this: You've got to look in the mirror and figure out where you are. In my case, because I was so much younger than the other first ADs, the only jobs I would get were the ones that nobody else wanted. My thought was that if they've got 15 years experience over me, then I wouldn't go for the same shows. I wouldn't even try for a show on a big network. I would wait for a smaller network like UPN or WB to announce their shows. Then I would pick whatever show was at the bottom of the barrel. And I always got the job that nobody else wanted. That was my mindset. And it worked. Every two and a half years, I flew up the ranks. When *That's So Raven* started up in 2001, I chased that first AD job down for six months. My guess was that if that show didn't get canceled, I would get a chance to direct.

I was the sort of first AD who was overly helpful. If any director ever came to me and said, "I need to do this shot, but I don't know how I'm going to make it on time," I would say, "Let's go for it." I never said no. I was always overly helpful because I was trying to figure out what they were doing. I was always learning, even while doing my job to the best of my ability. That was the key for me.

JP: As a director, do you prefer ADs like that?

EDS: Oh, yeah. Like, let's go for it. Let's try it. And then give me the cut-off point of when I'm getting into trouble with time. That means I'm totally trusting you. And if I get that extra shot, it's great, and you're part of it. And I'm going to thank you.

JP: When you were a first AD, the goal of directing was always in your sights. How did you take the initial steps to let the powers-that-be know that you wanted to get a chance to direct?

EDS: Like I said before, I was always helping out as a first AD. Also, I was always talking about directing. And then I went and shot a short and told everybody about it. But even before I shot the short, they had asked me if I wanted to direct. And I said, "That's all I ever waned to do." Then I asked *them*, "Do you think it's going to happen?" And they went silent. I was like, "Well, what does that mean?" And then you've got to figure out when you can ask again. It's truly a dance. You don't want to bug people. But I figured since they asked me, they knew. So instead of bugging them, I just focused on "How can I show them?" I thought that was a better plan. I never wanted to say, "You gotta give me a show," because nobody *has* to do anything. One way I never want to feel is *entitled*. My struggle growing up was too hard for that.

And by the way, invest in yourself. Go shoot a short. Every time I shot a short, it changed things. The original short that I did showed people I could do kids' stuff. And then the short I made that was based on my graphic novel *Legend of the Mantamaji* allowed everybody to see that I can do action. So go invest in yourself. Shoot a short, and edit it yourself. At least do that once. It teaches you everything about what you need, or don't need, when you're in crunch time as a director.

JP: Can you tell me about your first directing job?

EDS: I was the first AD on *That's So Raven*, and they gave me an episode to direct in the third season. It was my first time ever directing anything. For my first scene on my first day, it was just two people. I had my four cameras, and the actors were acting, and I heard the line producer say, "Oh, great! Every camera is shooting the same thing." I looked up and I went, "Oh, crap. They *are*." It was just that the actors were standing too close together. So I went, "Can you guys separate a little bit?" And all of a sudden, every shot looked different. Afterwards, when we took a five, I went to the bathroom and I was just sweating. I was like, "I can't do this. I'm gonna fail. It's too rough." And I looked up in the mirror and I was like, "Fool. This is your one shot. Calm down. Suck it up and go be a director." I took a deep breath, washed my hands, walked out there, and I was fine. I've never been nervous since. Part of my confidence is, I don't have any other options. This is it. This is all I ever wanted to do.

I always tell new directors this: There's a moment when you're shooting your first show that someone is going to challenge something, just because they can. In my first episode, they had this ice cream machine. And it's a kids' show, so of course it explodes and all this ice cream falls out. I wanted to get a shot where one of the actors pulled the plug out on the machine to make it stop. So I had the cameras move over to get this special shot. And the producer said, "We don't need that. We don't need to see it." And I remember just doing it anyway, even though he said not to. When we got into editing, we totally needed that shot to pull the scene up. There was all the ice cream coming out and the kids were falling, but there was nothing else to cut to except the shot I did. And it totally worked.

I remember thinking, "Why would you challenge me? We weren't behind. Why did you do that? Just because I'm new and you didn't understand what I was doing?" When you're new, they're going to think you don't know what you're doing. But you do know what you're doing because you prepared for it. So go get it. And later the producer said, "Well, I'm glad we had that shot because we were able to get the scene to time." But I didn't say anything.

JP: How would you translate that experience into advice for a new director?

EDS: Prepare. And if you believe in something, go get it. There's no guarantee you're going to get another shot at directing. So you've got nothing to lose. If you didn't get that shot, and the episode didn't come out good, you may not get another opportunity. It will be like, "He or she was okay, but they didn't get all the coverage." So just because you got the first job, don't think it's going to lead to 17 more jobs. You have to deliver each and every time. Remember, the first time you direct, they got your back, because everybody wants you to do good. The second time, you've got to show them something. By the third time, you're on your own.

The first time that I directed, they cheered for me. By the third time, when I was thinking "Here comes the cheer," everyone was just like, "Oh, it's Eric again." There was no cheering. On the first episode, the actors would say okay to whatever I needed. By the third episode, they would talk to me differently. They we would be like, "Oh, I don't really want to do that."

So they let me direct a few episodes on *That's So Raven*, and I was still the first AD. On my third show as a director, I got nominated for a NAACP Image Award, which was a big deal. Then at the start of the second season, I found out that they hired a couple of directors who had never directed before. As the show's first AD, I was expected to help them out. I had no problem with that. But the catch was that I didn't know these guys. They were friends of the executive producers. And one of them told me straight out that I would get them through it and fix things. But from that, I thought, what if they can't make it, and they say I wasn't helpful? I'm not the director, *you* are. I figure you can go up to a certain point, but then you can start to go downhill. I remember it was two days before we were going to start and I was in the shower. And I literally remember feeling like I was trapped and I didn't want to do it any more. I threw some clothes on and drove down to the show. I knocked on the executive producer's door and I said, "I'm so sorry to do this, but I have to talk to you guys." I said, "Listen, I don't want to AD any more. Will you still let me direct?" And they all kind of looked at me. I knew that one of the executive producers was going to direct that season. I was just thinking fast on my feet and I said, "Look, I'll start the show off as a first AD But after that, I don't want to AD any more." And I said to the executive producer, "I know you're going to direct, so if you ever need me, I'll come and AD for you." They were like, "Sure." And I stopped being an AD. That was 2008. So I made this big announcement to be a director. Then, three weeks later, the writers' strike hit, and I didn't work for a year.

JP: How did you learn the craft of directing, especially multi-cam?

EDS: Multi-cam is actually harder than single-cam, because you can only learn the four-cameras-at-once process while you are doing the job. Every day when I was an AD, I would write down the blocking of whoever was directing. And every night, for one hour, I would come home and do camera shots on their blocking. This is not an exaggeration. I would do it six days a week. After a while, I started doing blocking while I was watching TV. I would watch anything that James Burrows directed, or Mark Cendrowski, Rich Correll, or Joel Zwick. I would count shots. What I mean by that is, as I'm watching the show I would go, "That's camera A. That's camera B. That's camera X. That's camera C." As the show would cut, I would count in my head. And I learned camera shots by doing that over and over. I did that for two years. So I knew cameras really well from the first moment I got to direct. There are a lot of rules in multi-cam, but once you learn them, the job becomes pretty easy.

JP: Did you ever shadow?

EDS: No, because I was working. But when you think about it, I was shadowing every day in my job as a first AD.

JP: Your first directing jobs were opportunities you got on a show where you were the full-time first AD. After you announced that you were no longer going to be a first AD, how did you get that break to become a full-time director in your own right?

EDS: At that point, I had directed maybe 10 or 12 episodes, but I was still a new director. What usually happens is that if you're a new director, or a minority director, you might get episode 11 or 12, of a 13-episode series. You know, you get the episode later on in the line. It will be the one written by the writer's assistant. It might be a good script. But it might also be a script that needs work since it's the writer's first opportunity.

What happened to me was the weirdest thing. It was a Friday night, and I was getting ready to go to the movies. I had bought a ticket, but I was just too lazy to get off the couch. And luckily I didn't get up to go because the phone rang. The call was from a new Disney show called *Sunny with a Chance* with Demi Lovato. The producer called and said, "We want you to come in and direct." I said, "Okay, when? Like in a few months?" And she said, "No. On Monday." And I go, "Wait, you're still shooting right now and it's eight o'clock on Friday night? Someone's about to get fired?" And she said, "Sadly, yes." She asked me to come in on Sunday for a meeting with all the people behind the show.

The room was full of network execs, all the people behind the show. There were about ten people. And this is not an exaggeration, every one of them told me the show was about something different. When I left the room, I thought, "Holy crap. They don't know what the show is yet. They're still trying to figure it out." So I went home and started thinking. Basically, it was a show within a show. I had episodes of *30 Rock* on my DVR, and I started watching them, because that was also a show within a show. And I just started making all of these rules that we could go by, and I came in Monday with that list. For instance, since kids don't know the difference between fake and real, we're going to show them a guy walking by with movie lights. We're going to shoot off the sets, and when we come around a corner, we will show that it's a fake wall. The head of Disney asked me, "Are we going to be okay?" I looked him in the eye and said, "We are going to be great." And he said, "Okay." From that moment, everybody followed my rules, and over the years on *Sunny with a Chance* and the spin-off sketch show called *So Random*, I ended up directing 40 of the 60 episodes.

Afterward, I just kept trying to get jobs outside of the kid world but was having trouble. The thing I did not realize is that you get pigeonholed. I would say that I was probably one of the most pigeonholed directors at that time, ridiculously so. I say that because there were quite a few multi-cams on network TV, and not only could I not get the job, I couldn't even get a meeting on any of them. I got horribly pigeonholed because I had done kids shows. When I did get the meeting, I could tell in the first two minutes if I had a chance or not. If the executive I was meeting with had photos of kids on their desk, then they would have a concept of the world I came from. But if they didn't have kids, they wouldn't understand. The worst was a meeting at MTV with two young, hip, single male execs. I walked in and they go, "What's up?" And I go, "What's up?" And that was the best part of the whole meeting. They looked at my résumé and it went downhill from there. No one at MTV who was doing *Teen Wolf* was watching Disney Channel. So why would they hire a director from there? It was the worst meeting I ever had and I loved *Teen Wolf*. I had all these interviews and they would go nowhere year after year. It was a rough time, because I am very, very passionate about directing.

Finally, my first break-out of kid show world was on *Undateable* from executive producer Bill Lawrence on NBC. His producer, Randall Winston, who is black, took a chance on me and that made all the difference in the world. Bill Lawrence was so big, having his name on my résumé made people pay attention. Then I was hired for one of his other shows, *Ground Floor* on TBS, which led to *Dr. Ken* for ABC. It's a little different now, but at the time, I learned that executive producers didn't always really want to hire the people that the network execs recommend. Because if it goes wrong, their episode is messed up. Producers wanted to call their friends and see what their friends thought of you. And if their friends thought you were good, they would hire you. The perfect example is that I got booked on *Dr. Ken* and then I met the execs afterwards. Then I shot my own short for my graphic novel *Legend of the Mantamaji*. That finally made everybody take me seriously.

JP: What is the difference between directing single cam and multi-cam?

EDS: In multi-cam, you have no fourth wall. It's a proscenium. You're blocking a play. Multi-cam is all right to left. In single-cam, everything's coming toward the camera and moving away from camera. It's front to back, and then you turn around to look the other way. What I say to anyone from single-cam who has never directed multi-cam is to do everything you would normally do, but do it right to left. My method when I do multi-cam, is to stand in the middle of the set with my script, and I mark down the four cameras, A, B, C and X. I draw it on my script, so it's logical when you're looking at each direction. For instance, looking one way is A and B, and then looking the other way is C and X.

JP: There's an x camera?

EDS: Yeah. It's called A, B, C and X, because D sounds too much like C. If you want to learn multi-cam, go watch plays. The actors always open to camera, and never block themselves. And, they always go left to right or right to left. If somebody moves up stage [away from the audience], then the other actors are coming down stage too, otherwise they will get upstaged. In single-camera, the actor walks into a room right towards the camera, talking. Then the cameras have to turn around to get the opposite angle. Single-cam is easier, because it's what you learn in film school. You're doing single-cam when you go out and shoot with your phone. Everything you're already doing is single-camera. But you only learn multi-cam if you're doing a multi-camera show. That's why it's so hard.

Also the chain of command is confusing. On multi-camera you have camera coordinator, also called associate directors, who are supposed to be your liaison to the cameramen. But through the years, on a lot of shows, the directors have let the people who hold that position do their shots for them. It's has actually gotten to the point where producers will look to them to see if you got a shot or not. Or worse, tell them and not the director what coverage they need. The director would handle all the acting, and the coordinator would handle all the shots. It's kind of turned into a mess for new directors.

JP: A lot of the shows you've worked on seem to touch on social issues. Many had multiracial casts. Was that a coincidence?

EDS: When I was an AD, the only shows that I could get were shows with black casts. They would always hire the black AD to do the black show. They still do that to this day on a lot of shows. That is pigeonholing. But I was always about being diverse. I think my background as a kid growing up in an Orthodox Jewish neighborhood, and having my grandparents living in a low-income neighborhood, made me always want the rainbow coalition.

JP: I loved *Game of Thrones*, but it drives me crazy how white it was. The only people of color were slaves. It's a fantasy, after all. The characters could be any color.

EDS: We all see it. We accept it. With people of color, no matter what nationality you are, you know everything about white culture. People who don't have color don't know about other cultures.

Oddly enough, most of my directing career has been on shows where I'm the only black person. At the wrap party is where you get perspective. I did this one show, and the actress on the show had a baby in real life. So the whole crew put on white shirts with the baby's name and we did a video. It wasn't until I saw the video that I was like, holy crap. It was me, the DP and like two other black guys in the video with 100 other white crew members. And it wasn't a racist thing. It's just that there are so few black people working in the business. It stood out when I saw that video. I'll always remember that image. And I'm glad that things are changing.

JP: As an African-American director, do you ever feel that you have a responsibility to represent all black folks on set?

EDS: Absolutely. Every day. At the end of the day, people are still seeing this [*gestures to his own face*]. Many years after I had become a full-time director, I would still go to a show and people would be like, "Oh, you must be the first AD."

I was directing a kids' show and they had this giant alligator. The alligator could not be in the same shot with the kids, so it required a special effects shot. We started rolling on the shot when all of a sudden the editor walked in and in front of everybody he goes, "Stop! Cut! You can't do that. You're doing it wrong." So I went up to him and said, "Why?" And I told him what I was doing. Then I turned and walked away, and we did the scene. The show turned out great. But when I asked my agent about going back, he informed me that the editor told the producers that I was the most arrogant director he had ever worked with, and that he would never work with me again. I told my agent that the editor had confronted me in front of everyone and that none of the big-time directors would ever put up with that. But the editor actually won and I never did the show again. I realized that they're all looking at me. And even though I was 100 percent right, my execution was wrong. The proper way to handle that would have been to waste time by asking him, "Well, this is what I want to do," and not do it loud in front of everyone. Because all he saw was everyone looking at him. Even though he started it, I finished it and he looked foolish. It sounds crazy, but if you can always show respect, even when you are disrespected, you will always win.

That's what I tell everybody now. Those crew members, like that editor, are going to be there a lot longer than you. So now, I don't fight the battles the same way. I'm nice to everyone, even when they act a fool. As a matter of fact, I was shooting a show a month ago, and the boom guy missed a line. I said, "That last line was off mike." And the boom guy, who I've known for years, snapped at me in front of everyone. I said, "Wait a second. I've known you ten years, you can't yell at me like that. It's not that serious. We can always go back and pick the line up." That's the response you give. At the end of the day, I could have snapped at him and gone off. But then everyone would think, "Eric was so rough on this guy." And as soon as the moment was over, he came and apologized to me. Everyone didn't see that, but it doesn't matter. What matters is how I handled it, and I did it the right way. You don't have to destroy people when they mess up.

JP: What I'm hearing is that you have had to develop strategies to work around the ingrained racism of the industry. To do otherwise would damage your career.

EDS: Absolutely.

JP: Wow. Stories like this make me realize that some people have to deal with some really crazy stuff.

EDS: You do. And you can choose to do it a different way, but being personal works for me because it takes the wall down. Then I can get what I want and I can get it fast. Remember that even though we are working here in Los Angeles, a lot of people in the business actually live way outside of L.A. You don't know what their lives are like, or if they have ever come across any black people. My wife and I have been to weddings of some of the white executives that I'm close to, and we were the only black couple. And maybe there was one Asian couple. Are those executives racist? No. Not at all. It's just who they associate with. Shonda Rhimes said it: "Everybody is not racist. But people hire their friends and hire like minds." When people are not diverse in the people they are around, that ends up leaving you out. I have heard that a lot of white male directors are mad now that women and equality has become a real thing. They have no reason to be mad because they don't need to do six episodes of a single show in one season. Go get something else. And by the way, had there been diversity and equality from the beginning, they wouldn't have gotten all six episodes.

JP: I've also heard that the agents and managers of some of these white directors are telling them they can't book them because all the jobs are going to non-white directors.

EDS: Oh, they're totally telling them that, and it's bullcrap. It's creating anger and resentment, and it's wrong.

JP: One thing people need to read about it is how you actually get a job as a TV director. So touching on this whole issue of taking meetings and selling yourself in a meeting, what can you advise an aspiring director?

EDS: I tell people that every meeting is speed dating. Every executive wants to champion you. But they need a connection. So in that meeting, you have to find a connection. But do it from a place of honesty because you can get called on it. I did *The Mick* a few seasons ago. I needed them to know how much I really liked it. I walked in and they asked, "Have you seen the show?" I said that I had seen every episode, and I had. It was a really good show. I told them the ones I liked and why. And then they asked, "Tell us which ones didn't you like?" You get some curveballs sometimes.

Bethany Rooney

Of all the directors I interviewed, the one I was most excited to meet was Bethany Rooney. The book she co-wrote with Mary Lou Belli, *Directors Tell the Story: Master the Craft of Television and Film Directing*, is the most comprehensive and vital work on the topic of directing television I have come across. Bethany's dedication to mastering her craft is matched by her commitment to fostering the same passion in the next generation of TV directors. And she does it all without airs or pretense. As she says in her interview, Bethany is a "steady Midwestern girl."

I had the pleasure of working with Bethany as a camera operator on two occasions that were separated by a few years. It was remarkable that when I saw her the second time, she remembered me and told me that she was glad to see me again. At wrap, she thanked me for my work. This may not seem like much, but in Hollywood such a display of appreciation by a director to their crew members is a rarity. I never forgot it.

• • • • • • • • • • • • • • • • • • • •

BETHANY ROONEY: I was born in Columbus, Ohio, and I grew up in a farming town called Findlay. I would say that I come from the land of cows and corn. Findlay was relatively big when I was growing up, about 30,000 people, but very Midwest. Very basic. My father was an architect. My mother was an artist and stay-at-home mother. The fact that my mother was an artist, and also my father's architecture gave me a basis in aesthetics and beauty, which was important to me.

JACOB PINGER: What kind of artist was your mother?

BR: She worked in a lot of different media. She worked in fabric. She painted. She created weird sculptures. She was a very creative person who wanted to express herself but she had four children under the age of six. So mostly she worked on things at home. Then once the kids had grown up, she owned and operated a kind of craft store. It wasn't that she

A self-described Midwestern girl, Bethany Rooney bolsters her directing artistry with a renowned attention to the craft (Matthew T. Collins).

31

sold the elements to make art, rather she would go to art shows and buy unique and wonderful handmade stuff and then sell it in a retail setting.

JP: Was your mother a stay-at-home mom by choice or was that just the times she lived in?

BR: That was just the times.

JP: What do you think she would have done as a career today?

BR: Because she was passionate about art and because she was compelled to create, I'm sure she would show her art and sell it. But in that time it was just a form of expression for her. She belonged to the local art society and she showed her work in some shows. But if you were living in a small Ohio town and not going to New York it just was not a very sellable sort of thing.

JP: Do you think she was frustrated as an artist?

BR: Totally. But she accepted it because it just was what it was.

JP: What was it like growing up in Findlay? I grew up in L.A. so I'm imagining something like *The Andy Griffith Show*.

BR: Yeah, it was kind of similar to that. There was only one high school. Everybody knew everybody. There were the small town things like parades on holidays. We would play outside all day in the summer and go ice-skating on the pond in winter. It was a quintessential 1960s small town experience. It's something that I'm so grateful for because it formed me. It was All American. I still have that Midwest down-to-earth thing happening for me.

JP: What was the influence of your mother's artistic passion on you?

BR: I got grounding in art. Every once in a while she would drag us kids to the Toledo Art Museum, which was 50 miles away. I think she needed to be amidst beauty. Had I not had her as a parent, I doubt I would have ever gone to that museum. My knowledge of art history informs my work as a director all the time. You have to know how the perception of the world was reflected during each artistic period, and that influences your decisions about sets, colors and wardrobe.

The other passion that my mother had was movies. There was a channel at the time that came out of Detroit and would air old movies on Sundays. We would always watch them. They showed movies with Judy Garland and Mickey Rooney, or Bette Davis or Clark Gable. I got a really strong grounding in old movies, and I loved them.

JP: Did television play a role in your life growing up?

BR: No. We weren't allowed to watch television except for Sunday nights. I could watch *Lassie* and Jackie Gleason's show and *The Ed Sullivan Show*. That was it. Otherwise the TV was not on in our house. My parents were more in favor of being productive. They would rather have us read or do art projects than have us sit around like slobs and watch TV. Isn't it funny that that is what I do now? I make TV for other people to watch.

JP: Was your family spiritual or religious?

BR: Yes. I was raised Catholic and went to Catholic school.

JP: Can you tell me about your dad?

BR: He had his own business as an architect and he specialized in churches and schools. I think in another time, he would have been an artist also. Architecture was an aesthetic pursuit, but it was a business as opposed to being an artistic endeavor. He was raised to be very practical. He was one of 11 children. And, you know, you were supposed to do something that could make money and you could support your family. So he was an architect. I used to go with him to his projects in the evening or weekends because I was the oldest child. He would go to check construction. I still love the smell of freshly sawed wood.

He would talk to the contractor and I'd wander around within the half-built structure. The benefit of that today is that I can read floor plans really well.

JP: What role do you think the changes of the 1960s played for you as you were growing up? Was there an awareness of the cultural revolution happening around norms of sexuality and drug culture?

BR: I remember being in second grade when the Beatles first appeared on *Ed Sullivan* and what an explosion that was. It was a new time, but I didn't know that then. I was just radical about the Beatles, like everybody else. But you have to remember that I was in a very protected Midwestern town. I understood that there was this turn from '50s conservatism to hippies. And at the end of the '60s, the Vietnam War was on the news every night. But in terms of everything else, I was a goody-two-shoes kind of girl. There were no drugs. There was no drinking, really. There was no craziness. There was no rebellion. I have often thought about how different it was to grow up in a small Midwestern town vs. growing up in L.A. or New York. It was very protected. Very much in our own bubble apart from the world.

JP: What were your aspirations as a young girl?

BR: First I wanted to be a ballerina. Then I thought I would be a TV news anchorperson. I worked at a cable station out of my hometown when I was in high school. And I was the hostess of two shows. I got a national cable TV award as a hostess when I was 17. I also worked at the station at night. We used to run the old TV show *The Avengers*, and it came to the station in film cans. My job was to thread the projector. That's how we were showing it, from a projector.

JP: As you got into college, were you aware of the challenges facing a young woman in the world regarding sexism?

BR: No. I don't remember having those feelings at all, that the world could be against me because I'm a woman. Nope. Never crossed my mind.

JP: When did you first decide you wanted to be in TV?

BR: Starting as a freshman in college, I began working at the public PBS TV station. I started there in a division that had to do with going to classrooms in northwest Ohio, like elementary classrooms, and putting on shows or getting them to watch the PBS shows. It was sort of a traveling internship.

After working in the educational division, I began working as part of the crew. First I was running camera and then I became a producer and director of various shows and also an on-camera talent. I was part of the talent pool for everything the station did. Like if we were covering a parade, let's say. I was also the host of *The Chemistry Bowl*, which was like *Jeopardy!* only all about chemistry. I didn't understand it but somebody had to ask the questions. I also did the station's voiceovers.

Working there in college was a way for me to be in control of my own self and my contributions. That was the way that I saw it. I'm there alone in front of the camera or I'm there alone at the control panel with no input from anybody else. And I think that sense of independence and that sense of doing it on my own was hugely important to me. So I thought I'd be in television.

JP: So the PBS station work was a side job that was separate from your formal college education?

BR: Yes. The school and the station were affiliated but the station was two blocks away. My master's degree was in radio, television and film. But there really wasn't much schooling regarding that happening at the college. The whole education I received happened in the PBS station.

JP: It sounds like you were comfortable doing technical tasks. Was that unusual? Were there other women in the program at the time?

BR: I don't think so. But honestly, after all this time I've never asked myself that question. I'm sure there were other women there. I just don't remember other women running camera or anything. Truthfully, as I'm talking to you, I feel like, "Wow. I was really unaware of what was happening around me. I was just doing my thing." That probably wasn't very smart. Or maybe it was smart because I wasn't letting anything stand in my way. I was just doing it.

JP: You grew up in a place where the role of women was probably more traditional and conservative than in the world of Hollywood where you ended up. At that moment in time as a young person, did you ever feel that your future was limited by being a woman?

BR: No, I didn't. My parents were very supportive. They always said to me, "You can do anything." And when I look back on it, I think, "Wow. Why did I, this young girl from Ohio, think I could make it in Hollywood?" I think I just didn't know any better. Honestly, I never even thought that as a female, the deck would be stacked against me. I just kept going. I think it was ignorance more than anything else. I didn't realize that there was discrimination against women in Hollywood. And I had a boss, Bruce Paltrow, who was way ahead of the times who gave me my shot. He was known for giving people their opportunity to jump ahead.

JP: You mentioned a friend who played a role in your move to Hollywood. Was she another student?

BR: Yes. It was through my college work at the PBS station that I met a woman who had moved to Hollywood about three years earlier. Her name was Michele Gallery. It's a fantastic story because Michele wrote a fan letter to Mary Tyler Moore, and it must have been great because out of that letter she weirdly got a job in the accounting department at Mary Tyler Moore Enterprises [MTM]. Then she worked her way up to become a story editor on *Lou Grant*.

Three years later, when I was getting my master's degree at Bowling Green, Michele came back to work on a documentary out of the PBS station. I went to see her in person and said, "I'm coming to California. Can I call you?" I owe her a great deal because when I landed in Los Angeles in 1978, the first thing I did was call Michele. She put me on hold and called the H.R. person at MTM and said, "Could you meet this friend of mine?" Then Michele came back on the line with me and said, "Okay, you have an interview at three o'clock on Monday." So I interviewed with the H.R. person about being a secretary. Today they would call it a PA, but then it was called a secretary. I also interviewed that day with Mark Tinker, one of the producers of *The White Shadow*. Bruce Paltrow was the boss but he was out of town at the time. The next Wednesday, a secretary quit and Mark hired me to start the following Monday. So a week after I arrived in California, I was the secretary on *The White Shadow* for CBS, produced by MTM. Honestly, that was just one phone call. It's not even like I got here and struggled. A week after I got here, I had a job. When Bruce Paltrow returned to the office, I was the new person sitting at the desk. And I was Bruce and Mark's secretary for the entire run of *The White Shadow*, which was three years. I learned so much there. I answered all the phones, I hand-typed all the scripts. The office was very small for the first 13 episodes. It was Bruce, Mark, a writer named Marc Rubin, an associate producer named Scott Brazil and myself. Abby Singer was the production manager, but his office was down the hall. Isn't that amazing? I made $175 a week as a secretary.

JP: Was that enough to live on at the time?

BR: It was a little challenging because my husband was in law school. He didn't work so I supported us.

JP: What was behind your decision to come to L.A. in the first place?

BR: The summer I graduated from graduate school, I married my high school sweetheart, and he wanted to apply to law schools. During the winter before I graduated, we had a big blizzard. We were snowed in for days, sitting around talking about possible law schools for him to apply to. And we said, "Let's go to California." For me to work in television, the two choices were New York or California. So we came to California and he went to law school at Pepperdine. We had a thousand dollars and a 1966 Mustang. We moved into somebody's house in Malibu where we just had a bedroom and a bathroom. But we weren't there long because there was one of the big Malibu fires in 1978. So we moved into an apartment in Reseda.

JP: You mentioned that you were typing scripts. Were the writers handwriting them and then you would have to type them out?

BR: Yes. It was pre-computer. I actually played a big role in MTM's move to computers. This was probably 1981. I went around to various companies and had them show me how their computers worked. They were called word processors then. I remember that the text was green on the screen. But I never got to work with them because by then I had moved on and I wasn't typing scripts anymore.

JP: So you did three years as a secretary on *The White Shadow* and then Bruce Paltrow promoted you.

BR: Yes. It was a big leap to associate producer. That meant I supervised all of post-production. And at that time, it was just me. A secretary in the office could type up things and print them out for me. But otherwise it was just me. I didn't have final approval of picture editing. That was Bruce and Mark, but I did everything else. I supervised ADR and the loop group. I did the spotting session with the composer. We had a full orchestra for doing the score and I was the one in the booth saying, "Could you do this? Could you do that?" Good thing I took piano lessons for ten years. I supervised the sound mix. I would supervise the color correcting at night. I would start at seven o'clock and usually get out around midnight. Everything in post-production was mine. Bruce and Mark would see a final picture cut and then they wouldn't see the show again until it aired. They didn't really want to participate in it once they had approved final cut. I guess they trusted me to supervise all the post work myself. It was crazy.

JP: Your credit was associate producer. Would that now be called post-production supervisor? Or would you even be getting a solid producer credit for doing those tasks now?

BR: Probably a solid producer credit. I'm sure I made a billion mistakes, especially at the beginning because I had to learn the craft. I just jumped from a producer's secretary to associate producer who was supervising the entire post-production of a network show. At the time, there was no training for it. They supervised me for, like, the first four episodes. But after that, they were like, "Okay, you do it."

JP: Was that unusual?

BR: I'm sure it was.

JP: You went from being a secretary to being an associate producer supervising post-production and being in charge of a lot of men. Was there any pushback against you?

BR: No. I think I was just so focused on what I was doing. Along the way, there were men who were resistant, especially when I started directing. But I would say that as an associate producer, I never felt I was being disrespected. I don't remember that at all. When

I started directing the very first episode I did of *St. Elsewhere*, one of the actors was completely offended that a young 28-year-old woman was his director. And he was very hard on me. To this day, it was probably the most difficult experience I have had because he was an alcoholic and was so rude and horrible. But I knew him well because I'd been an associate producer on the show for three and a half seasons.

And then there were some crew people along the way, you know, older grips and stuff like that, who were questioning of me. But actually the worst one was a DP that I worked with. And this was only, like, five years ago. He was just a jerk and he treated every woman director on the show the same way. He was very disrespectful to the point that the A-camera operator apologized for the way the DP behaved. But it wasn't about me at all. That was just the way he was.

JP: What did you want to do when you first came to Hollywood?

BR: Anything. I wanted to be in the movies but not as an actor. I wanted to be a producer or a director or a writer. I tried writing. Scott Brazil and I wrote a script for *The White Shadow* and it was probably okay. But writing was sort of a dead end for me at that time and place. So then I turned my attention to directing. If I can't be a writer, maybe I can be a director. And it suited me way better because of who I am. I'm not good at sitting in a room by myself typing away.

When I came to L.A., I didn't really know what directors did. I didn't know what anybody did. I mean, I would watch old movies and I would see the credits, but I didn't really know what was involved. When I was a secretary on *The White Shadow*, I got to observe directors for the first time. The director at the beginning of *The White Shadow* was a man named Jackie Cooper who had been a child actor and worked his way up. He was a really old-fashioned Hollywood male. He was loud and brash. He smoked cigars and wore cowboy boots and had this commanding way on set. When he directed *The White Shadow*, he would be very tough on the young men playing the basketball players. Jackie Cooper was my example of what a director is, and how a director behaves.

So when I first started directing, that's what I thought I had to be like. Clearly that wasn't going to work for me because I wasn't anything like him. It took me a little while to figure out how to be as a director. I didn't have any mentors or anybody to look up to. Eventually I figured out that I had to be the best version of myself that I could be. My modus operandi was love, not fear, to be kind and sweet and nice but also decisive. There is nothing about being kind, sweet and nice that belays being a decisive, clear and visionary leader. It just took me a while, but I got around to understanding that's the way I had to be as a director.

JP: How did you get your first opportunity to direct?

BR: I just kept bugging my boss, Bruce Paltrow, for years and years. After *The White Shadow* ended and we were working on *St. Elsewhere*, I was still working as an associate producer in charge of post-production. I started saying to Bruce, "I want to direct, I want to direct." I took an acting class for five years while I was an associate producer to better understand the actors' point of view, vocabulary and the process they went through. I wasn't a director in the class. I acted. I was not very good. However, it let me walk a mile in their shoes, which to this day makes me an actor's director. And being the associate producer in charge of post-production was a fantastic education because I saw every frame of every episode a hundred times. What did the director shoot that worked? What didn't work? Can we manipulate the film to make it work or not? What was visually interesting? What wasn't so good? It was an education in camera that at the time I didn't realize I was getting.

In season four of *St. Elsewhere*, I was 28 and Bruce Paltrow gave me my shot. He left me completely alone. Everybody did. I was on an adrenaline high the whole time. It was the best seven consecutive days of my life. When my episode was done, Bruce called me into his office and closed the door, which was a very bad sign. He paced up and down and yelled at me for not being a good director, for not assuming the mantle and not leading people, as I should have. In hindsight, I think Bruce was saying, "This is a tough business, little girl. And if you want to stay in it, you have to get tougher. This is what happens. People will yell at you." But two things happened. First, I saw my episode and it was really quite good. And secondly, I went in the next day and told Bruce, "I'm really sorry I did such a bad job. Please give me another shot." And later that same season, Bruce gave me another episode.

The next season, which was season five, I directed another episode but I was still the associate producer on the show. At that point, I went to Bruce and said, "I would really like to have a producer credit. I've been associate producer for five seasons. I really think a bump up is appropriate." And he said, "No. I already have a producer. If you're doing post-production, you're the associate producer." And I, being quite full of myself at that point, said, "Okay. I think I have to leave then." And he said, "Okay, I'll give you a directing slot for next season so everybody knows that we like you. Goodbye and good luck." And I thought, "Oh my gosh. What have I done?"

Now this is really a strange thing, but here's what happened. Bruce had been a best friend with a producer named Jay Tarses. And at that time, Jay had created this show called *The Slap Maxwell Story* starring Dabney Coleman. It was partly because their friendship had broken apart, but when Jay heard that I had left, he called to ask me if I wanted to direct an episode of *The Slap Maxwell Story*. It was like Jay's "F you" to Bruce. You know, if you're not gonna hold onto her, I'm gonna take her. The show was a half-hour single-camera, and it was a very sweet show. It felt like it was in the 1950s. It shot in a warehouse in North Hollywood. After day four of dailies, they asked me if I would do another one and I ended up doing eight episodes that season. It was my first season as a freelance director.

Jay and Dabney Coleman had a falling out, so there was no producer on set. It was just me alone directing. This is the one time where being a woman was in some ways not to my advantage because Dabney could be really hard on directors. He just didn't have patience for people who weren't completely on their game. So one day pretty early on, he was really rude to me and he made me cry. The next day, he apologized and never did it again. And I never cried on set again, never in all this time. That's not cool and I wasn't going to do it. But after that, because Dabney in his heart of hearts was a Southern gentleman, he was kind to me and horrible to the other male directors. We were a good fit in that regard. And the fact that there was nobody on set allowed me to make a billion mistakes, but also to learn.

JP: It sounds like Bruce Paltrow really saw something in you and believed in you.

BR: Yes. But he did that for a lot of people. There were three actors on *The White Shadow* who wanted to direct, Tim Van Patten, Thomas Carter and Kevin Hooks. Bruce gave all of them the opportunity and was a mentor to them.

JP: After you did *Slap Maxwell*, was your career a pretty steady trajectory?

BR: Well, there are some years that are better than others because there are a lot of factors. In fact, there was one year where I hardly worked. I think I only did one episode. But at that time, all the shows I had worked on the previous season were cancelled and my agent left the agency and I was starting over with somebody else. But also at that point, my son was going into first grade and there was a big part of me that didn't want to be away while he was going to first grade. So I think my own intention played into that as well. But the next year, I got a different agent and I was ready to go back to work. Overall it's been pretty straightforward and pretty even. I usually direct between eight and ten episodes a year. My career has been very straightforward and very profitable for me and very satisfying. But I am in this middle ground of doing broadcast television, which in this day and age has sort of been left behind by streaming television. It's just where my career is and where it's gone. And the only regret I have is that traditional network shows are sort of seen as mediocre television, and I would like to feel like I'm doing superb television. I guess I'm doing superb television within the boundaries of where I'm working. I think the industry perception of me is not as an innovator but rather as a steady continuing director. But that's not sexy or exciting to anybody. So I don't get hired for the new stuff. And it sounds like I'm complaining. I'm not really because I love what I do. It's just that there are other directors who are exploding in terms of industry perception and excitement. I'm not that, I'm just the steady Midwestern girl.

JP: Thanks for sharing that. It's important for people to understand that there's always a space for development and analyzing your career and figuring out if this is where you want to be right now. I think you have a sense of the industry as it's changed over time. What are the changes you've seen?

BR: Well, when I started it was a business of white men because that's who started it and that's how it continued. It's funny because even though it was a business of white men, I didn't see why I couldn't do it. But there were a lot of other women who felt like it wasn't a cool thing to be a woman in this business and that they were being prejudiced against. So they began banging on the doors. In the beginning, I didn't have a lot of patience with that because I had been successful. And actually it had served me really well because very often on a TV series roster of 22 shows, I'd be their only woman director. It was beneficial to me to have that be the case. I also wasn't a big fan of being a victim, which I felt women and people of color were being, victims of the business that doesn't open the doors for them. Again, because I had been successful, I was just sort of impatient with that. But starting about ten years ago, I began to be very active in the DGA. And so I could see other people coming in and what they were saying and how difficult it was for them.

And then I had an experience where the DGA Women's Steering Committee was so raucous and crazy, and was demanding so much because, as they saw it, the business owed it to them. They were playing the victim and that kind of thing. So I became a co-chair of the Women's Steering Committee because I felt like somebody had to get everything back on track. In my opinion, they were harming themselves because of their hysteria. So over the next couple of years, we sort of became more professional. And then eight years ago, I became the teacher in charge of running the Warner Brothers TV Director's Workshop. And that was because my friend Mary Lou Belli and I had written a textbook called *Directors Tell the Story*. The book was motivated because there were so many bad television directors and I would hear it all the time when I would walk onto a set. Crew people and actors would say to me, "You wouldn't believe what the last director did." It was things that were not appropriate behavior. Or the directors just weren't good at the craft. It upset me so much because I felt like I was being tarred with that brush. If the director before me was terrible, they're going to assume the next director coming in is terrible too.

Mary Lou Belli and I talked about it. She had already written some textbooks for actors. I said, "What can I do? I don't want to complain and be another victim." What I thought I could do is write down what I know and share it so other people could be better at it. The first edition of the book came out in 2011 and then in 2013 I started teaching the

Warner Brothers TV Directors Workshop. In 2015, I became the diversity co-chair at the DGA with Todd Holland and we created a program to educate and nurture rising directors in the DGA. I teach the craft workshop and Mary Lou does it with me so the directors can go out better prepared to do the job.

I guess it became clear to me at a certain point that TV directors needed help, and particularly women directors and people of color. My way of helping them was to teach them so that they could be successful in the job. Four years ago, John Landgraf at FX said, "We're going to have a 50-50 roster next year of white males and women and people of color." That was pushing the door open violently because there were not that many people to call upon. But now, because of all the studio and network diversity programs, especially I think the two that I teach, people are better prepared. And most shows are required or encouraged to have a 50-50 directing roster. The show that I'm producer-director on this year didn't make 50 percent. We made 37 percent because the type of show that we have needed for the directors to not necessarily be so new. Sounds like I'm making excuses, but it's the truth. Anyway, point being, there was myself and a few other women who worked in the '80s, '90s and early 2000s. Not a big group of people. Now there is a larger group, and industry wide I don't think there's a prejudice against women or people of color because it's all about, "Are they good? Do they have the skills? Is the show safe in their hands?" Particularly for the actors because they need to feel that the directors know what they're doing.

JP: I know you've been a mentor to a lot of people both directly and indirectly through your book. If there's a 15-year-old girl growing up in Ohio today who wants to be a director, what would you tell her?

BR: I would say that there is a worldview that we pick up. And that worldview might say that your chances are not very good for you to succeed in the way you want to. But just because that's the worldview doesn't mean it has to be *your* experience. Your experience is your own experience. And that happens to me all the time. Say I go on a show and they tell me that some actor is difficult to work with. I take that in, but then I'll let it go. Just because that was someone else's experience doesn't mean it has to be my experience. And the same thing happens for anything that you do. Take in all the wisdom that's given to you but know that it is other people's perspective. It doesn't need to be your perspective. Go your own way and have faith that it will all work out. They call me Pollyanna on set all the time, but I believe in goodness and I believe in positive thinking and I believe in love. And it works for me.

JP: You wrote a blog post that was inspiring and also a little surprising. It was about the feelings of anxiety and uncertainty that you can have when things come to an end. It spoke to me, but I was also surprised because it was written by Bethany Rooney who has done a gazillion episodes, and yet she still has those anxious feelings that come up when you're not sure what is next.

BR: Yes, I do have those feelings. That blog post was inspired because we were coming to the end of the season of *Bull*, which I was the producer-director on this year. When we wrapped, it felt like there was this chasm of not knowing what comes next. Even though I have faith that if the show gets canceled, I'll still work and my career will go on and life is good, I'm still standing at the edge of that precipice going, "Where does that road go? That road just dropped off. Now what do I do?" I don't care how experienced you are, you are still going to feel that way. And it requires faith and it requires trust and it requires self-confidence to say, "I will be okay no matter what." But you're still going to feel those feelings. That's why I wrote it. I knew that if I, as this extremely experienced person, was feeling those things, then everybody else who was along the same path would feel it too.

JP: Does your faith still play a role in your life?

BR: Yes. It's a spiritual faith. I would not characterize myself as Catholic so much anymore. But Christian, yes. I have a very strong relationship or belief in a higher power. For me, it's a very positive thing to have that higher power behind me, supporting me, raising me up, because if I had to feel like I was doing it on my own, it would be so much harder.

JP: I think that's important for people to hear because Hollywood has this reputation for being a sort of atheist hellhole.

BR: That's not me. And even though I've been in this business for 40 years, I can't be turned into that. I can't be turned into a loud, cynical, sarcastic, bombastic person because it's not me.

Payman Benz

The first thing I realize about Payman Benz is that he is funny. His smile, his laugh, his self-deprecating manner—it all draws you in and sets you at ease. Comedy has been such an integral part of his life for so long that it seems embedded in his DNA.

Payman is undoubtedly the most prolific filmmaker I interviewed. The sheer quantity of sketches and short films he has created is stunning. If he were never paid a cent to direct, he would still be doing it every single day. He would forgo food, water and air before giving up his true passion.

· ·

PAYMAN BENZ: I was born in Iran during the revolution. When I was six months old, my whole family left. Then we went back again because one of my dad's friends was, like, "It's cool now." But actually it wasn't cool. When I was four, we had to leave for good. I grew up in Silicon Valley, in Mountain View. I grew up obsessed with comedy. The way I assimilated was making kids laugh.

JACOB PINGER: Do you remember living in Iran?

PB: I remember they woke me up to say we were leaving. It was the middle of the night. And they said, "We're going to your aunt's house in England." I remember I had *Jungle Book* wallpaper.

JP: Growing up in Silicon Valley, did you feel different because of where your family came?

PB: I definitely felt different. The kids embraced me because I could make them laugh. That was my ticket out of being bullied. Kids would make comments here and there, but I was always funnier than everybody else. And not to say that I'm hilarious, but the kids I was around weren't that funny. So it was easy for me. I was watching a lot of adult comedy when I was a kid. *Cheers* was my favorite show in second grade. I would recap it to my friends at school. In the seventh grade, I was into *Seinfeld*. I was always into comedy that was ahead of what my friends

Payman Benz cut his teeth writing, directing and editing hundreds of short comedy videos before landing his first "real" directing job (Robyn Von Swank).

were watching. The times I really felt different were when I would go to a friend's house. That's when I realized, "Oh, I'm the weird brown kid." People were nice but you knew there was some unspoken uneasiness. Los Altos was a pretty liberal area but it was also a wealthy area. I knew a lot of kids whose parents were loaded, and we weren't. I felt that difference a lot, but I could have grown up somewhere more difficult.

JP: Was your family religious?

PB: My parents say they're Muslim. But I'll be honest. The only time I ever saw a Koran growing up was if somebody in the family was sick or dying. Then they would dust it off. They're not religious. I think they believe in God and treating people well and stuff. But I don't even know how many times Muslims pray per day. That's how little I know. It was all about figuring out our new country and surviving. My dad was working and then my mom started working, and my brother and I were in school right away. I think they tried to retain some traditional values, but it was difficult because I was four and my brother was nine. We came here and thought, "This place is awesome! The toys are better. The TV shows are better. The music is better. Everything is better." My parents were trying to hold on and be proud of where they come from. I was too young to fully understand that. My brother and I were just like, "No way, dude. This place is great. And we don't have to run away from here. We ran *to* here. So this is my home." It had to be difficult for my parents even though they were already pretty westernized before they came to America.

Even today, the majority of Iran loves America. The people you see in that footage chanting, "Death to America," they don't represent the majority. Everybody else is just afraid.

JP: Was the community you grew up in largely white?

PB: Yes. The Bay Area has always been pretty diverse, but there was nobody in my elementary school that was Iranian. There was one other Iranian kid in junior high and on the first day of school the teachers were, like, "You two should meet." It was almost forcing a friendship on us.

JP: What did your family think of your interest in adult comedy at such a young age?

PB: They didn't really mind. I learned English so quickly, way faster than my brother, way faster than my parents. We got here on a Thursday or Friday and by Monday, because I was watching *Sesame Street* all weekend, I was able to translate at the grocery store for my mom. Basic stuff, like lettuce and water. I was four. I was a total sponge.

JP: You learned English from *Sesame Street*? That's so awesome.

PB: Yeah. And *Mister Rogers* too. We had the TV on PBS and I was just ingesting it all weekend. I was able to translate pretty well. If my parents were watching *Cheers* with me, I don't think they understood. Even in the second grade, I understood all the innuendos and got why it was funny. I got that Norm was obsessed with beer. At night I'd be in my room watching sitcoms. We had this old wooden box TV in the living room. And then my dad decided to replace it with a big TV. This was the mid–80s. He gave me the old wooden box TV, and it was the type that when you turned it on, it made that crazy sound. It was so loud. I loved *Saturday Night Live*. Even when I was in sixth grade, I was into it. So on Saturday nights after my parents went to bed, I would turn the volume down on that big wooden TV and put my ear against the speaker to watch *SNL*. That was the show that I didn't want them to know about because it was past my bedtime.

JP: So you went from watching *Sesame Street* to *Cheers*.

PB: Yeah, almost straight away. That's funny.

JP: In an American family, there are people who can play the role of introducing you to

American culture. But in your family, maybe it wasn't the case. It sounds like you absorbed those cultural lessons through TV comedy.

PB: It's weird how much I learned about life through sitcoms. I learned that the characters that are good to people have things work out for them, and if you're bad, things don't work out for you. I learned about family structure, what a sibling relationship is supposed to be like and what a parental relationship is supposed to be like. I was teaching my parents more about the culture than they were teaching me.

JP: What did they do here?

PB: At first, my father had a gas station. He worked in it every day. My mom was doing daycare at the school I was in. Eventually she started working at a boutique. She loved that. When the owner decided he wanted to sell the store, he sold it to my parents. My mom still owns it and works in it every day. She's had the boutique for 30 something years now. Eventually, my dad bought a building and was renting it out, and he bought a car wash. Now he's in real estate development. They've been working nonstop. Even at their age, in their sixties and seventies, they won't stop working. I think that's where my work ethic comes from.

JP: At what point as a kid did you realize that you could employ comedy in your own life?

PB: I think it was as soon as I got into pre-school. That was just the way I assimilated. I started making kids laugh. A lot of times it was regurgitating the stuff I had seen on TV, or doing impressions or just being silly. That's the way I survived and learned how to navigate school.

JP: Were you good at school?

PB: No. Well, at first I was. Through third grade, I was so good at school that the principal met with my parents and told them how well I was doing. And then they gave me an IQ test. This tells you how cocky my parents were, my test score was apparently so high that my parents threw a party for the family. What a horrible idea! Imagine the shit-talking everyone did after that party. Then in the fourth grade, I got introduced to baseball and I just stopped giving a shit about school. Also, that's around when I started getting into *SNL*. By junior high, I knew I was going to work in comedy one day, although I didn't know in what capacity. I should have had a backup plan but I didn't. I was a solid C student all the way through high school and even college.

JP: How did you come to the conclusion that you would work in comedy one day?

PB: The first time I thought that comedy would be fun to do was in the fourth grade when my family took a vacation in New York City. We didn't have HBO at home, but the hotel did. Howie Mandel had a stand-up special on HBO and he was so silly and absurd back in the day. He was doing fart machine jokes and stuff. I had never seen an adult be silly. I remember watching that and thinking, "That's his job? That's what he gets to do? Man, that looks fun." I didn't even know he got paid a lot of money. That's when I first started thinking about the idea of working in comedy.

In junior high, I was a weird kid. It wasn't that I was unpopular exactly, but I was kind of a dork. When Adam Sandler and that group got on *SNL*, it made me proud to be weird. His whole thing was being this kind of uneasy guy who was barely getting his words out, but he was funnier than everybody. I wanted to be Adam Sandler.

JP: So was your initial thought to be a performer?

PB: That's what I thought I was going to do. I would do little bits for my friends. I would write songs about the other kids at school, but only perform them for my two best friends. I wanted to do stand-up. That was the original hope. After high school, I went to a junior college that was five minutes from my parents' house. I knew some guys in the school who were coming up in the hip-hop scene and they were having this big showcase at the school. They asked me to emcee it. That was actually my first time on stage. They knew I wanted to do stand-up and this guy basically called my bluff. I had to do this 15-minute opener and also stuff in between the music. I did really well at that first show. Then I started doing open mikes and did pretty well. I never bombed, I never killed, but I was always able to make it go pretty okay. But the thing I couldn't get over was the anxiety in the 24 hours leading up to a performance. I would drive there and have to convince myself not to make a U-turn. Once I got up there and started talking, I'd be fine.

The other thing I didn't like about stand-up was just how bummed the other comedians were. I didn't know about the "sad clown" side of comedy. I knew comedy as something light. You just make people laugh. Now I know there's a definite dark side to it. But all these guys were like, "Wait until you have a drinking problem. Wait until you have a drug problem." It was a really sad environment. So I told myself, "I'm just going to be a writer."

JP: So the performing thing didn't last that long.

PB: It was less than a year. I got my AA from community college and then I decided to drop out of school entirely. I was just kind of working odd jobs. One day I was hanging out with an old buddy and he happened to be watching *The Big Lebowski*. It was the scene where John Turturro is bowling in slow motion. I had never seen a comedy scene that looked like that. And I lost it. Up until that point, I didn't really know what the job of a director was. My buddy explained the Coen Brothers to me, and I thought, "That's what I'm going to do. I'm going to write and direct." It was that moment. It was that scene.

I looked at a bunch of schools in the Bay Area to study film. I called San Jose State, which was 15 minutes away. I asked, "Do you guys have cameras that students can check out?" And they said yes. So I signed up and went to San Jose State. Then my grades skyrocketed because now I gave a shit about what I was learning. I got Adobe Premiere and was filming my old dog and just taught myself how to edit one night. I started making shorts. It was all comedy and it was getting a great reception in my film classes.

Right when I finished school, the last short I made got into the 2005 Newport Beach Film Festival. The short was called *Needle Anus*. We were the talk of the festival. It showed to a full house and there was a roaring response. I still get chills thinking about it because it was the first time I had really experienced that. That was when I realized, "I think I can maybe work in this industry." I moved to L.A. and lived with my brother. This was January 2006. Six months later, my buddy Sean from San Jose State came down and moved in with me. We got his shorts and my shorts and put them together to create a quasi–production company.

JP: What were you doing to make rent?

PB: I had saved a bunch of money but it was going quickly. I got a job at this small company that would shoot little web series. They were also filming stand-up at the Ice House Comedy Club. They would broadcast it on different cell phone networks. My job was programming, basically data entry. I was paid $350 a week and working about 70 hours. But something told me I was supposed to take that job. There were just three or four other people in the company. One of the guys I worked with was friends with Nick Swardson and a bunch of other comics. One night, he invited me to the Improv. We went to the show and hung out with some of the comics afterwards. I really got along with those guys.

At that time, my buddy Sean and I were putting our stuff on YouTube and MySpace Comedy. At first our friends back home were seeing it. Then L.A. comedians started seeing our stuff. After a couple of months, Nick Swardson asked me to shoot a sketch for him that he wanted to show the next night at the Improv. I went to his place and shot for three or four hours. I drove back to Hollywood and cut it on my laptop. The DVD was burning in my passenger seat while I drove to the Improv to deliver it. Nick showed it as part of his set and it killed. A week or so later, Nick told me that he showed the piece to Adam Sandler and that Sandler loved it. I couldn't believe that Adam Sandler saw a thing that I shot. It blew my mind. Then all of a sudden, comedians started asking me to shoot their stuff because everyone knew Nick. That project with Nick was the first time I got paid to direct. He gave me 300 bucks. I couldn't believe it. I just got paid! Then other people started paying me to shoot or edit stuff for them.

In 2007, there was a magazine called *Moving Pictures Magazine*. I don't know if it still exists, but when it started Sean and I entered a short film contest that they had, and we won best narrative short. The magazine decided to have their awards ceremony at Sundance in Park City, just to get some exposure. So they flew me, Sean and our DP Chris Darnell to Park City and gave us the award. It was really fun. We ran into Gregg Schwenk, the head of the Newport Beach Film Festival. We had known him for years. I had a couple drinks that night. (Side note: I never drink.) And I was feeling a little confident. So I said to Gregg, "Hey, man, we have a bunch of shorts no one's ever seen. And there's a lot of really funny shorts on the Internet. What if you just gave us a program in the Newport Beach Festival?" And Gregg shook my hand and said, "You got it." And we were like, "Oh my God!" So Sean and I started scouring the Internet for some shorts to screen. The final program we put together ended up being eight shorts that we made and four that we found. A friend sent me a short that starred this kid, Tyler Spindel. I selected it for the program and a few weeks before the festival, my friend told me that Tyler is Adam Sandler's nephew. So all of a sudden there was this other connection to Sandler.

The day of our program at the festival arrived and I was a nervous wreck. One of my buddies came in and told me, "I just saw Adam Sandler in the parking lot." And I was, like, "Oh no." I wanted to leave. I was freaked out. Then Sandler walked in. I went up and introduced myself. I said, "It's really great to meet you. You're my hero and this is like meeting Mickey Mantle." And then I said, "I also did that short for Nick." And Sandler says, "You did that short?" And I go, "Yeah!" I was freaking out.

All our shorts screened during the program, including some that I acted in. We had a Q&A afterwards and I thought Sandler had left. But when it was done, I was walking up the aisle and Adam was walking towards me. And he said, "Come here, I want to talk to you." He took me aside and I was shaking. He said, "You're really fucking good, man. The directing, the cutting, the writing, the acting. You're really fucking funny, man." I'm so bad at talking to people, and I was so intimidated that all I said back to Sandler was, "Thanks, man. You're good too." And he chuckled because he knew that I beefed it. But then we started talking. He goes, "Let me ask you a question. Can you do a Palestinian accent?" And I said, "No, but I can learn one." And he said, "I'm doing a movie and I'm gonna have Nick call you." I didn't know what he was talking about. It ended up being *You Don't Mess with the Zohan*. So it happened to be that he was filming a movie that summer about a bunch of Middle Eastern guys, and he just happened to watch a Persian guy make an audience laugh. So it was perfect timing. I didn't think anything of it besides Adam Sandler loves my shit.

The next morning, Sandler's cousin Tyler called me and said, "Before I fly home, I have an idea for a sketch. Do you want to come over and shoot it?" So I got my camera and drove over and we shot it. Then right as we were wrapping up, Tyler got a call and he said,

"Hey, my uncle is going to come by." And fucking Sandler shows up. He sees me and he goes, "Hey, Payman, I showed your website to everyone in the office today. Everyone thinks you're really funny." I was just really comfortable with him. I was cracking jokes and making him laugh. I'm not a networker, so I didn't want anything from him. I was just thinking, "Whatever. I'm just gonna make this dude laugh." Ever since I was a kid, if someone intimidated me, I always tried to make them laugh.

So Sandler said, "What do you want to do? Do you want to direct or do you want to act?" He was basically asking me what career I wanted. And I said, "Well, I want to direct but I just want to make comedies." So Sandler said, "I'm producing this movie and we haven't met with a director that we're excited about yet. Maybe we'll call you about it." At this point, I'd now lived in Los Angeles for 15 months, and so I was not thinking much of it. Later, Tyler called me and he said, "My uncle loves you. Call his office tomorrow." By the time I got home, there was an email from Heather Parry's office. She was the head of development at Sandler's company. In the email, the assistant told me that Heather would like me to come in for a general this week. I didn't even know what a general was. I had to call somebody and ask, "What's a general?" Five days later, I was driving to Sony. It was the first time I'd ever been on a studio lot. I pulled up and the guy thought I was making a delivery. He was being really shitty to me. I walked in the offices and there were pictures of Chris Farley and Kevin Nealon. It was my childhood of *SNL* on the walls. And I was losing my mind. I went to Heather's office and she told me, "Adam really loves you. And we think your stuff is really funny." She said, "We have this movie and he wants to consider you for it." It ended up being *The House Bunny*, and they didn't have a director yet. And then she said, "Adam wants to see you before you go." So we went to this little outdoor area and Adam was out there learning how to cut hair for *Zohan*. There was a mannequin head on a pole and he's cutting hair. This old lady stylist was looking over his shoulder telling him how to do it. Adam said, "I want to talk to you about directing *The House Bunny*, but I really want you to audition for *Zohan*. I want you to punch the script up. I want you to send me some jokes." So now it was the first time in my life that I was holding a real script. And I looked down at it and it said, "Written by Adam Sandler, Judd Apatow and Robert Smigel." And I said, "You want me to punch up these three guys?" And he said, "You're fucking funny. Do it." So I went home and wrote a bunch of jokes and sent them in. I don't know if anything got in. But it was just this trust he had in me.

About a week later, I went in to audition for *Zohan*. I was like, "Whatever. I don't want to be an actor. I don't care about this." And the second they called my name, my mouth went dry, my voice started quivering and I forgot everything. I went in the room and said, "Guys, I'm not an actor. I should not be here. Let me explain how I got here." And I told them the story and they were laughing in the room. I did the audition and I didn't do that well. Obviously, I didn't get the role. Then a month or so later, Heather called me and asked if I wanted to read the script for *The House Bunny*. Within minutes, a messenger showed up at my door with the script. I read the script and it was really funny. I called her back and I said, "Obviously I'd like to direct this." And she said, "Okay, great. You're going to meet with me, Jack Giarraputo and Doug Belgrad tomorrow." And she hung up. I Googled Doug Belgrad because I didn't know who that was. He was the head of Columbia Pictures. I was losing my mind. So I called Chuck Martin, the only friend of mine that had directed anything real. He was a writer and supervising producer on *Arrested Development*. I called Chuck and said, "I'm meeting for a movie tomorrow. What do I do?" He gave me a bunch of pointers and I went into the meeting the next day. It was me, Heather, Jack and Doug Belgrad.

Doug Belgrad said, "We've seen everything you've done." And, again, the website was just five or six of my shorts. And I was, like, "The head of Columbia Pictures watched that awful short I did in college?" So we had this meeting and they said, "Tell us your story." And so I was telling them my story. At the end of the meeting, Jack Giarraputo said, "All right, Doug. Tell Payman how he did in his first director meeting." And they said, "You did really great. I can tell you're a great director. I know that you have a bright future. Adam loves you, and that holds a lot of weight here." Then he gave me one note that I'll never forget: "Don't be afraid to tear the script apart next time." And I said, "Really? I was told not to do that." And they said, "No. Do that."

After the meeting, I went outside and I was talking to Heather. Jack came out and said, "You know what? No matter what happens here, you're one of our guys now." And I was, like, "What? I'm one of your guys now? This is crazy." They asked, "Who's your agent? Who's your manager?" I said, "I don't have any of that stuff. I have three friends in this city." So Heather Parry called all the agencies and said, "Adam loves this guy. You have to sign him." CAA called me, UTA called me and ICM called me.

As time went by, I knew I wasn't getting *The House Bunny* because the budget had gone up and the studio was like, "Who is this guy?" I kept hearing from other people that Adam wanted me to do it and was really pushing for me. But at some point, the studio pointed out that this guy has literally never worked with a production designer. Actually, I didn't even know what a production designer was. And they couldn't give a $25–30 million movie to the guy who didn't know what a production designer was. I would have ruined it for sure. But a year and a half after moving to L.A., my producing partner Sean and I signed with UTA. If anything was a confirmation, it was that. I knew how lucky I was. But I also remember in that first meeting with UTA when I said I wanted to direct TV and movies, and they were like, "Slow down. You do stuff online. You do stuff on YouTube. There's a stigma attached. You have a long way to go before you can do real TV." I never forgot that.

JP: Not to get too off-track, but what does it mean when an agent "hip pockets" someone?

PB: Hip pocketing is when an agent does not technically represent you. You're not actually their client, but they will represent you in a specific deal. They might help get you a meeting, and still take ten percent of the deal, but you're not really their client. It's a way of keeping you at arm's length, but still making a little money off you in case you happen to land something.

JP: So what was the intended role of your agents at UTA?

PB: We had a digital agent who was sending us out on meetings with companies that had money for a web series. At the same time, we were also going on generals at TV studios and movie studios. But that was just so people could get to know us. We pitched a sketch show called *Comedy Gumbo* to Crackle, which was called Sony C-Spot at the time. It was basically a show with a bunch of our shorts. They bit. We could have hired a crew but it was literally three of us making the show, just me, Sean and our DP friend, Chris. We were doing everything. I was holding the boom, picking up food, directing and producing. I wrote the majority of the show. Sean and I shared the directing and editing. We ended up delivering a ten-episode show that had about 60 sketches in it. They didn't know we were giving them that much. They actually said, "We should've paid you guys more." That show really started the movement for us.

JP: And at that point, you were actually making a living as a filmmaker.

PB: Yeah. It happened quick. Around then, I started meeting comedians who were performing at UCB, like Daveo Mathias. I started shooting a bunch of sketches with them and I felt like I found my sensibility. It was really dark, super-smart, subversive comedy. Some of the sketches we did had great comedy people. Harris Wittles was in one of them. Dave Horwitz, who is a TV writer, Michael Blaiklock. I started directing videos for a sketch group called the Midnight Show. There was zero budget. It was all running around asking for favors. But I started to really find a different level of joy in what I was doing. I was now working with people who were so much funnier than I could ever be. I was looking at things differently and I became such a better director through working with them.

Their videos were getting a lot of views. So all of a sudden there was a new set of eyes on my work. It wasn't just the YouTube eyes. It was industry eyes. That's when stuff really started to accelerate for me.

JP: How were you making a living at this point?

PB: I was sporadically doing branded stuff for Funny or Die and College Humor. I'd also get work as an editor from time to time. I was in L.A. at the perfect time as a comedy director because there were so many companies putting out money and paying people to make short-form stuff. It was the heyday of websites like Funny or Die, College Humor and YouTube comedy videos. There was no shortage of work, it was just a matter of how often you could get it. I would have good months where I could eat out at El Pollo Loco once or twice. And then there were months where I'd be, like, "Holy fuck. How am I gonna pay rent?" It got terrifying many times.

JP: You weren't getting a couple of grand a month from your parents? You were supporting yourself this whole time?

PB: Right. There was one time I asked my parents for money because my dog had an eye surgery and I didn't know what to do. But I was racking up a sizable credit card debt. I lived a really simple lifestyle. I was single for a big chunk of the time. I was like, "It's going to suck now, but this will be worth it later. I'll have a nice dinner in ten years." I decided that I was just going to work. Every year felt like I would get a little closer, but then I would take another step back.

Then I did a web series with this comedian, Dan Levy, for Atom.com, which was Comedy Central's old website. The web series was called *Dan Levy's Laugh Track Mash-ups*. It was the worst title. It was supposed to be directed by Todd Strauss-Schulson, who I had known for a few years. When Todd got hired to direct *A Very Harold and Kumar Christmas*, he told Dan Levy about me and I got hired to direct the web series. Then that summer, Todd recommended me to the writing team of Evan Mann and Gareth Reynolds, who were doing a pilot for MTV. I was already a fan of those guys because I would watch their shorts. I remember it was one of those nights where I was just sitting home thinking, "Man, am I going to just be doing this online shit forever? I'm just going to be doing these sketches." I got a Facebook message from Evan Mann. He said, "I'm doing a pilot presentation for MTV, and Todd said we should look at you. Do you want to read this script?" I read the script and I was freaking out because it was single-camera comedy. To that point, I had only been doing sketches, nothing more than four or five minutes. I met with Evan and Gareth and it went really well. So all of a sudden I'm directing a single-camera comedy pilot presentation for MTV. It was called *Evan and Gareth Save the World*.

My agent called and said, "You have to join the DGA to do this. The problem is that the amount you are getting paid to direct the presentation is less than half of what it costs to join the DGA." To join the DGA was like $9800 then. And to direct this pilot presentation, I was only getting five grand before taxes, and before the agent and manager commissions. So after taxes and commissions I only got $1800. That's what people have to realize. You have to make a lot of money in this industry to make money. Financially, I was fucked.

JP: You couldn't borrow money from your family?

PB: No. It was too much. In the end, the DGA let me do a payment plan, so I got to shoot the presentation. It was my first time with a real crew. I even had extras. MTV loved it. They were over the moon. They gave it to Tony DiSanto, the head of the network, and they told me that Tony yelled out, "They reinvented the sitcom!" We were positive that we had a show. We were going to go out to this big, expensive sushi dinner that night but we had to delay it for some reason. And thank God we delayed the dinner. The next morning, *Deadline Hollywood* reported that Tony DiSanto was leaving MTV. Our showrunner, Jim Biederman, informed us that the new person in charge of a network never takes the old person's shows. So MTV ended up passing on *Evan and Gareth Save the World*. We were devastated.

My 2011 was really slow. I was just getting enough work to pay the bills. It was like, "What the fuck happened? I was right there in television." That was the first time I actually started to get a little bummed. I started thinking maybe I should be further along. I think it took me about a week to shake out of it. An early lesson that I learned in L.A. is that your career is a wave. When it's down, it's going to be up again at some point. And when it's up, it might go down again. So don't get ahead of yourself. There are a lot of people celebrating before they even get to the end zone. My thinking was, "Don't be celebrating. Be getting better. It will be fine. Just go with the flow and keep working. It will work itself out." In 2012, Evan Mann and Gareth Reynolds got another show at MTV called *Failosophy*. It had recreations in the vein of *Drunk History* and they needed a director for the recreations. I got hired and went to New York for a month. It was my first time traveling to direct.

Meanwhile, I was still doing stuff for the UCB Midnight Show. But the branded work I was doing for Funny or Die and College Humor was really paying the bills. All of a sudden, people in the industry started to know who I was. I was hearing from people, "Oh, I heard your name in this or that room." I could feel myself getting closer.

Then in 2013, I got asked to be a segment director on *Jimmy Kimmel Live*. It came out of nowhere. It was because of a producer friend named Daniel Kellison, who had previously brought me in to work on the YouTube channel JASH. Daniel is one of Kimmel's close friends. Jimmy went to Daniel and said, "I need a director who can handle branded content. I'm having trouble finding someone that can make the brands happy but can also make it funny." Daniel told Jimmy about me. I went in for a test run and they said, "We want you to come on full-time." I started in August 2013. And now all of a sudden, I had a day job.

This was the first time I would shoot something and know it was going to be on television. It was a weird feeling. Jimmy was great to me. But it was a bummer because I was still doing branded stuff. I was there about five or six months when my friend, director Peter Atencio called me, and said, "I want to talk to you about *Key and Peele*. When the final season starts in a few months, I will have to bring in another director. Do you want to do it?" I was like, "Are you serious? I'd love to."

So I went to the executive producer, Jill Leiderman, and said, "I think it's time for me to move on. I feel like this branded stuff is starting to get to me." She said, "We knew the day you arrived that you wouldn't be here long." It was hard to leave, but I knew that it was time for another leap because I could feel myself getting too comfortable. I realized I made my best stuff when I was terrified about how I was going to pay rent. The fear of the unknown just made me work harder. I liked that hunger.

JP: Give me a ballpark figure of how many sketches you had directed by this point.

PB: At least 200. A majority of those I wasn't paid for. But that's the stuff that made the biggest difference. The free stuff is what really put my name out there. I left Kimmel and then directed over a dozen sketches on *Key and Peele*. It was an unbelievable experience because I was inside my favorite sketch show. I ran with it and for the first time I felt like a director. I got a different level of confidence. One day I was in post and I ran into Jay Martel, who was one of the *Key and Peele* showrunners. He had this other show that had just been picked up by TV Land called *Teachers*. He asked me, "Do you ever want to do single-camera half-hour?" I said, "Dude, that's the only thing I want to do." Later that day, my agent called me and said, "TV Land wants you to meet with the girls who created *Teachers*." I was thinking that it wasn't going to happen because I had already met for a couple single-camera shows and didn't get them. But I still went in to meet on *Teachers*. Afterwards I hear that they really liked me, but because of budget and scheduling issues, one director would have to do the full season, so I was probably not going to get it. It was a long shot. And I was thinking they were going to go with a veteran director. Then one day Jay Martel sends me an e-mail that said, "Get ready to not sleep. You're getting the whole season." I remember I was on my way to pick up a friend to go to a Clippers game. I didn't say anything to him the whole night because I was thinking, "Holy shit. I'm going to direct a scripted single-camera TV show."

Three or four months later, I directed nine episodes in just seven and a half weeks. We cross-boarded everything. No hiatus. Also, we had no money. *Teachers* was boot camp for me. I learned so much. The crew was teaching me every day. It ended up being the best education of what it is to be an episodic director. You're making someone else's show.

JP: The thing you encountered is that as a TV director, you have to direct somebody else's vision. How did you come to terms with that?

PB: You have no time to because you have to just do the work. It's an awesome job and you realize quickly that you need the experience before you can attempt to curate what you do. The great thing is, there's a million shows out there so something is going to fit at some point.

That's when *The Last Man on Earth* started airing on Fox on Sunday nights. I thought, "Man, wouldn't it be cool to direct a show like this?" By the time I finished *Teachers,* I was obsessed with *The Last Man on Earth*. It gave me hope because I felt, "At least this exists out there." Then I got an email from an old friend, Seth Cohen, an executive at Lord and Miller, which produced *The Last Man on Earth*. I met Seth back in 2007 in a general meeting I took with Comedy Central. Seth was so cool, and I remember wondering if all TV executives were that cool. They're not. Through the years, he would check in to see what I was up to. But at that point, it had been two or three years since we had talked. So he hit me up out of the blue. I went into his office and he was like, "Have you seen *The Last Man on Earth?* I'd love for you to direct an episode." I'm freaking out. He said, "The crazy thing, though, is to jump from cable to network TV. It's such a hard jump for a director to make." From Internet to TV sketch was a hurdle. Then from TV sketch to cable half-hour was a hurdle. Now he was telling me that from cable to network is another hurdle? I was like, "This is crazy." And he said, "I want you to meet with the studio and the network at the same time. I don't want to stagger those meetings. I'm going to set it up." So Seth set up a meeting with both Fox and 20th Century. By the time I met with them, I'd watched the series three times.

And it's a great meeting. A few of the executives there had actually seen a bunch of the weird stuff I had made over the years. A few weeks later, they had me meet with John Solomon, the show's executive producer. Apparently they had called Peter Atencio to ask how

I was on *Key and Peele*. Peter praised me like crazy. At one point in the meeting, John said, "Tell me some stuff that you liked from season one." I just started vomiting random moments from the show that I liked, but I was blabbering. It was the most incoherent answer I have ever given. At the end of my rant, John smiled and said, "Literally everything you just said was Will Forte's pitch." And then I thought, "That was the best answer I've ever given."

But I was positive I wasn't going to get an episode of *The Last Man on Earth* because this was a new level. In my eyes, I was still the guy that was just doing sketches a couple of years ago. I still didn't think I was in the game to get *The Last Man on Earth*. Everybody was fighting to get that show. A couple months went by and I saw the cast members were tweeting that they're already shooting, and I thought, "All right, I didn't get it. Whatever." I wasn't that bummed because I really didn't think it was going to happen. And then I woke up one day to an email from my agent that said they were offering me an episode. I was like, "Okay, now I'm directing on my favorite show. I can never complain about anything again." They liked what I did and I ended up doing three episodes in one season. Then I got a call to meet on *Brooklyn Nine-Nine*.

JP: Going from directing little sketches to network episodic is a big leap. How did you learn the basics of how to behave on set like a TV director so that people would accept you?

PB: Before I shot on *Key and Peele*, I shadowed Peter Atencio. Actually, a lot of the terminology and even the hand gestures that I use go back to that first time I watched Peter. I remember watching him and thinking, "Oh, shit, that's what you're supposed to do?" I was taking notes like crazy. When I did *The Last Man on Earth*, they had me shadow Jason Woliner. I ended up being successful on that show because of Jason. He gave me so many insider tips. "This is how you get what you need out of the DP. And if this is happening with the AD, here's what you do. Here's how you get a line out of this actor." What he taught me made a lot of things I had experienced on *Teachers* make more sense. I had shot so much stuff up to that point that I just kind of knew how to direct. But in terms of knowing how to carry myself on set as a director, it was from watching Peter and Jason. I'm so worried about not wanting to hurt anybody's feelings. But Peter showed me that there's a way you can ask for something directly without being too direct. I refuse to be a yeller on set. I just will not do it. We're making comedy. It seems weird to yell at people.

And by the way, it's really bad to go over schedule as a director. It really hurts your career. Everybody finds out, including your agents. And then they won't pitch you for certain shows because it makes them look bad. If you don't make your days, the studio will judge you, the network will judge you and the producers will judge you. I've been on shows where they might have a directing slot open and I'll hear another director get mentioned. And then the script supervisor or one of the writers will say, "I've worked with that dude and he is slow as shit." Then they producers are like, "Okay, never mind." And that director has now lost a job because three years ago they were stubborn about a set-up and they went into overtime.

You have to make your days and be prepared. I've heard crazy stories about guys not showing up with shot lists. I don't know how many shows I've been on where they are shocked that I have a shot list and overheads. I'm like, "Well, yeah, I have shot lists and overheads. We have a stunt. Why wouldn't there be overheads? Why wouldn't there be a shot list?" And they tell me, "There's guys that come in with their Tommy Bahamas shirts and they're just winging it." My anxiety would never let me just wing it. You really have to do your homework. So I come in with every question answered.

But what I also learned from Peter Atencio is that every now and then, the creator, or a writer, or an actor is going to say something that will flip your whole plan around. Working with sketch people helped me prepare for that. It's about being able to improvise and change stuff on the fly. It really helps me in the episodic world because I already directed in a scenario where it's always "best idea wins." You have to be flexible. You might have a dope idea for a sequence but sometimes you get in there and it feels clunky. So forget it because it doesn't work. Sometimes your idea is just not meant to happen.

I've been lucky to work on a lot of stuff, but even now I don't feel that far removed from when we were running around Studio City shooting sketches for no money. There's still a part of me that thinks this could end any day. What if I don't get another job? I'm still the same idiot I was all those years ago. It's just that I got a bunch of luck. Timing and circumstance played big roles so I still don't get ahead of myself. I still get coupons every month from Ralph's supermarket and I definitely use them. I won't buy anything that doesn't have the yellow on-sale thing. It's that old Kramer quote, "Retail is for suckers." Man, I feel like a fool paying full price for literally anything.

JP: I love that you're still taking coupons to Ralph's.

PB: I will never stop. Stick it to the man!

Hanelle Culpepper

Sitting in Hanelle Culpepper's office is like hanging out inside a graphic novel. The walls are lined with photographs, drawings, sketches, diagrams, magazine clippings and notes that lay out her creative process for various feature film projects she is developing. The display creates a powerful sense of dedication to her craft, and I get the impression that Hanelle Culpepper has never been caught unprepared on a film set.

I asked every director I interviewed how she or he learned the nuts and bolts of directing. For some directors, like Hanelle, it was self-taught. Having excelled in higher-level academics, she took the approach of giving herself the best film school education she could create. She learned by doing.

. . . .

HANELLE CULPEPPER: I was born in Montgomery, Alabama, and grew up in Troy until I was six. Then I lived in Birmingham until I left for college.

JACOB PINGER: What was the community like where you grew up in Birmingham?

HC: Until my parents separated, I grew up in a very suburban part of Birmingham that was predominantly middle to upper middle-class African-American. But, oh the horror, we were in a one-story house when everybody else had a two-story house. We lived on an older street, so the houses were not as nice or as big as the ones in the newer section. Then, when I was about 14, my parents separated and my dad moved to New Jersey. I went to live with him for my ninth-grade year. I hated it in New Jersey, and came back to Alabama to live with my mom and finish high school. She had moved to a much more urban setting, still mostly black and definitely more of a lower middle-class area. I went to a private school with kids that had lots of money and came from the upper-class parts of Birmingham. So I was always a bit embarrassed about where I lived. Everyone else at the school got a car when they were 16. We couldn't afford that kind of thing.

JP: What did your parents do for a living?

HC: My dad worked for the telephone company. He was an executive there. He started off as a telephone

Even without going to film school, Hanelle Culpepper built upon the success of her short films to get an independent feature off the ground (Jacob Pinger).

pole climber and worked his way up. My mother was a stay-at-home mom. Once they separated, she started working as a bank teller. I had two sisters and one brother.

JP: What did you want to be when you grew up?

HC: It changed. The Hollywood answer is that I wanted to be an actress. But before that, there was a point I wanted to be a computer programmer. I was in high school when the first little Apple Macintosh computers came out. I was learning math CAD and it was kind of cool to be able to program things. My aunt worked in computer programming and I spent a day at work with her. I decided it was too boring.

JP: Where did the desire to be an actress come from?

HC: My parents say that I always wanted to tell stories. When I was a kid, I would do little plays and stuff. I would record radio dramas on cassette tapes. I think there was always this inherent desire to tell stories. It first manifested itself as wanting to be an actress. We went to the movies all the time. It was definitely a way of bonding with my father. I always loved movies and wanted to be a part of it. I didn't know anyone who worked in the industry, and so the thing that you respond to as a kid is the actor. I think that's where it came from.

JP: How long did your desire to act last?

HC: I had always auditioned hoping to get cast in one of our school plays but I never did. In my senior year, I took this directing elective class because as part of the class, you would get to act in another person's play. I basically took the directing class to guarantee myself an acting role. It was in that class that I discovered how much I loved directing and how much I really hated acting.

JP: What were the movies that you responded to as a kid?

HC: Definitely genre stuff. I loved action and thrillers. The movies that I remember clearest were *The Black Hole*, followed by *Logan's Run*. I loved *Star Wars* too.

JP: I feel like your directing credits defy expectations in the sense that you're a woman doing genres like thrillers and sci-fi. What was your connection to genre movies as a kid?

HC: I don't know. Maybe it was just being able to live in another world. Maybe it was just an escape for a little girl who was going to school and feeling so different from all her classmates. They all had money. And I was raised in a religion that contributed to my feelings of being very different from my friends and schoolmates. So maybe it was just a little bit of that escapism. But honestly, I don't think I can verbalize why I liked those kinds of movies. It could just be that my father's taste rubbed off on me. He loved thrillers and sci-fi and action.

JP: Growing up, did you have an awareness of the history of Birmingham in the Civil Rights movement and fighting Southern racism?

HC: I felt like, while growing up, I didn't really have any experience with racism, except for one blatant thing that happened during my high school years. I feel like I was able to see Southern racism more clearly once I had left, especially later when talking to white people who had moved to the South. They would tell me, "Oh my God! It's so racist here!" They were able to see the true face of everybody. I'm sure my experience would be different today because unfortunately everyone feels like they can just say whatever they want to now because of Trump.

JP: Were your parents political?

HC: No. Political views were frowned on because of our religion.

JP: It's interesting that you were raised with religion because I think a lot of people see Hollywood as a godless place where faith plays no role.

HC: I'm always surprised when I meet a friend in Los Angeles who goes to church every Sunday. I don't practice any religion right now, and so I don't go to church. I think it's partially because of my upbringing. But there is a lot of faith in Hollywood. And it's authentic faith. People think Hollywood is just producing these faith-based movies because they make a lot of money. There is some of that, but there are also people making those movies because they believe in the messages they are sharing.

JP: Many directors have had to learn how to live in two different worlds in their lives. That could be culturally, racially, or with economic class or religion. What signifiers made you feel separate?

HC: I guess it's the way I spoke. People in the South always said I sounded like I came from an island or something. I didn't have enough of an accent to sound Southern. That was probably the biggest signifier. And when I went to New Jersey, they would always laugh at the way I spoke because I would use words like "y'all." The way I speak right now is the way I've always spoken. I never had a thick Southern accent, but I used key Southern words. To someone in New Jersey, that was a funny thing.

When I came back from New Jersey and went to a private school in Alabama, I experienced being black in a predominantly white school. And that has kind of been the case for the rest of my life. College was predominately white, and then obviously being in Hollywood, you're in a predominantly white world.

JP: When did you start being aware that you and your family were seen as different?

HC: I don't remember. In the first grade, I used to sing this little song with one of my good friends who was white. The song went, "I see your heinie! It's so black and shiny!" One day we came to school and I wanted to sing it, and my friend told me that her mom said she shouldn't sing the song any more. I think it was because of the line, "so black and shiny." I also remember this joke that Martin Mull did in his HBO show *The History of White People in America*. The joke would not fly today. He showed all these different smiley faces for various cultures. He started out with the regular smiley face. And then he did the Chinese smiley face, so he changed the eyes to be slants. And then he did the black smiley face, so he took the smile and he went around it again to give it thicker lips. I remember asking my mom about it, and also the "black and shiny" song. And that's when the awareness of skin color really came into place for me. Other than that, I guess I just always felt different. I don't remember when that feeling really started. I think it may have been once we left Troy and moved to Birmingham.

JP: What was it like to come back to Birmingham, after that year in New Jersey, and start attending a predominantly white private school?

HC: It was very tough. Partly it was coming from a public school to a private school. The workload was just huge. The first day in history class, they piled up the books that we had to read. One of them was about the Spanish Armada. I remember opening up that thick book and all the print was tiny. So there was the academic part of it and there was also the, "I'm poor and everyone here is rich" part of it. And there was the "I'm black and everyone is white" part of it too. Also, a lot of the kids came from schools in the area, so they knew each other. I came there not knowing anybody. Tenth grade was quite a rough year for me. I had a mix of friends that was predominantly black, but I definitely had white friends as well. Also, I am a perfectionist and I really wanted A's. I had come from public school where I had gotten A's all the time. And here in this private school I was getting C's. And that was a little demoralizing. I had to work super-hard to get A's.

JP: That school was 10th, 11th and 12th grade?

HC: Yes. That first half of tenth grade was the hardest. I was 15. My black friends had nice long hair that they could get straightened all the time, but my hair was breaking off. My mom made me cut my hair. In my yearbook from tenth grade, there is this picture of me looking miserable with my hair cut off. Eleventh grade was easier. I would say that by twelfth grade, I kind of figured it. What was cool about my high school is that it had a very liberal vibe. We had classes outside. They called it Learning Through Living. Ultimately I really loved my high school.

JP: What did you draw upon to get through that?

HC: I think it was just my own inner drive to succeed. I just wanted to be successful. Maybe there was a part of me that knew my mom was making a huge sacrifice to send me to that school. I had a scholarship but it didn't cover 100 percent of the costs. Like I said, we were living in a lower middle-class part of town. It wasn't like my mom had the money for a private school. I had to do well for her.

JP: But it must have also taken a lot of discipline and good work habits.

HC: I think the school created the right work habits. It's kind of like what kids who go to college have to learn in freshman year, especially if they come from public school. You have to really learn how to focus and dig deep. You develop that work ethic. I did very well in college, even in my freshman year, probably because I had to figure it all out in high school.

JP: Many of the directors I interviewed had experiences that correlate to what you went through, learning how to exist in multiple cultures at once. Was high school the first time you had been around a predominantly white status quo in your daily life?

HC: I think so. The older neighborhood where I lived was probably 50-50 black and white. When you drove through the newer, upper middle-class subdivision, it was mostly black. My elementary school was about half black and white. Going to school in New Jersey was definitely a cultural mix, probably a lot more Spanish. But going to Indian Springs in Alabama was definitely my first time in a predominantly white environment where being black was very much a minority.

JP: Did your consciousness of race become different at that point, or did you just kind of flow with it?

HC: I actually feel that it's always been the socio-economic differences between me and other people that were more dominant in my life, more than race. I think that I felt more isolated from the kids in my high school because of their socio-economic status than because they were white. In college, we always called ourselves the international table because there were so many ethnicities all hanging out. But we were probably all of a very similar socio-economic status.

I feel like as black women directors, we probably feel what white women feel, which is a constant need to show that you're smart enough, and have the stamina and emotional stability to do the job. Also, that you're creative enough to work in the sci-fi and action genre, and not just do emotional stories.

JP: Can you tell me about that high school class where you discovered your passion for directing?

HC: For the theater class, you had to pick a play to direct. I picked *If Men Played Cards as Women Do*, a comedy. I remember how much I enjoyed the process of choosing the play, finding the right people for the roles, working with the actors, and hearing the audience laugh where I wanted them. It was thrilling. That's when I knew I wanted to be a director. But as an actor, when I actually went on stage and had to be vulnerable, I realized I didn't enjoy it because I was too reserved.

JP: Even though you initially thought that you wanted to be an actor?

HC: Yes. Sometimes you want to be something and then you try it and you're like, "Oh, no. I don't want to do this." When I finished high school, I thought that I wanted to direct commercials, so I went to Lake Forest College in Chicago to get a business degree.

JP: I'm trying to understand how you knew at 17 that you wanted to be a commercial director. That's such a bold decision.

HC: I always loved good commercials. I loved movies too, so I don't know why I initially chose advertising. Maybe this was part of it: I always wanted to move to Los Angeles, but I had a little fear about going there. Commercials were in Chicago or New York, which for some reason seemed like an easier move than making the leap all the way to L.A. I chose Chicago even though Lake Forest did not have film-directing courses. My plan was that I would earn a business degree and then get a job at an advertising agency where I would direct all their commercials, which is completely not how it works. But I didn't know that then. What I tell young people now is that when you know what you want, you need to talk to people who are doing it and learn the smart way to go about it.

Anyway, when I was majoring in business at Lake Forest, I ended up taking my first econ course. I loved economics, so I changed my major to econ and French. When I graduated from Lake Forest, I got a fellowship to do a Ph.D. in economics at University of California at Riverside. I was only halfway through the first semester at UCR and I was, like, "Wait a minute. What happened?" I loved economics and I was good at it—but I really wanted to direct movies and TV. And so I had to right the path. I transferred to Annenberg at USC to earn a masters in communications management. I wasn't in the cinema school, but I took a lot of film classes and I worked on other people's school projects.

JP: Why didn't you just major in film at USC?

HC: That's a good question and I do not have the answer. What I suspect is that there is a part of me that wanted security. And so, whereas some people take the risk and go for it as a director, knowing that when they move to L.A. they are going to starve and sleep on someone's couch until they hopefully make it, I was not quite ready for that instability. I always made choices that allowed me to have a fallback career. Earning a masters degree in communications management at Annenberg meant that I could work as an executive at a studio. I would still be working within my love of telling stories, but I would have a stable job.

It wasn't until after USC when I was working at Sundance and was so inspired by the filmmakers there that I decided to stop playing it safe. I realized that if I wanted to be a filmmaker, I needed to start making films. I used a bunch of savings, bought a camera and I made my first short. Once I fully committed is when the opportunities started to slowly open up. So I'm about eight years behind in my career because I didn't just go for it from the start. If I had been brave enough, I would have applied to USC Cinema School straight out of high school. I think I've always had a little bit of an inferiority complex about not having gone to film school. I didn't take a class and get an A in directing. So I've always wondered, "Am I doing it right?"

JP: How did you pay for USC?

HC: Student loans.

JP: Was that pretty heavy?

HC: Yep.

JP: What was your plan after getting your masters at Annenberg?

HC: My plan was to get a job at a studio as an executive.

JP: Is that what happened?

HC: No. After graduating I did the temp pool, and that led to getting a job for Kathy Kloves. I worked full-time for her while she had a deal with New World Entertainment and DreamWorks.

JP: You got that job with Kathy Kloves through temping?

HC: Yes. I temped for her and then she hired me full-time. I was her assistant, and did whatever she needed. All the general duties. Part of what made that job cool was that we did this show called *Weekly World News*. I was involved in reading the stories they were writing, and making suggestions. I didn't get on set that much, but there was a lot of development. Then Kathy's deal at DreamWorks ended and I needed a new full-time job. That's when I started working at Sundance as the assistant to the executive director, Kenneth Brecher. After about a year at Sundance is when the inspiration hit me and I decided to pursue directing 100 percent. I realized that I needed to do it and not keep hoping that someone was going to give me permission to do it. At that point, I got back in touch with Kathy and told her that I was looking for part-time work. She was friends with Callie Khouri, who was looking for a new part-time assistant. I ended up working part-time for Callie, which allowed me to spend more time developing my craft.

That's when I wrote the script for my short film *The Wedding Dress*. It was inspired by something that happened in my own life around 1998 or '99. I knew that somehow I needed to make that film. I met the person who produced it through one of my jobs and she knew an up-and-coming DP. We just did what people do to make a short film. We asked for favors and got money however we could. I paid for a lot of it with my savings.

JP: And it did well?

HC: It did well. I could have made it better. You grow and learn, but it was my first thing. And it felt really good. I'm still proud of it.

JP: You directed plays in college, but you didn't go to film school. Where did you learn how to direct cinema?

HC: Theater trains you to analyze stories and work with actors. And then for the technical part of filmmaking, I learned from all the different times I volunteered as a P.A., or producer, or grip, or did wardrobe, or art department on various student and indie films. I was in a group called Filmmakers Alliance and we always helped each other make our films. That was my film school.

JP: So you were really proactive about getting out there and being part of other people's projects. You created your own curriculum to teach yourself, with the aid of other people.

HC: I guess you could say that. It wasn't that planned. Then *The Wedding Dress* got me into AFI's Directing Workshop for Women [DWW]. That was the first time I had any kind of formalized film school training. It was a year-long program. You took three weeks of courses and then over the rest of the year you produced, shot, edited and presented a short film.

JP: At that time, did you want to do features?

HC: Yes, I wanted to do features because it felt like the easier way in than TV. In television, there were so many gatekeepers, but with features you could raise the money and make it yourself if you had to.

JP: In the late '90s, when you were an aspiring filmmaker in Los Angeles, I remember that there was no real awareness in the industry about the fact that women and people of color were not getting opportunities to break into the business. It wasn't on the radar. So you were kind of a lone soldier in that battle. Were you aware of those issues at the time?

HC: No. I just knew it was hard for everyone. I always blame myself and my lack of film school experience for it being so hard. I never pointed to being a woman or being black as the reason why. I don't remember when issues of accessibility became a thing. I feel like it was probably after my first feature, but before my first TV show, when they started talking about all those bad statistics. I remember thinking, "Okay, I'm going to be the exception to the stats." I feel like if you wallow in that negativity, then you become very bitter, and then who wants to work with you? I can't walk around with a chip on my shoulder that everything that goes wrong is because I'm black or because I'm a woman. That could be my own naiveté. But even generally in life, I don't go around thinking that any negative interaction is because I'm black. I know that there are lots of people who do that, especially in the South. They often see that as the first reason. And I just don't. There are times where I'll think back on an interaction and wonder about it. But you can't get too caught up in things that you cannot change, and I cannot change that I'm a woman, and I cannot change that I'm black.

JP: You made your short film *A Single Rose* through the DWW program, and that also did well. Was that an exciting time for you?

HC: It was. It was cool that it went to Cannes as part of Kodak's International Cinematographers Guild showcase. I adapted the feature script that I was pitching all over Hollywood at the time. I had written it based on a book that my father wrote. I was having meetings on the script, but no one would greenlight it because I hadn't directed anything. Also, it starred black women and was a period piece, which was everything that Hollywood didn't want in a movie at the time. For the short film, I condensed the script and was super-proud of it. I wish it had done even done better. I think it was just too long. It was 19 minutes. If it had been 14 minutes, I think it would have done even more festivals. But it was a good, exciting time. I traveled a lot. My husband was very supportive and I definitely feel like one key reason I am where I am now is because he supported me and allowed me to spend our money to do what I was doing. Traveling, going to film festivals, only working part-time. He had a stable job and I acknowledge that it is hard for someone who doesn't have any kind of financial rock to stay with it for as long as I did.

JP: How did you get your first feature?

HC: *A Single Rose* got me into the Berlin Film Festival's Talent Campus and there I met Rebecca Sonnenshine. The Berlin Talent Campus brings together writers, directors, producers, composers and editors from all over the world. The idea is that you'll meet people and create international co-productions. Of course, I ended up meeting a writer from Los Angeles. When we got back to L.A., we had lunch and she pitched me some stuff. I had decided I wanted to do something low-budget that I could get the money together for and shoot. I really loved this one story she had. It became my first feature, *Within*. It was set in the '80s and so I worked with her to rewrite it to be set in the present. Then I brought it to Filmmakers Alliance and they really loved it. They also loved my work ethic and felt like I had talent from what they saw with my short films. At the time, they had a deal with a production company called Big Foot to produce low-budget genre. So they bought *Within* to Big Foot and they really liked it too. But of course their question was, "Why should they hire Hanelle Culpepper to direct?" My response was that it was a combination of the fact that I was attached to the film, so you're not going to get it without me, and also here's *A Single Rose*, which shows the stunning visuals I can give you. And in addition, here's another short I made called *Six in the City* which shows you I can work with kids; the feature starred two nine-year-old kids. And so Big Foot gave us the money to do it, and that's how my first feature came out.

JP: I've got to say that for an independent movie, that is the easiest story I ever heard.

HC: It definitely was, and it spoiled me. It's never been that easy since. We shot *Within* in 2006, and finished it in 2008. Lifetime bought it and aired it. It did well on their channel and they were happy with it, so they introduced me to these producers who were looking for a director for another feature. I got that job and went on to do two more Lifetime features with those producers. Technically, they were independent films that Lifetime acquired. But Lifetime still had cast approval, director approval, etc. They came through the acquisitions department and were not officially made-for-Lifetime movies.

I was kind of lucky with how that first feature happened. It took a while to finish and was difficult to sell because it didn't do as well on the festival circuit as I would have hoped. It did get into a few, and it won a few awards. It was a supernatural horror movie with kids. It was almost too scary for the kids' festivals but didn't have enough horror for the horror festivals. So it was in this weird space. But then *Within* led to three thrillers for Lifetime: *Deadly Sibling Rivalry*, *Hunt for the Labyrinth Killer* and *Murder on the 13th Floor*, which starred Tessa Thompson.

JP: What were the budgets of those films?

HC: *Within* was just around a million. And the three Lifetime movies were under a million. They were in that $750,000 zone.

JP: Can a director make a living at those budget levels?

HC: Maybe. I guess if you make enough of them in a year. They don't pay you that much. So if you do four a year, I guess you'll be surviving. You won't buy a house or a fancy car.

JP: So if you do three independent movies a year, you're still going to struggle?

HC: Well, actually, if you do three a year, you'll do fine. With each one, I upped my rate. But really, who is going to make three features a year? It's practically impossible.

JP: I think that's something that would shock a lot of people. If they see your name as the director on a movie, they're going to assume you made a million bucks on it.

HC: No. That's not the life of a lot of feature directors. And even if you did get paid a real wage, like 100 grand or something for a feature, if that's the only feature you do for five years, then that's not enough. I'm trying to do another feature but I will never stop working in television. I enjoy television. You actually earn money, your work gets before an audience, and you don't have all the heartbreak that features have where you get so close and it's about to go but then it all falls apart.

JP: Talk about getting into TV.

HC: The Lifetime movies had enough different material, with the VFX, major stunts and stars, that I was able to put together a reel. The reel got me into NBC's diversity program. At the same time, I was going on various general meetings and they would always say, "You did movies. How are you going to handle a TV budget and a TV schedule?" So I had to constantly tell people, "I did not have a lot of money or days to make those movies." On *Within*, I think I had 20 days, and that was a luxury because the number of days kept going down. I think I had 18 days on the next movie and 17 on another. As hard as those schedules were, I was able to point to those experiences to show that I could do a TV budget and a TV schedule.

JP: So you were pigeonholed as a feature director when you were trying to get into TV?

HC: Yes. That was the case then. Hollywood loves an easy way to say no to you, and so for anyone who's trying to go from features to TV, that was the easy way for them to say no. Convincing them that I could do TV was the challenge. It's changed. A lot of shows like to find independent filmmakers now.

JP: Was it after you made those three Lifetime movies that you decided to go into TV?

HC: Not exactly. I got my manager just after I got my first Lifetime feature. Once I directed my second feature, my manager set up various meetings to break me into the TV world. I also started to do some shadowing. When I got into the NBC diversity program, I was selected to shadow on *Prime Suspect*. Then my third Lifetime movie came up, and so I was in the dilemma of whether I should do the NBC program or direct another Lifetime feature. If I did the Lifetime movie, I wouldn't be able to shadow on *Prime Suspect*.

Jonas Pate, who was the *Prime Suspect* showrunner, and Karen Horne, who ran the NBC diversity program, talked about my situation. They felt it was better for me to do the feature. We didn't know if *Prime Suspect* would get picked up after season one; I would not get to direct if the show got cancelled. So I did my third Lifetime movie. That decision turned out to be a lucky thing. I was lucky because I did the movie and then *Prime Suspect* did get cancelled, but *Parenthood* ended up picking me to shadow. And when *Parenthood* got another season, I was given a shot to direct an episode. That was just the luck of what happened.

JP: One of the things that I think these interviews will do is help relieve people of the idea that diversity programs are bringing unqualified people into the industry. I have found that it's the contrary. The diversity programs are in fact finding very qualified people who just don't have access to the gatekeepers of television. They are basically taking very qualified people, putting them through a process and then gradually providing them access. Then it's on them to get the job or not. I think your case illustrates that because you had directed four feature films before you completed the program at NBC, people will clearly recognize that you were qualified to direct an episode of a TV show. What is your feeling about the diversity programs?

HC: I feel like they're a good thing. The NBC program I did was different than the other diversity programs. At the time, NBC only accepted four participants. And the show you shadowed picked you, which meant that the showrunner already had a vested interest in seeing you succeed. The NBC program also had a financial incentive for any show that hired you to direct: The network would reimburse the show for the cost of that director. ABC did not have that. So I feel like the NBC program gave you a better chance at getting an episode.

All the programs are so competitive that you have highly qualified people getting in. People also do multiple programs at different networks. It's all to finally get a showrunner to say, "Okay, they are getting in all these programs. They're clearly good. We have no more excuses not to give them an episode." So I feel good about the programs, but I also don't want people to think that's the only way to get in. The programs have made it harder in a way to shadow the independent way. I shadowed on 13 shows, but I only shadowed on one through an official program. It becomes harder to do the independent route when a show says they would love to let you shadow but they can't because they are already committed to whatever studio program they are part of.

JP: After shadowing on 13 shows, how did you end up getting offered an episode?

HC: The first show that offered me an episode was *Parenthood* on NBC. When I was offered the episode, the showrunner of *90210* was able to go to CW and say, "NBC is giving her an episode of *Parenthood*. So certainly CW could give her an episode of *90210*." That's how I got that one. I had shadowed on *90210* twice before. So *90210* ended up being the first thing I directed and *Parenthood* was my second episode.

JP: I've been told that television is a club, and when you're not in it, you're not in it. But once you're in it, you're in. Was that your experience?

HC: I guess you could say that. I would say there are several clubs. You have your Shonda Rhimes club, and then you have your ABC club, your CBS club, etc. I think once you get into one of the network shows and they really like you, then you're in for doing other shows at that network.

JP: I imagine that you had to start going in to meet network and showrunners to get hired. Can you tell me about the process of meeting and getting a show?

HC: Well, one thing that I've learned is that when you're going to meet on a show, it basically means that they want to hire you and they're just making sure that you understand their show and you're not an asshole. If you come into that meeting with passion for the show, having watched as much of it as you can, having read the pilot if it's new, having looked up the producers' credits and watched their other stuff so you can be passionate about that too, I think that's what they're looking for. To make sure that you know their show, love what you're seeing, will be collaborative and not be an egomaniac.

JP: It sounds like you don't put a ton of pressure on yourself in those meetings.

HC: No. I put tons of pressure on myself. The meetings are getting easier now. But I prep really hard for every meeting I have. My agents might propose a meeting date, and I'll say, "No. I already have a meeting that day." They're like, "It's just a general," and I'll tell them, "No, you don't understand. That still means four to five hours of prep work because I'm not going to just walk in and wing it." I really try to learn as much as I can about the person and the company and what they have done, or what they have coming up.

JP: Just from all the research materials on the walls of your office, you look like a person who really dives in and prepares for their directing jobs.

HC: For any job I get, I try to watch every episode that came before mine, unless it's something that's been around for so long that there's just too many episodes. In that case, I'll watch the season opener, the finale and whatever seems to be the key episode in the middle of every season. At a minimum, I'll read all the descriptions of every episode. I want to walk in knowing the storyline of all the characters. I don't want to be caught blind or unfamiliar with all the episodes and character development. If it's a new show, then I'll read the pilot, but I will also ask the showrunners to tell me the types of movies or shows that convey the correct tone or shooting style, and I'll watch all of those. Yes, I do a ton of prep.

JP: I'm sure you shot-list.

HC: Yes, but I don't shot-list until I'm there in prep. You only get the script the day before you start prep, if you're lucky. Some shows are giving them really late, and you're getting them like two days before you shoot. Anyway, I don't know how you come in to start your first day of prep with a shot list. I come in to prep having ideas of what I want to do, but until I see the locations, until I talk to the writers and make sure that I'm envisioning this the same way that they are, then it's a waste of time to come into prep with a shot list. During the course of my official prep days, I develop my shot list. I block everything.

JP: So by the time you get to shooting day number one…

HC: I have a shot list. I always send out a shot list the night before I start shooting.

JP: The directors I've been interviewing are very well prepared.

HC: I think that those directors who just wing it are generally the older directors. There's probably some younger ones too. But just based on what I've been told when I've been prepping with ADs is that it seems to be the older white guys who just come in and wing it. I'm always flabbergasted by that. One AD told me, "Wow, it's so nice that you actually want to prep and have these meetings." My response is, "Of course you have these meetings!" But for some of the older directors I've heard of, it's just about, "What can we do by 11 a.m. so I can go and play golf for the rest of the day?" I'm just shocked. Or the tales you hear about directors who show up to shoot and they're clearly reading the scenes for the first time. I just cannot believe that.

I feel like there's a backlash against the industry wanting to give more jobs to women and people of color, but what I feel is really happening is that the people who were just phoning it in are getting pushed out to make room for the directors of all types who are coming in, working hard, and appreciating the opportunity.

JP: If you go home for your high school reunion and see an old friend, how would you define the role of a TV director to somebody who has no idea what a TV director does?

HC: Well, I never call myself a television director. I call myself a director. It's actually interesting, the extent to which people don't realize how much a director does. When someone asks me what a director does, I ask in return, "What's something you've seen that you liked? Well, the director received that script and brought that story to life. So whether it be casting, choosing wardrobe, choosing locations, figuring out how the actors move through the scene, working with the actors to get the emotional tone, that is what the director does. She takes the words off the page and creates the way that you will see them. She brings the script to life."

JP: You mentioned that you had not experienced racism except for one incident. Are you open to talking about it?

HC: Sure. It was so random and just silly. I was in a car with my aunt—I was probably 16 or 17—and we were at a light, and some white teenage guy zoomed up next to us and yelled, "Nigger!" and then zoomed off. We were just like, "Okay...?"

JP: That was in Alabama?

HC: Yes.

JP: Well, thanks for being willing to talk about. I feel that people who read this should know that even successful Hollywood people aren't immune from these sorts of things.

HC: Yes. I don't look like a director in most people's minds because I'm a black woman. And there are little things that happen, like when you park in the director's spot at base camp, and the security guard really wants to make you go to general crew parking. So you have to actually convince them that you're really the director. It always seems like it takes a little bit extra to do that.

Here's another example. One time I came to the studio on a Saturday to block a complicated scene on a set that I hadn't seen during my prep because it was still being built. When I arrived, art department's construction and set dressing teams were there working. I sat down in a chair on the set to do my work and a worker snapped at me to get out of that chair. I did and continued with my blocking. That Monday, when the same worker saw that I was the director, he was very apologetic and changed how he related to me. He said, "I wouldn't have said that to you if I had known you were the director. I thought you were the script supervisor or something." And I'm wondering, what script supervisor comes in on a Saturday and sits on set to do her job? So you still experience stuff like that because people aren't used to seeing someone like me directing.

JP: Imagine some young person in the world who has no connection to Hollywood and wants make movies and TV shows. What kind of advice might you give her?

HC: My main advice would be to seek someone out to talk to who's doing it and get as much information as you can, as much guidance as you can about the smart way to pursue it.

Jay Karas

I first met Jay Karas when he directed an episode of *Parks and Recreation*. I remember that he seemed to have so much fun on set. So I was surprised to find out that the episode had been his first network half-hour episode. I couldn't believe Jay had been so relaxed.

A few years later, I had the opportunity to shadow Jay when he directed another show. Not only did he remember me from *Parks and Recreation*, but he went out of his way to make me feel welcome. He introduced me to the entire crew and told them that I was already an excellent director. And then he shared his entire process with me and kept me involved throughout post-production. I couldn't have hoped for a better person to shadow. It was a great experience, but the one thing I hope I learned from Jay is that if you're not having fun on set, then you're doing it wrong.

· · · · · · · · · · · · · · · · · · · ·

JAY KARAS: I was born in D.C. and lived in a nearby city called Rockville, Maryland, until I was almost eight. When I was five, my parents split up, and then when I was eight, my mother and I moved to Virginia Beach, Virginia, for five years. Then we moved north to Bloomfield, Connecticut, which is where I went to high school. So growing up, I lived in three very different places, and all three are in my bloodstream.

Rockville, Maryland, in the '70s was a tolerant and diverse community, whereas Virginia Beach was decidedly not. Even though it's only about four or five hours drive south of D.C., it's very Southern in its mentality. Southern accents. Southern food. Southern attitudes. I was one of the only Jews in my school. Living in Virginia Beach was an interesting experience.

Bloomfield, Connecticut, is in New England. When people hear Connecticut, they automatically think uptight and rich. But Bloomfield bordered Hartford, so on one side of the town it was literally projects. The result was that my public high school was 75 percent African-American, ten percent Puerto Rican, and also a lot of Jews. My school even had Jewish holidays off because they couldn't get enough substitutes. When I moved to Connecticut in 1985, it was amidst the emergence of both hair metal and hip-hop. You would walk into school and these guys over here would be smoking cigarettes in their jean jackets with Led Zeppelin on the back and these other guys would be blasting Public Enemy.

I feel like Bloomfield was a really interesting place to live during my formative years. It made me very comfortable going anywhere. I hadn't really thought about this, but a big part of being a guest director is that you have to bounce around to all these different places and be able to fit in. I wasn't one of the popular, cool kids in high school, but I had friends in every group.

JACOB PINGER: What did your parents do?

JK: My dad was a computer programmer. He worked at Honeywell, which does a lot of government contracts and aircraft engine design. My mother had a masters in social work and when I was little, she worked part-time doing senior adult programming and other sorts of social services. After my parents split up, my mom had to get a full-time job. She started working in the Jewish community running the senior adult program at a synagogue. When I was eight, we moved to Virginia Beach so my mom could run the senior adult program at the Jewish Community Center [JCC] there. Later she shifted into being a school social worker. She ended up being a school social worker for K through eight at a district in Connecticut for about 26 years.

Jay Karas figured out how to leverage his position as an executive producer in order to gain invaluable experience as a director (Jacob Pinger).

JP: When your parents split up, did you live with your mother?

JK: Yeah. I was an only child.

JP: How important was Judaism in your young life?

JK: Extremely important. I lived in a fairly religious home. We used electricity on Shabbat, but we went to shul every Friday night and Saturday morning. We wouldn't eat meat in restaurants unless it was kosher. My parents practiced a staunchly conservative Judaism. So religion was a pervasive element in my life. At a really young age, I learned about some pretty horrific things. I started learning about what happened in World War II at about eight. I definitely feel like learning about that dark history was a contributing factor to me leaning into comedy. Another factor was what was going on in my home life. When I was five, suddenly my world got turned upside down and laughter was an escape. I didn't realize any of that then, but as an adult I look back and see it. Even when a bunch of family was around—and there was yelling and screaming and fighting—five minutes later, we would all be together on the couch as a family laughing at a sitcom. TV comedy was an escape and a real place of refuge.

JP: Judaism has a great tradition of finding comedy in tragedy. Was that something that you were consciously aware of as a kid, or was it just kind of ingrained in your DNA?

JK: I think it was just ingrained. I definitely wasn't aware of it. I liked things that made me laugh, but it wasn't anything, like, "Oh, I need to laugh so that I can numb the pain." It was something I gravitated towards naturally.

JP: What were some of the shows you liked as a kid?

JK: Early stuff was *Happy Days* and *Diff'rent Strokes*. I used to watch every episode that I could of *The Andy Griffith Show*, *Green Acres*, *The Brady Bunch*. TV was a huge part of my life. I was a bit of a latchkey kid, and living with a single mom who worked full time, I ended up in front of the TV a lot, and I loved it. I remember when we first got cable, it was amazing. All of a sudden you went from four or five channels to 15. I also used to watch dramas, soapy stuff like *Dallas*, *Falcon Crest*, *Dukes of Hazzard* and *The Incredible Hulk*.

JP: What was it like to be a Jewish kid in the Southern town of Virginia Beach between the ages of eight and 13? Those are pretty formative years for developing an identity.

JK: We lived in a very Christian area and there was not a lot of understanding of Jewish people. I think in my public school of several hundred students, there were five or six Jewish kids. But I was the only one that observed Jewish holidays. I ran up against a lot of stuff that I now realize was blatantly anti–Semitic, whether conscious on their part or not. I used to stay out of school for all the Jewish holidays, not just the big ones like Rosh Hashanah and Yom Kippur, but also for the smaller ones like Sukkot, Passover and all the Yontif days. I remember being out for a holiday in the fifth grade. When I came back to school, my teacher said, "Where were you this time? Another Jewish holiday?" It was this attitude of, "Why weren't you in school? What the fuck kind of crazy thing are you doing now?" And I was ten!

Every Sunday, the other kids in my school went to church. I remember being at school on the Monday after they all were told that the Jews killed Jesus. I also remember the Monday after the kids learned that all Jews are circumcised, although most of those kids probably didn't understand that they were circumcised as well. They did a lot of things at that school that they probably should not have. We did an art project that incorporated the Lord's Prayer, and I was the only one that didn't know what that was. Once I found out what the Lord's Prayer was, I was like, "I don't want to make that." It wasn't out of disrespect; it was just something that didn't apply to me. And this was a public school—and there's supposed to be a separation of church—and it was not there at all. It was crazy.

Every time I was out of school for something related to being Jewish, I would get ostracized by at least one kid. It actually caused a lot of inner conflict for me in terms of being raised in an observant Jewish household. Being Jewish made me different, and it made me unpopular. It made me all these things that I didn't want to be. I would dread having to be out of school for Jewish holidays. In addition to sitting in synagogue all day, I would have to make up tons of schoolwork.

JP: In that kind of environment, being labeled as different is a real burden.

JK: For sure. There's one other ridiculous thing I just remembered. At the end of every school year, they would have a pizza party and I would have to order the cheese pizza because the pepperoni wasn't kosher. I remember one time my pizza came and it had pepperoni on it. I went to the teacher and said, "I can't eat this." And she goes, "Just pick it off." And I said, "No, you don't understand. I'm not allowed to. It's cooked with pepperoni and the juices are in there. I can't eat this." It became this whole thing and no one understood.

Everything was always a thing. Like on Passover, I couldn't bring a regular sandwich to school. I had to bring this crumbly matzo sandwich that looked like a disaster. All the time there was something. It was just comedically endless.

JP: Who were your friends at the time?

JK: I had a couple friends in school that I would hang out with. It wasn't like I was completely isolated or anything. I was kind of living a dual life. I had my Jewish friends that I would see every weekend at the synagogue, and I went to the JCC Summer Camp in Virginia Beach. Actually, there is a great story from JCC camp that plays into my comedic upbringing. So you didn't have to be a Jewish kid to go to the camp. And the summer after fourth or fifth grade, there was this Christian kid there, also named Jay. Jay was one of my best pals. I started going to his house after camp every day because my mom worked and couldn't pick me up until six. It was a whole different world at Other Jay's house. Their house was big and they had a VCR, which was a huge deal at the time. One day, Jay asked me in this shady voice, "Hey, man. Do you want to watch *Richard Pryor Live on the Sunset Strip*?" I didn't know what that was, but based on the way he was asking me, I knew that it was some sort of clandestine activity. So of course I said yes. And he popped the VHS tape in. I was probably ten and Richard Pryor was talking about all sorts of stuff that you're not supposed to hear at that age. But it was funny. It was incendiary and eye-opening and I was laughing my ass off. So every day for the rest of the summer, we would watch *Richard Pryor Live on the Sunset Strip*. That Pryor VHS tape was an early influence on me. I don't think I told my mother about it until I was 35.

JP: Your mom finally left Virginia Beach and went to Connecticut.

JK: In Connecticut, no one cared if you were Jewish. But I hated moving to Connecticut because, right at the time we moved there, was when things were starting to turn around for me in Virginia Beach. All that weird stuff from the earlier years was going away and I was coming into my own a little more. I had more friends and was riding my BMX bike and skateboard around with them. And then we moved and nobody had a skateboard in Connecticut. I was the only kid who had one, and I had a Southern accent at that point. So I was this Jewish kid with a Southern accent who rides a skateboard to school. Being Jewish wasn't a big deal, but there was all this other stuff that made me different. Everyone else in that community had been together since kindergarten. I was one of the only kids to move into the school system later, which presented its own host of issues. But by the ninth grade, my Southern accent went away and I started to turn around.

JP: Did you continue to have an interest in TV during high school?

JK: My love for watching TV never went away, and I consumed as many movies as I could. All I wanted to do was go to the local theater and watch movies. We would get our friends' moms to drop us off. We would buy tickets for one movie and then sneak into three others. I saw as many as I possibly could. I was a teenager and living with my mom in a small apartment. Going to the movies was my escape. I didn't care what it was.

Actually, one formative experience for me was when I was about 11 and my mother took me to see *Beverly Hills Cop*. That was my first R-rated movie. She was actually really conservative, so looking back, I'm not clear why she took me. But I'm forever thankful that she did because it was Eddie Murphy. Even with all the language and the F-bombs, it just made me laugh. I loved it. And I love my mom for being cool enough to take me to that movie.

Another formative thing was visiting my dad when he was living in Cincinnati. I was probably about ten. We were browsing the aisles at the video store for a movie to rent. I remember I was articulating to him that I was thirsty for something different. My dad is also a pretty conservative guy, but he did this thing that I will never forget. He pulled this VHS off the shelf and said, "If you want watch something really different and really interesting, you should watch this." It was *Harold and Maude*. I asked, "What's it about?" He said, "Why don't you just watch it? If I say what it's about, it's going to sound weird." I was intrigued. I watched it and it was a real disrupter for my brain. It was a love story about this young guy and this old lady. It told me that you could tell a story about anything. It was great. I feel like that was one of the things that helped inspire my desire to see more independent cinema, and it was also incredibly illuminating about how things could be darkly comedic in a decidedly not laugh-out-loud way.

In high school, I went to the mainstream cinemas, but there was also an art house theater in Hartford that I would drag my friends to. I was trying to see everything. I didn't really like school, which meant that I would do well in the subjects I liked and terribly in the ones I didn't. But in senior year, I had a really wonderful English teacher named Mr. Lowd who helped legitimize film as an art form for me and also as a potential profession. He was one of the only teachers that inspired me to actually read. I would read anything that he wanted us to. We read *The Natural* by Bernard Malamud, and then watched the movie in class. Then Mr. Lowd went back and we re-watched the movie and analyzed it scene by scene. He was the first person who illustrated cinematic things for me, like when you put a strong backlight on someone, it's a metaphor for being angelic or godly. That class awakened my senses in terms of paying attention to literature and film and what you can do visually to manipulate the audience and tell your story. I already knew at that point that I wanted to make movies and television. But Mr. Lowd's class was when I realized that it wasn't a crazy idea, but a real thing that you can do and be respected for. Before that, everyone's parents were saying, "TV and movies is not a real profession. You need to have something stable." Mr. Lowd was the guy that made it seem like it was okay to pursue it.

JP: After high school, you went to college at the University of Maryland. At that point, it sounds like you already had this idea of becoming a filmmaker.

JK: That idea started to develop around sophomore year of high school. By the time I went to college I wanted to be a director and make movies. I wanted to go to California, but I was only 17 when I started college and it was a little too daunting to move all the way from Connecticut to California. I couldn't quite put that together, so I applied to schools in the D.C. area.

I enrolled in the Radio, Television and Film program at University of Maryland [UMD]. At the end of my first year, there was a recession and the school had major budget cuts. They announced that they were going to be phasing out the TV and Film program, so I took it as a sign that I should go do what I wanted to in the first place. During my sophomore year, I put together a plan to get myself into a real film school. I cut back to just two night classes at UMD and began working full-time to save money. I applied to NYU, UT Austin, UCLA and USC.

JP: What was your full-time work during your sophomore year?

JK: All through high school, I worked in a pharmacy. I got a job there right after I turned 15, right when it was legally possible. I started as a cashier, and then got trained as a pharmacy technician. So by the time I was 16, I was filling prescriptions. The owner gave me a lot of responsibility at a young age. When I got to college, I worked in two different pharmacies. I also worked at the university bookstore and I started making and selling t-shirts. I had three jobs. Later on, when I transferred colleges and moved to L.A., I got a job at a pharmacy on Bedford Drive in Beverly Hills. Steve Martin, Norman Jewison, Cathy Moriarty and all these noteworthy names would come in as customers. I once rang Steve Martin up for some saline. He was wearing a bike helmet.

JP: Where did you transfer to?

JK: I didn't get accepted to UCLA or NYU. I also didn't get into the USC film school, but they accepted me in general admission. USC was so damn expensive—and I didn't have any parental help with costs—but I just needed to get to Los Angeles. I said to myself, "I have a credit card, I have student loans. I'll just figure it out."

JP: Since USC didn't let you into the film school, what did you do to learn about film and TV?

JK: I ended up doing a make-your-own major, where I could still take the bulk of my upper division classes from the film school, so I ended up taking cinematography, editing writing, and several critical studies classes.

JP: So how did you learn to direct films?

JK: I didn't have access to check out film gear. But I got a job in the USC business school helping other students in the computer lab. The business school had a VHS camera that I would borrow every weekend. I would shoot with my friends, just recording life and getting used to having a camera in my hands.

JP: You put yourself through one of the most expensive schools in the country and kept pursuing your dream. That's pretty amazing.

JK: Going to such an expensive school was part of the drive I had early on when I started working. I wanted to get rid of my student loans. For better or for worse, it forced me to look at filmmaking as commerce. I still have a very fraught relationship with art vs. commerce. When I finished USC, I had to work. Five years after USC, I was debt-free.

JP: One of the stereotypes about the USC film school is that you go there for the connections. But you graduated with a social sciences degree. What was your experience with getting TV and film connections at USC?

JK: I didn't get that at all from USC, partially because I wasn't in the film school. For me, it was all about making my own connections. But being at USC did set off a series of events. The summer between my junior and senior year of college, I couldn't get a job to save my life. I thought, "Well, I've got one more year of school left and if I can't find paid work, I might as well start interning in this business." So I cold-called MTV and ended up speaking with Kallissa Miller. She said, "I don't really have anything but my friend Lesley Chilcott might need somebody. Call her."

So I called Lesley and I got hired as an intern at this boutique production company called Tenth Planet Productions. I ended up interning that whole summer. In August of 1993, they were doing the *MTV Video Music Awards*. I went to my boss, Dave Cunningham, who I am still very close friends with, and I said, "Is there any way I can get to work on the show as a PA?" So Dave called the exec in charge and got me on. All of a sudden, I had a nine-day paid job as a PA, but it meant that I was going to miss the first week of my senior year of classes at USC.

I was the parking lot PA. I was stationed at the guard gate with my list of who was allowed in. That was my first paid job in the business. The rest of my senior year, I was getting called by MTV to do more PA gigs. So I would leave school for a week at a time to go work. By the time I got out of college, I had a little client base going.

JP: I can still hear your excitement and enthusiasm about that first job.

JK: It was a really exciting time. After USC, I ended up working at Tenth Planet Productions for five years as a staff producer. I worked my way up from post super to associate producer to coordinating producer and it was great. I was in my twenties and was working 16 to 18 hours a day, six or even seven days a week. I just wanted to work and learn and move up. I had this thirst for the fun of it but also the knowledge. At one point when I was a PA, Dave Cunningham asked, "What's your short term goal, and what's your long term goal?" I said, "My short term goal is to never drive a cube truck again. My long term goal is to direct." Not long after that was the last time I ever drove a cube truck.

When I left Tenth Planet Productions after five years, I got an offer to run the *VH1 Vogue Fashion Awards*. I had worked on it for three years as a lower level producer while at Tenth Planet. Lauren Zalaznick, the head of VH1 at the time, called to offer me the job. I remember being on the phone with her and pulling over on Sunset Boulevard and saying, "Are you sure about this, Lauren? You know there's a lot that I don't know." She said, "I know. But I know you can do it." I was, like, "All right. I'm in. Let's do it." So at 27, I was running a show that was a two-hour live broadcast with a four million dollar budget and 25 A-list celebrities.

And what I had learned from my boss at Tenth Planet was that I could hire myself to direct the single-camera short films that were being incorporated into the live show. So I started utilizing my awards show producing jobs to give myself the opportunity to direct single-camera comedic shorts. And that's how I was able to build up a director's reel. I used that reel to eventually get other people to hire me as a director.

JP: Were those awards show short films the first scripted projects that you directed?

JK: Yeah. As the executive producer on those shows, I was in charge of running the writers rooms, and then I would hire myself to direct the shorts.

JP: Did you ever make a scripted short in college?

JK: Nope.

JP: So the first scripted thing you ever directed was literally something that aired for the *VH1 Fashion Awards*?

JK: Yeah.

JP: Do you remember what that first short was?

JK: There were a few in that first show I produced. They were shot on super-16mm film. One was this thing with Billy Zane and Henry Rollins called *A Fashionable War*. One was with Tim Meadows as his *SNL* character, *The Ladies Man*, which had just been released as a feature film. Some were better than others. That's what kicked off directing for me. But once I started turning down awards show work, it was actually really hard to get into story-based shows. I did a stint as a producer in reality TV with Mark Burnett because I thought that would demonstrate that I could tell a story.

Then luckily my friend Donick Cary, a writer and showrunner of some amazing half-hour comedies, called and said, "You know that Naked Trucker and T-Bones comedy show they do at Largo? I'm turning it into a variety series for Comedy Central and we have to do all these short films. Would you want to produce and direct them?" At that point, I had a director's reel with the Tim Meadows and the *Fashionable War* shorts from the *VH1 Fashion Awards*. I only had three or four things on a VHS reel, but it got me the job as the co–executive producer on *The Naked Trucker and T-Bones Show*, and I was directing all the single-camera shorts. That led to more Comedy Central work and then I got to do some *MADtv*.

But it still took years to get my first half-hour episode. There was a point at which I had Jack Black, Paul Rudd and Will Ferrell on my reel from *The Naked Trucker and T-Bones Show*. All marquee movie actors, the biggest guys in comedy at the time, but I couldn't get a half-hour show to save my life because no network or studio exec wanted to give a half-hour to a guy who had never done a half-hour. The line I was hearing was, "We can't give you a half-hour until you've done a half-hour." Well, how am I going to get a half-hour if no one will give it to me?

Then I did a whole sketch series for TBS called *Frank TV* with Frank Caliendo. I tried to shoot as many of the sketches as I could like little movies. That was something I learned early on, when I was working on the *MTV Movie Awards*: Anything you shoot, try to make it look like a little movie. So with limited resources, I would do all these really funny little sketches and try to make them as cinematic as I could.

JP: What got you your first break on a half-hour scripted show?

JK: One of the guys I was fortunate enough to work with along the way was Troy Miller. When I was an associate producer at Tenth Planet Productions, Troy directed most of the single-camera shorts on *The MTV Movie Awards*. Troy was at the cutting edge of using technology to figure out how to do stuff. He was the first director I saw to use video capture on a Mac. He had all these adapters and cables to figure out how to hook it up. And he would take stills from the actual movies that we were parodying and storyboard out where we had to cut our shots in with existing footage. Because I was dealing with all the post and was in on all the edits, I got to watch and learn a lot. I was just learning and soaking up all the info. So Troy gave me my first break. It was for *Eagleheart* with Chris Elliott on Adult Swim. They brought me in for a meeting and Troy vouched for me.

I did two episodes of *Eagleheart*. Then right on the heels of that, I got a call from Chelsea Handler's producing partner at the time, Tom Brunelle. They knew me because I had produced a special called *Comedians of Chelsea Lately*. Tom Brunelle called and said, "So you've done all those single-camera things, right? Chelsea really likes you and we're doing this series called *After Lately*. Would you want to come and talk to us about running it?" I went in and got the job running a single-camera half-hour show. Suddenly I had to learn on the job really quickly. From the time I was hired to run the show, I had five weeks before we started shooting. I cross-boarded all eight episodes and directed half of them.

Once I had done a cable half-hour, I still couldn't get a network half-hour. So that was another hurdle. I always look at a hurdle as something where if I'm told that I can't do it, I want to do it even more.

JP: Were you able to use *After Lately* to get more opportunities to direct and transition into being a full-time director?

JK: While I was running *After Lately,* I was able to duck out occasionally to go direct other things. Promos, commercials and episodes of other shows. I ran *After Lately* for three seasons and continued to build other episodic work as much as possible.

JP: You basically became a showrunner as your way into directing.

JK: I was a showrunner who hired himself to direct as a way of showing other people that I can do it.

JP: How did you get your first network half-hour?

JK: Of all the network half-hours to be your first, mine was this massively successful show called *Parks and Recreation*. I got that because of bugging my friend Dean Holland. I used to hire Dean as an editor when I was doing awards shows. In our twenties, we would sit in editing for 18 hours a day and became really close friends. We used to go to parties and play poker together. So when Dean was an executive producer on *Parks and Recreation* and it was season six, I finally asked, "What can I do?"

He had tried on a few occasions to get me in there. But it's hard. They usually bring in people that they know already. Mike Schur has accumulated a long list of people he knows. Dean had mentioned me as a possible director. But then my friend Donick Cary from *Naked Trucker and T-Bones* got on the show as a writer and co–executive producer, and he also mentioned me to Mike Schur. Then someone from the show asked the *Eagleheart* guys about me. After a bunch of people vouched for my acumen, I went in and had a meeting with David Miner and Mike Schur and I got the job.

So that basically came about from harassing my friends. I didn't want to ask Dean or Donick for help, I just wanted to get the job because of my work. But I remember thinking that if I don't ask, then I won't get to do it. So I always try to be helpful whenever anyone asks me for help. You learn that it's just part of the whole process.

For a while, the next hurdle I had was that even though I had done my first network half-hour, no one was going to give me an episode on a brand-new show, especially one of the first 13 episodes. Because it's a season one show and it doesn't know what it is yet, they typically want more established directors for the first 13 episodes. Then what about getting an episode on the back nine? On the back nine, they want to hire people that they feel comfortable with from the first 13, or the people that the showrunner already knows from the 20 years they've been in the business. So how do you get an episode on the back nine? It took years to get over all those hurdles and truly break into doing network half-hour shows. This past year was the first season where my whole season was just network half-hours and it's been almost nine years since I did my first cable half-hour.

JP: I think it's easy to look at a successful TV director and think, "They made it." But there's a sense I get from everyone I have interviewed that the hustle never really stops.

JK: I say that all the time. It was made clear to me a couple of years ago. I was at a Directors Guild breakfast and there were guys there who have done five times as many episodes as I have. They were saying that every time a show gets announced, they get on IMDb to research all the people involved. They're still doing the hustle. Making the phone calls, sending the e-mails, telling their agents about it. They're doing exactly what I'm doing and they're 20 years further along than I am. I came home and told my wife, "The hustle never stops."

JP: As part of hustling to crack into one-hour network shows, you do a series of general meetings. What is it that makes a good meeting?

JK: As I shifted into directing, I found that there is a desire on the part of the showrunner or execs to just have a real conversation as a human being. They want to hear your story, they want to see what you're about and what you gravitate towards. Once in a while I'll get a very specific sort of director question like, "What's your approach to this?" But it's typically just a conversation, a little bit of personal story, and then some dialogue about work experience. For me, the best meetings are when they are as conversational as possible. When I go into a meeting and they're asking me questions like, "Where are you from, and how did you get into this?" I always ask them about themselves as well. "How did you end up working at NBC? Where did you come from?" I actually really want to know because I find it all interesting. The best meetings are when it's a real conversation and you find that there's a mutual respect. I don't like going in and just talking about myself and leaving. It feels weird.

JP: It's been explained to me that by the time you're doing a meeting, they've already been convinced that you know how to direct.

JK: Pretty much.

JP: So it's not about them grilling you over if you know how to cover a scene because that's been established.

JK: It's never that kind of question. A lot of it is that they want to make sure you're not crazy. They want to feel out your temperament and make sure that you're someone who can handle all the big personalities on set and the dynamic of that particular show. The showrunners are empowering you to get what they want and also to bring some of your own flourish to it. There's a tremendous amount of trust that has to be there. That's the biggest thing. You have to show people that they can trust you to get what they need. Part of the job as a guest director is that you have to understand that it's not your show. I think some directors come in and they don't quite understand that. The role of a TV director is to direct, but you also have to make sure you get what the showrunner wants and what the studio wants and what the network wants. You need to have collected all of those facts during prep.

I put notes in my script referencing what I need to ensure I get for the showrunner, and also what I want to get for myself. Sometimes I'll give a note to an actor and they might have a reason that they don't really want to do a take that way. In that situation, I may even say, "Well, in the tone meeting, the showrunner said he wanted to get a take this way." That's a way to help me get a read on a take that an actor may be slightly reticent about. If you say that something came from the showrunner, it can be a tool to help get different performances. It ends up being about the intentionality of the scene, from the show's creator's perspective.

JP: Would you define "tone meeting" and "concept meeting"?

JK: Oftentimes, at nine a.m. on day one of prep, you have a concept meeting. The concept meeting is when everyone goes through the script scene by scene to conceptually discuss all of the elements. Where is the scene taking place? Is it on an existing set or is it on a location that has to be found? Are there props involved that don't exist yet? Are there things that refer to another episode that they need to make sure are there? Is there is a scene with the actor getting out of a car? Does the car actually have to move? It's typically a very practical, brief meeting, just a quick overview. Sometimes the showrunner is there and sometimes not.

You just jump right into the practical details during the concept meeting, so you need to have read the script and done some of your own prep work at home before your official prep starts. You need to be prepared to talk about it and ask questions. The concept meeting is typically led by the first AD. After the concept meeting, you will scout the sets and locations. You start to digest all the material and come up with your own ideas and questions for the showrunner.

The tone meeting is the opportunity for the showrunner to creatively go through the script with the director page by page, and vice versa. They usually tell you the intent of the episode as a whole and what it's trying to say. They share what they want about the characters and their backstories. A lot of times, the showrunner will tell you about specific traits the regular actors might have. For instance, this one prefers to do their takes last if you're not cross-shooting. This other one needs more time to ramp up, or he's better right out of the gate, so get his coverage first. Or you should do his closeup first because he burns out, and then you can do the wide last. It's all the little details a director needs that you'll never be able to know from watching the show, even if you've watched every episode. It's all insider stuff. The tone meeting is your final chance to get answers to any questions that haven't been addressed yet, like, "In what way is this character meant to say such and such line?" Or, "For this prop, did you want the yardstick or the ruler?" There's a lot to absorb very quickly when you step into a show. Sometimes it can even be info about the dynamic between two actors and how they are getting along. The editor can be helpful with that as well.

JP: What's the worst mistake a director can make?

JK: One of the worst mistakes is missing a piece of coverage, or just very specifically ignoring a showrunner's request. That's one of the most egregious things. If you have your tone meeting and the showrunner tells you very specifically that he wants something a certain way and you don't get it, then you haven't done your job.

JP: Is there something that you wish you had known when you started?

JK: Yes. I learned this lesson the hard way when I was still running big, multi-cam live variety shows: You have to let the network be right. I was running a show for VH1 and I was digging my heels in on a creative element. Looking back, I wonder why I cared so much. I cared, obviously, about what I was making, but I cared too much about a detail that I should have been more indifferent or at least compromising about. It was a real awakening. I should have just told the network, "Sure. Whatever you want."

As much as you want to think it's your show, it's not your show. It's not your money. You're working for a big conglomerate. This lesson definitely carries over to directing. The showrunner is right. It's their show and you have to recognize that. I know of a director who went in on a show and he wanted to do his thing, what he does, in his style. But it wasn't matching the style of the show. It got to the point where the showrunner was on the phone with the network saying, "He's not getting closeups. He's not getting the coverage we need." And the network said, quote, "Tell him to get the fucking coverage." They had to have this conversation with the director: "The network wants to make sure that you get a closeup on everything." And the director was saying, "But that's not how I do it." In the end, he didn't get asked back. Actually, he went from a guy that I saw directing a lot and now I'm not really seeing him that much. It's not your position to do that when you're a guest on an existing show. The showrunner is always right. You can think of ideas and pitch them, and sometimes you can even ask a question about the story where the showrunner might think, "Oh, my gosh. I hadn't even thought about that." But ultimately you have to get what is required of that show. And then figure out how to add your own stamp on top of that.

Jude Weng

Working on an episode that Jude Weng is directing is more than just a job, it's a life experience. She's part teacher, part life coach, part guru. Her style of leadership on set involves starting a party and making sure that everyone is invited. There is always dancing on a Jude Weng set.

When I decided to undertake this book, Jude was the first person I reached out to. Not only did she agree to my interview request, she also set me up with the connections to find more directors. In addition to everything else, after the interview she insisted that I stay for lunch and proceeded to whip up a killer chicken stir-fry. When Jude decides to give, she gives her all.

· ·

JUDE WENG: I have a weird and complicated story for how I got into this business. I come from a working class, immigrant, Taiwanese-American family. When I was three, my parents came to the U.S. on a tourist visa. Then the visa expired, which meant that we were illegal immigrants. So it was all very strategic. I grew up in my family's diner in the San Francisco Castro district in the mid–70s when it was becoming a gay mecca. It was also the epicenter of the hippie and radical revolution. That provided a lot of stories. My mom abandoned our family when I was very young. So all of a sudden I was this dirty little kid with no mom that was always covered in blood because I did a lot of butchering and food prep for the diner. I grew up dirty because I didn't have a mom around to tell me to take a shower. I probably looked feral.

The Castro also had a lot of straight, Irish, working-class, Protestant folks who hated immigrants. But they hated gay people even more. There was a lot of racial tension and a lot of violence. They would attack us in the diner parking lot, me, my dad and my sisters. They would

The experience of working as a kid in her immigrant family's restaurant gave Jude Weng the strongest work ethic in the business (Jacob Pinger).

75

ambush us and spraypaint, "Fuck you chinks. Go home chinks. Die chinks." And then it became, "Fuck you, you fag-loving chinks. Die fags." Stuff like that. It was my job to paint over the graffiti every day. It was a crazy childhood. There was lots of graphic violence. I would see my dad getting attacked. But they didn't know who the fuck he was, and he would beat their asses. I'll give you this highlight: In Taiwan, my father was a lieutenant colonel, and worked for the Ministry of Defense. There were things in his past he didn't want to talk about. Things he was hiding from. He spoke of a "friend" who trained spies and assassins, and I frequently wondered if he was actually talking about himself.

JACOB PINGER: Your father was a badass.

JW: And being a former military guy, his biggest thing was that I should not be an artist. He would say, "Artists die poor, so don't be an artist." He used to tell a little story: He had an army buddy who after the military decided to become a professional painter, an artist. And he could barely make any money. He had a wife and kids, and he got really sick. He couldn't afford the medicine, and eventually his widow came around asking my dad for money to buy a coffin. And so that was literally the steady drumbeat in my head as a kid: Don't be an artist.

JP: How did he react when you first told him you were going into show biz as your career?

JW: When I got my scholarship to the American Film Institute's Directing Workshop for Women program, he was more impressed with the statistics of it—that I was one of only eight women chosen for this prestigious program. He visited Los Angeles, and I walked him around the AFI campus. We walked down the long hallway filled with framed photos of AFI's many luminaries, and he said, "So you're going to make movies? I would have liked being a painter, but all I know how to do is kill." That was as close to a compliment as I'll ever get from my father. I like to think he was a little happy and maybe even envious that I was on the path of becoming an artist.

JP: You have quite a story.

JW: I do have a story, but I used to reject my childhood. I was very embarrassed growing up poor, being an immigrant, and not having a traditional upbringing. I didn't even get to watch TV. Other kids would talk about *The Brady Bunch* and *The Monkees*. And I didn't know what the fuck that was. People would laugh at me. I was the weirdo immigrant kid.

The only time I got to watch TV was once or twice a week when it was time to count the cash at the diner. On Friday, I had to count all the cash and prepare it for the bank. Cash-counting night was a huge treat because that's when we got to watch TV. But we got home so late from the restaurant that all the channels were already off except for PBS. So I grew up watching *Fawlty Towers*, *Benny Hill*, *Monty Python* and Mutual of Omaha nature documentaries. I still love British shows.

We had two restaurants. The second restaurant was in a worse part of town called the Tenderloin. And again, this was like the height of meth and the porn industry and cocaine and heroin. It was a crazy time, and for whatever reason my dad thought I could manage that restaurant better than the first one, which was in a much nicer neighborhood.

JP: How old were you?

JW: Twelve. I would let all the other employees go and then I would lock up. I would mop the floor, and sometimes I had to kick people out of the bathroom because they would be in there shooting up, or there would be prostitutes giving blow jobs to their johns. I had to kick down the door. But then it would be like 11:30 at night. I'd lock up the restaurant and I would have to wait for a bus, the Eight and Market, to ride it up to the Castro where my older sisters were working at the nicer restaurant. I had such a weird, un-relatable childhood.

My graphic and violent upbringing really informs who I am as a director. And it informs the kinds of stories I want to tell. It informs the kinds of characters that I gravitate toward. And because I actually survived my weird, fucked-up childhood, I think that's why I'm drawn to comedy. What helped me survive was that I could laugh at shit. I've seen so much weird shit. One time I found a redheaded, gay dwarf in a tailored plaid shirt and ass-less chaps floating face down in a public fountain. I think somebody beat him for his welfare money. I think he was a male prostitute. I knew him. He would walk around, and I would recognize him. I would try to be nice to him but he would yell at me. He called me a chink too. I found it really fucking weird and funny.

Another part of my story is that our diner wasn't far from the SFPD special ops building. So a lot of our customers were cops, snipers, bomb squad guys, K9 unit and cavalry. All those badasses would come eat at our diner. So when I was done with my restaurant work, I would go do my homework in the dining area and sit there with these guys. They would be telling their stories and I literally grew up like in the middle of a *Law and Order* episode, every fucking day. I would hear them talking about cases and crimes and bodies they found. And I grew up with this entire cop lingo. I was sort of adopted by those cops. Once one of them saw me eating a pancake, and I didn't know how to use a knife and fork. I took the whole pancake onto the fork, just skewering the whole disk, and I was trying to eat it. This cop walked behind me and he put his arms around me and he showed me how to use a knife and fork to cut the pancake. I was raised in a cinematic world but I didn't appreciate my story until recently. And that's a big part of my evolution as a director, actually. One thing I tell a friend who is an emerging writer is, "How can you be hired to write other people's stories when you don't value your own?" I think that's very true for directors as well. You have to value your story. You have to really be clear about who you are.

By the way, when I take a meeting, these are the things I talk about. People ask me, "What do you think you bring to the table as a director?" I really think I understand how people behave and think and what really makes them tick. I think a good director has high E.Q.—emotional intelligence. All of my life experiences have helped me develop high E.Q.

JP: How is your dad today regarding your choice of career?

JW: To this day, my father really doesn't understand what I do for a living. Other than *Benny Hill* reruns and old Mutual of Omaha documentaries, he doesn't watch any TV. That said, I once had to direct some pickups and interviews for an ABC show in San Francisco, and after watching me work for an hour he said, "You're like a field general. Good." My father was a man of few words.

You know what kind of pop-culture hole I had in my life? All the kids at school were talking about this movie called *Indiana Jones* and how amazing it was. Well, I had never seen a movie before.

JP: How old were you when you saw your first movie?

JW: I was 11. I had such a weird, small life. It was just work and school. So I kept hearing about this movie and how amazing it was. Well, I had some balls, man. I stole some money from my dad's restaurant, and I cut school. I took the bus to this theater on Van Ness Street. I didn't even know what to do, I had never even been to a movie before. So I was like, "Ummm, I heard there was a movie." They're like, "Yes." I said, "How do I see the movie?" and they're like, "You pay for the ticket." So I paid money, walked into the theater and sat in the front row. There was nobody there but I still sat in the front row because I didn't know better. I thought it was a live show. And then that movie [*Raiders of the Lost Ark*] came on. And it fucking changed my life. You remember that movie? It was the first one with the rolling boulder. When I saw that, I jumped out of my chair and ran up the aisle. But it was incredible. One of these days I'm going to write a letter to Steven Spielberg and thank him.

But even at that point, I wasn't thinking that I wanted to become a director. I didn't know what a director was. All I knew was that the experience of seeing that Indiana Jones movie moved me. It changed me. Cinema became deeply engrained in my subconscious. Over the next few years, I found ways to channel that. I started writing and I put on some plays.

JP: Was this through school or on your own?

JW: It was very self-generated. I was reading above my age because I had older sisters, and I was really obsessed with Greek mythology. Susan Story, an English teacher, encouraged me to put on a play of my favorite Greek myth, which was King Midas's Touch.

I started an Asian-American sketch comedy troupe in my late teens and early twenties, and it was successful enough that I started touring colleges around the country. I wrote and produced and directed. So I always found a way to be a storyteller, and create content.

JP: Once you were in that world, especially in that era, L.A. and New York City were the places to go.

JW: Yes, exactly. I was 24 when I moved to L.A. I was desperate to pay rent, so I did all these temp jobs. I've worked on so many different things. When I first moved to L.A., I worked the graveyard shift at a Donna Antonia's Pizza. I worked as a matchmaker at a dating service called Together. I helped order condoms on Princess Cruises. I worked as craft services for a Christian music video company. I've had a bunch of weird jobs.

JP: Did you move to L.A. to pursue a career in the entertainment industry?

JW: Yes. And I didn't know anybody here. I wanted to work in the film industry in any capacity. I'll get coffee. I'll wash cars. I didn't care. I had no ego. There was no job too small for me to do. I was so determined to get my foot in the door. The first real job that I had in the industry was at New Line Cinema, I worked in the music department for a guy named Toby Emmerich, who is now the president of New Line. My other boss was Paul Broucek, who I still consider like a father figure and mentor. When I left New Line in 1999, I got a scholarship to attend the AFI Directors Workshop for Women. I had New Line's blessing, and they gave me money to help me make my short.

Right out of the AFI program, I made two shorts. One was seen by Nancy Jacoby. She has a really deep history as a producer. She worked at Discovery Channel and CNN and is just a really lovely, kind woman. She was looking for talent, looking for people who had an eye. This was early 1999. *Survivor* didn't exist yet. She hired me to do travel interstitials. I would go to exotic destinations and figure out how to write, create, produce, direct and edit 20 spots. I was what you call a preditor now. A preditor is somebody who produces, directs, writes and edits. They do everything. And it was the best training ground for me as a director. But because I was traveling, because I was a multi-hyphenate, somebody said, "Oh, you'd be really valuable on this new show. They really need people who are going to be multi-hyphenates." That was the first season of *Survivor*. I started out as a challenge producer, and then I got promoted to co-head writer. And I was writing all of Jeff Probst's copy.

JP: Your reality TV career really took off. You worked your way up to being a showrunner. At what point did you say, "I'm going to leave the unscripted world and get into scripted TV"?

JW: It was so hard. It was as if my work in reality TV was a scarlet letter around town.

And there was a part of me that for quite some time really minimized it. I didn't bring it up. But it was really hard not to, because I had developed so many skills from it. I felt like in some ways I was not honoring my own experience. That was actually really hard. But now I'm at a point in my career where I feel like I can talk about it, and it's not a scarlet letter anymore.

JP: It used to be worse than having porn on your résumé.

JW: Yeah, it really was. But how did I do it? I was very tactical. I'm fucking tenacious. I will keep going after what I want. Once I set my sights on becoming an episodic director, I just knew I was going to be tireless about it. I had to get out of reality TV. And that was really scary on a personal level because I was making a certain income as a showrunner, and all of a sudden my husband was like, "Are you having a midlife crisis here?" It coincided with me turning 40. So I think there was a part of me that said, "In life, we only regret the choices we didn't make and the dreams we didn't pursue." I think philosophically, I needed to go and really try. But coming from reality, I didn't know anybody in scripted at all. And people in scripted protect their relationships very carefully. Now that I work in the scripted world, I really understand why. It's because the people that you refer really reflect upon you. For example, I thought, "God, how hard could it be to get somebody to let me shadow them?" It was impossible. And then I heard about the ABC Directing Program. I applied and was really fortunate that I got in. The program certainly helped open some doors. But it doesn't give you everything. The onus is on you to make the most of it. I shadowed through the ABC program three times, and then on my own. Once I started making relationships, I started to ask different directors to allow me to shadow them. I was able to shadow probably 12 directors. And they were all so different.

JP: How long did it take to become a director? From the point you decided to get out of reality TV to booking your first directing job?

JW: Six years almost to the day. You want to know something really weird? When I first got into the ABC Directing Program, there was a big general meeting with all 16 of us directing fellows. There was somebody from the DGA and ABC and they were welcoming us. They said, "You all come from some aspect of the entertainment business, and what we've seen is that on average it takes five years to make the transition to director." So technically, from when I got into the program to when I got my first directing job on *Fresh Off the Boat* was five years. But I had already spent a year before that trying to make a short film. I finally got to shadow on *Fresh Off the Boat*, and it was super-exciting. Then they offered me another chance to shadow. And my husband was almost at the end of his rope with me shadowing. He was like, "You already shadowed on *Fresh Off the Boat*, why do you need to go shadow the same show again?" When you shadow, nobody is paying you. So between pre-production, production and post, that's almost a three-week commitment.

I did it as thoroughly as I could. I'm not sitting there on my cell phone. I'm blocking. I'm preparing. I've gotten together with other emerging directors, and several of them were bemoaning how boring it is to shadow. I didn't want to criticize those people to their faces, because who am I to do that? But my thinking was, if you're shadowing and you're bored, then you are not shadowing properly. Wherever you come from in the business, it doesn't hurt to be a little humble. I think that humbleness keeps you open. It keeps you emotionally available.

JP: How did you get your first job as a director?

JW: For my first directing gig on *Fresh Off the Boat*, I got that job because I was shadowing. Apparently I was the first *Fresh Off the Boat* director who got hired from shadowing.

But the first part of getting the job is being in a meeting. You have to be in a meeting where somebody likes you enough to want to send you to another meeting. You go to that other meeting, and *they* have to like you enough to send you to *another* meeting. On average, you can take one to ten meetings to book a single job. I think I took nearly 16 meetings for my first job on *Fresh Off the Boat*. For that show, I had to meet with studio people, and sometimes the studio people are not all there at the same time. So you might meet with somebody who can't be the decision-maker, but then recommends you to their boss. So just on the studio side, it's maybe two or three meetings. Then on the network side, it's the same thing: two or three meetings because not everybody can meet at the same time. And then you've got to meet the production company. Then you've got to meet the showrunner.

After I directed that *Fresh Off the Boat*, they hired me back almost immediately in the same season. And that was the game changer.

JP: How would you describe the job of a TV comedy director?

JW: My job as a TV comedy director is to make sure that I understand the writer's and the showrunner's vision for that episode, and to help elevate their story cinematically.

JP: How is that different from the traditional film auteur or Hitchcockian idea of what a director is?

JW: The difference is that as a traditional director, I wouldn't need to ask the writer or showrunner for permission to do certain things. Like, "Hey, can I have this character do this even though it's not scripted?" So you really have to make sure that the writer and the showrunner are on board with what you want to do. Your job is to execute their vision. It's not to say that you don't have your own vision or that you aren't bringing your own ideas. But in my opinion, you must check your ego at the door and sublimate your vision for theirs. And some people don't like that. In fact, very candidly I would say that 80 percent of the directors I talk to attribute that to why they are burned out. Day in and day out, they feel so tired of not being able to even suggest a line or pitch jokes lest the writer feels like, "Oh, the directors trying to fucking write the show now?" On some shows, there is actually disdain for the guest director. If the guest director says, "Hey, we already got that take, what do you think about trying this other thing?"—in my mind, that's respectful. But on some shows, that's a big fucking no-no. So who are you then, as a TV comedy director? You're a traffic cop. That's a frequent complaint of working directors, they feel reduced to being a traffic cop.

JP: There are a lot of bosses for a TV comedy director to answer to. How do you navigate that?

JW: First of all, I want to give you a little context. I am relatively new to episodic directing. I was a showrunner for 15 years and I directed competition game shows. So I've probably directed over 300 hours of reality TV. But none of that matters. In the scripted world, I'm seen as a new director. So, that said, I think one of the reasons I'm getting booked so much now is that I bring so much enthusiasm and so much happiness. I'm not bitter and unhappy. And I think my joy and my passion shows. My mentor Beth Rooney has directed over 180 episodes of TV. She still prepares and she's still passionate. Every time I talk to her, what I hear is gratitude and recognition [of the fact] that what we get to do is a privilege. I very much come from that same school.

Keep in mind that you are a guest on every set you go to. And that's the weird part. You're the new kid on campus. Everybody else is a part of the machine. You're being judged and evaluated the moment you show up. People are deciding not just if they like you, but also if they are still going to like you after five really stressful shoot days next week. They're evaluating you on that human level. But more than anything, are you the kind of person who communicates, expresses and plans in a way that's going to make their lives more difficult or easier? So from a self-defense perspective, that's how you're getting evaluated by people. I've shadowed a lot of other directors and it's interesting how differently they approach the prep period. To me, your prep is where you figure out who your bosses are. It's true that you have multiple bosses, and if anyone says otherwise, I would think they're delusional. That's especially true for episodic TV because, again, you're the guest. So I think you walk in and you have to be deferential to a point. You need to have a point of view, and you need to know how to get what you want. But you also need to listen and collaborate, and hear what people have to say.

On some shows, you walk in and they say, "We never do one-ers here. We never do Steadicam shots. Don't ask for a crane. Don't do this, don't do that." And that's great to know, but at the same time when you look at your script, you have to recognize when there may be times where you explore. Is there a good reason to maybe break one of the rules? Here's what I do to prepare as a director: I talk to as many people in prep as I can. I don't go in and judge anybody. I just go learn what I can, especially from the editor. The editor is the closest to the showrunner and the writers, so the editor really knows what they like. The editor knows all their little peccadillos. I ask, "Can you give me the top ten things to do or not do or to be careful of?" For example, when I was a showrunner, I would tell my camera person that I would never use a snap zoom. If they were doing an establishing shot of a sign and they did a snap zoom, I would never use it. So I would tell them, "Please don't do that." Those are the kinds of things I want to know. And what I find amazing, show after show, is that I've had editors turn to me and say, "You're the first director to come meet with me before you shoot." And I don't understand why. I don't think I'm like a hero for doing that. But I find that confusing.

So perhaps as an episodic director, I can't help but wear a little bit of the showrunner hat when I'm directing. And I don't know if that's beneficial or damaging to me. But maybe sometimes I'm thinking too much as a producer. I'll be like, "Fuck, I really want to wrap by 11 hours," instead of saying, "You know what? So they're going to have a meal penalty. So they have to call grace. Don't worry about that. Make sure you get what you want to get." They always say that you only regret the shots you didn't get. But then how much do you push it? And then, of course, there's the working director voice in the back of my head: "Shit, if I go over-time or over-budget, will I get invited back?" There are so many priorities and thoughts and insecurities, and questions that are bubbling in your head, every second of the day. It's really, really intense.

One of the first shows that I shadowed on was *Happy Endings*. I became really friendly with the editor, and she invited me to come observe her in the edit bay. She said, "I'm going to show you what kind of director gets invited back or not." Then she opened up her computer to show me the episode she was currently working on. All the shots were categorized in columns of where the footage was. And there were a number of gaps where certain shots should have been. She said, "This particular director will not be invited back. Everybody on set loved them. But I'm telling the showrunner they did not get enough coverage, and this person will not come back because of my recommendation." And she was right.

JP: Sitting with the editor in prep seems like a great idea. Don't other directors do that?

JW: I'm certain some directors do. But the editors that I have met with have said to me that other directors don't. I also ask them to give me screen grabs that illustrate how the show frames their shots. What framing do they use for a closeup, a medium and a wide? What's important is to learn the lexicon of each show because every one has its own personality and style. If you were to look at ten different shows, none of those shots would match. In other words, a closeup on *The Real O'Neals* is what somebody would call a medium shot on a different show. So in an effort to make sure that I nail what the show wants, I will sit with the editor because they can literally give me screen grabs of the different shots, and then I use those to build my "decks." I think the term "decks" comes from the marketing world. It comes from developing concepts for people to go pitch at networks. A deck is a kind of power point presentation that has images and text. It's like a look book. I build it in Key Note. Some people call it a power point because it's a combination of visuals and text. Look, there are directors out there who do shot lists on the back of a napkin, and they get great stuff. And good for them. I don't know how to do that.

JP: For a new director, first, second or third episode in a career, what are some of the poison pills that can come up? Is it like offending an actor?

JW: On certain shows, certain actors have a tremendous amount of power. And it can be that simple. Offend an actor, and you're not coming back. Every show has different power dynamics. On some shows, the DP is so powerful that if they don't like you, you're not coming back.

Know the actors' names. That really goes a long way. It's amazing but that can demonstrate that a director doesn't really know the show, and that it's just a job to them. If you show up and treat it like it's just a job, people feel that. It's already a reason not to like you because everybody on a show cares so much. It's like going to somebody's house for the first time and you tell the hosts that their children aren't very attractive. Are you an idiot? That's not to say that you should be a phony and overly complimentary because I think people can tell if you're disingenuous.

JP: Tell me more about your directing philosophy.

JW: I don't put on airs. I've seen other directors do that, and maybe that works for them. But I find it confusing. With some directors, I think there's this perception of, "I'm the captain of this ship. I'm the pilot of this plane. I'm the leader." I take a totally different approach. I try to be more Socratic in my method. I don't think I appear weak if I pose direction as a question. For me, it gives the actor an option. Actually, it's kind of Chinese. For example, when Chinese people ask something, they don't just say, "Do you want to drink tea?" Rather, everything is posed as offering an option. They will say, "Do you or do you not want to drink tea?" I do something very similar when I direct. I say to an actor, "What do you think of this?" And most of the time, the actor will be like, "Oh, yeah, it's really cool." By posing it as a question, it gives me the opportunity to create a dialogue.

JP: What is the role of relationships in a director's career, and can you talk about the difference between shmoozing and relationships?

JW: I can understand why your initial word is shmoozing because there's this perception of, "Hey, who are you? What do you do? And what can you give me?" But I've never been that kind of person. I'm even a little jealous of people like that. I kind of wish I could be more nakedly ambitious in terms of the relationships I build. But I've always been somebody who really believes in quality of life. I want to surround myself with people that I genuinely like. I want to always be genuine with the people that I'm with. And therefore I'd rather be with people that I like rather than people I "need."

Relationships are incredibly important. But I think that building a genuine relationship means being your authentic self and having a true connection with somebody, so that no matter where you are in your career, you can always connect with them. So what is a relationship other than a genuine, deep connection?

It sounds like a cliché but you should be kind to everyone. Every person that you meet, you have no idea where they could end up. I have a friend who is a TV executive. Her former assistant is running a studio now. So don't discount where people are currently at regarding their role and position.

JP: What roles do you think age, race, gender and sexual orientation have in getting work as a director?

JW: I actually wanted to get into directing TV back in 1999 when I finished the AFI Directors Workshop for Women [DWW]. What ended up happening was so soul-crushing: I had completed the DWW workshop and finished my short. So I thought I would join the DGA and instantly get hired. I had pretty unrealistic visions about getting into the industry. I had a meeting at the DGA and the rep there said, "Congratulations, what do you want to do now?" I said, "I want to direct TV." The rep said, "Wait one second." And then he turned around to the computer and printed up this dot matrix print-out. He slid this piece of paper across to me and said, "This is our analysis for the current year. One percent of television is being directed by women." That was 1999.

JP: So was he doing that as a way of saying, "You go in there and get 'em because we gotta change this?" Or was this more like a reality check?

JW: It was a reality check. What he was telling me was, "You may not want to do that." The message was that women tend to break into commercials a little easier, or music videos.

JP: So it was like friendly advice?

JW: Yes, friendly advice.

JP: Friendly advice can be the worst form of sexism.

JW: It can be. But I'm very aware that people look at me and think that I represent other women. I don't like that responsibility, but I'm aware of it. I don't want to have to represent all Asian women and all women in general. But I understand that. You will hear people say about a show, "Ugh, that was not funny. Well that's why you don't hire women!" People will say shit like that. But if a bearded white guy came and directed an episode of *Life in Pieces* and didn't do a very good job, do you think anyone would ever say, "This is why we don't hire bearded white guys"? That sounds absurd. Yet it's okay to say that about women. You know what I mean?

Here's another quick anecdote: So I finally joined the DGA after 18 years. Over all that time before I joined, I used to drive past that awesome DGA building on Sunset and I would literally put my hand up and be like, "One day I'm gonna get in there." I finally joined in January of 2016. And a few months later, I attended my first event at the DGA. I was over the moon. I actually came out from the parking garage and as I walked in, I had little tears. My eyes got all watery. It felt so amazing. I was finally a card-carrying member of the Directors Guild of America.

They were doing some panel, which was awesome. Afterwards there was a general mingling session and a stranger, a white guy, walked up to me and said, "Hey, I heard you're booking a lot of episodes this season." I said, "Yeah, I am." He said, "You're one of the reasons why I can't get hired any more." My jaw hit the floor. I wasn't fast enough with a comeback. I didn't know what to say, and he walked away from me. What that guy said to me at the DGA hurt my feelings. But then I take a step back and say, "He doesn't know who I am. He doesn't know that I grew up in a family where we were starving, and that I've eaten out of garbage cans. If he knew me, he'd probably be really happy that I'm getting this work. But I'm just symbolic of something. So I'm not going to let that come into my body and my psyche." My mentor said something to me when I was having trouble on a particular show with some particular personalities and I called her for advice. She said, "Jude, kill them with kindness."

JP: What is some specific advice you would give as a mentor to people reading this book?

JW: When you hear people talk about, "Oh, yeah, I want to be a director but I don't have the money to make a short," I call fucking bullshit on that because I made my short for $500. It's not the best-looking thing, but it tells a story. And that's what people really pay attention to. When you know how to tell a story, people are very forgiving if the light is not perfect and the production values are not high. The question is, can you carry a story with a beginning, middle and end? That's what people are really looking for.

If you apply to any of these directing fellowships, they actually say it in their application: Please send us a narrative short that has a beginning, middle and end. Why do they have to say it? There are a lot of people who make mood movies with no character arcs. And they may be very beautiful and experimental. But that's not TV. Don't make a mood film.

I also tell people, "Don't go to film school." I look at all these people coming to set who are still in debt from film school and they don't even know what an apple box is. That actually happened. There is so much you can learn by doing it. Keep creating, no matter what, at whatever stage you are in your career. Don't give yourself excuses to not create. So whether you're writing or directing or shooting, you need to be making something. Give yourself your film school.

JP: I think that's never been truer than now.

JW: And I would tell all those young directors who read this book, "Don't fucking rush it. Bide your time." I know so many people who really weren't ready. They got their first job and it wasn't great. And then they went to TV jail. TV jail is real! I have a friend who finally got out of TV jail. It took them six years. They got one episode and did not do a great job. It wasn't horrible, but they didn't impress. And they annoyed enough people that they were sent to TV jail for six fucking years.

I also find that a lot of the people I've been mentoring over the last couple of years don't know how to handle themselves in a room. They actually don't know how to keep the conversation going. I have the most wonderful mentor. She is an executive at HBO named Kat McCaffrey. And I said to Kat, "Everybody wants to work at HBO. You must meet the cream of the crop of writers and directors. How do you make a hiring decision?" She said, "I make a hiring decision based on people I want to continue the conversation with." I fucking love that line, and I say it to everyone I mentor now. How are you going to prepare yourself to walk into a room with a studio executive, or a network executive, or a showrunner, and share things about yourself that make them want to continue the conversation with you? Because even if they don't hire you for that show, they might think, "Wow, this is a person I really want to continue the conversation with." But a lot of people actually don't know how to do it. Guess what? There's no science to it. It really is an art. But if there were any science to it, I would say this: Don't spend your time sharing your résumé when you meet because people can just pick up your résumé and read it. Share something about yourself that opens up the world of possibilities of how this person sees you. Share stories that make people want to continue the conversation. I don't mean to sound so hippy, but we really are all snowflakes. We're all so different and individual. Sometimes it's lying right under your nose, and you don't even realize what's special about you. I'm talking about somebody who is a fully formed person.

There are so many young people who are like, "I want to be a director." And the reason they want to do it is because it seems glamorous and they want be in charge. They want to be a storyteller, and make a lot of money. Sure, that's all well and good, but for people who really want to become a director, I would say, "Go be a fully formed human being first." At that point, you have far more value on a set.

Diego Velasco

The journey of a television director can be tough. Sometimes it's not clear if you are moving forwards or backwards. But regardless of where you are on that journey, you have to create your own happiness in life. I don't think anyone embodies that idea more than Diego Velasco.

When I walked into his house in Silver Lake, I knew that it was a happy home. First of all, it looked like one of those magazine spreads where a creative person has taken the bones of a beautiful old house and turned it into a hip, tasteful haven. In the backyard, Diego's office is a custom-designed wooden structure filled with memorabilia from his career. As I heard his story, it occurred to me that, like his unique home, his career has been a remarkable construction cut entirely from the whole cloth of his creative mind.

• • • • • • • • • • • • • • • • • • • •

DIEGO VELASCO: I grew up in two different worlds. I was born in Buffalo, New York. My mom is from Venezuela and my dad is a Cuban doctor. They divorced when I was 11, and I was transplanted to Caracas, Venezuela, to live with my mom.

JACOB PINGER: What do you remember from your early life in Buffalo?

DV: Cold as hell. But I don't remember that much from Buffalo. My first seven years were there, and then we moved to the suburbs of Miami where I lived for about four years. I was in the fourth grade when my parents divorced. I went to Venezuela to live with my mom. That was 1984 or '85.

I got a wake-up call really fast when I went from the quiet suburbs of Fort Lauderdale to Caracas, which is very urban and people are more combative and aggressive. I was this 11-year-old American kid who had grown up on pop culture. In Venezuela, I was always daydreaming about American movies: *Raiders of the Lost Ark*, *Goonies*, *Back to the Future*, *The NeverEnding Story*. But I was living in the world of Caracas where sometimes the truth was way stranger than fiction. I spoke the language because my parents had taught me Spanish, but in Venezuela I was still the gringo kid with the American accent. That always made me an outsider, and I had to work hard to fit in. From that point on, for pretty much my entire life, I've always been on the outside looking in.

JP: What was that transition like?

DV: I went from being an upper middle-class doctor's kid, going to a private Catholic school, two cars in the garage and never having to worry about anything, to being stuck in a Venezuelan apartment that my uncle lent to us, and going to a public school which had so many kids they had to run it in shifts. So one set of kids went to school in the morning from 7 a.m. to 12 p.m., and then a different set of kids went to school from 1 p.m. to 6 p.m. Usually the kids who were in those afternoon shifts tended to be a little more trouble because they stayed up late. They put me in the afternoon shift. After seeing the teacher get bullied out of the classroom on my first day in a Venezuelan school, I was like, "What the fuck am I doing here?" I wanted to cry, but I knew that I could not show fear. So I grew up fast.

JP: That's a pretty intense change for such a young kid.

DV: My mom did the best she could. But she took it really hard. She went from never having worked a day in her life to becoming a secretary. Thank God she knew several languages. She started working as the president's secretary at a multinational pharmaceutical company. But it was not the same as being a doctor's wife. My mom was amazing at always sheltering us, but we all had to chip in. We had to learn how to cook and do

Diego Velasco's self-made journey to directing has represented the epitome of perseverance and never losing faith (Carolina Paiz).

things to help out. I had to go pick up my younger sisters and brother at school. I think that my fear of confrontation comes from seeing my mom needing desperate help and turning to her kids to be, in a way, their own parents. It took a toll on me. It made me even more quiet and scared to voice things. It made me escape more into my own reality.

The flip side was that back in the States, I had been the kid who never felt special. When I arrived in Caracas, I was immediately the gringo outsider with the Nikes and the Levis and the things that nobody else had there. All of a sudden I was special, and that gave me a status that I had never experienced. And it helped me. People wanted to meet me. They would shout to me, "Hey, gringo!" Then it was like I was everybody's friend. That experience kind of fed into how I responded to things as I grew up. I was the outsider trying to fit in, which became something unique to me.

Later, when I returned to the States and arrived in Mississippi, the same thing happened. I was this Latin guy who was a metal head, so I was hanging out on the reservation with the Choctaw Indians, who loved metal. The Indians didn't hang out with the whites but I could. The white guys were into rock'n'roll and we listened to Lynyrd Skynyrd. I was also hanging out with the African-American brothers because I was Latin, and they were like, "No, no. You're different. You're not white." I could hang out with everybody. And every group would say, "You're different. You're not like the rest. You're one of us." It was interesting to be the outsider but also to be flexible in being able to do all that kind of stuff with each group.

I think those experiences prepared me to be a director. My leadership skill is that I can make everybody feel really comfortable and encourage them to do their best. I think that quality came from all the situations I was forced to deal with as an outsider.

In Latin America, there's a saying: "You suffer through life enjoying every minute you can." People really live their lives to the fullest, for good or for bad. So I learned to enjoy life in that way. I think that's the thing that changed me the most in Venezuela. I learned to overcome my shyness. Then every time I moved to a new place, like Mississippi, or California, or New Orleans, I would always make the effort to be, like, "Nobody knows me here, so I'm going to start from scratch and be the person that I want to be." I do that every single time I move to a new place. I even do that every time I step on a new set as a director. I say, "Nobody knows me here. So I'm going to come across as the director who knows all their shit, even though on the inside I may be freaking out." It gives you the opportunity to always present that image, you know? And whatever director doesn't tell you they get nervous is not telling the truth. I shadowed Bill Purple, and he told me that he still gets nervous on the Sunday before he starts shooting. He told me, "If you don't get nervous, you're not doing your job." And he's done a ridiculous number of episodes, and he's super good at what he does. He's super-fast and everybody loves him.

JP: Tell me more about your life in Venezuela.

DV: In Venezuela, I was a horrible student, and a horrible athlete, and a frustrated musician. I was never going to have enough talent to be the next Jimi Hendrix or Lars Ulrich, like I wanted. Daydreaming was the only thing I knew how to do. Actually, I failed the sixth grade because I was a horrible student. I failed by not going to class. I was just not a good student. Never did homework once. Never studied. So my grades were not great. My mom did everything she could. But she never really sat down to check in with me or do homework with me. I just slipped through the cracks. And my other two sisters were brainiacs. So because they were doing well in class, I think my mom was surprised when they held me back. "What do you mean, you have to do sixth grade again?"

JP: She just figured all her kids would be smart?

DV: [*laughs*] Yeah. *Surprise!* There was this huge mountain in front of the school. We would just ditch class and create things there. We would build forts and all kinds of things. We were reenacting scenes from *Goonies* outside the school.

JP: Were there any other movies that you and your Venezuelan friends were obsessed with?

DV: All those '80s movies, like *Gremlins*. Very early on, I was always messing with a camera. I was in literature class in high school and the teacher said, "Okay, we're going to put on a play." I said, "Can I just make a movie instead?" And they were like, "Yeah." My high school friends were all the sons of high-ranking military officers in Venezuela. So we had, like, 15-year-old kids who had access to things that they shouldn't have. Army uniforms, and an airport, and battleships, shit like that. So we're like, "Let's go do this!" We studied all those American movies that we worshipped, like *Platoon*, *Top Gun* and *First Blood*. We were doing crazy stuff trying to imitate those movies. We were shooting in private airports and doing all these chase sequences without even knowing what a script was, or what a low angle shot was, or what a dolly was. It wasn't so much that we wanted to make movies. We just wanted to be the cool guys who were *in* them.

JP: What made you decide to make a short film in high school?

DV: It was because I thought it would be fun to do. To this day, filmmaking has been the only thing in my life that came naturally to me. With everything else I've done, I felt like I was faking it. My friends never studied, but they would still pass. If I studied, I would fail. I had to practice the guitar way harder than my friends who were good at music, and I still couldn't do what they did. I was never great at soccer. I was always like the last person picked on the team. When I came back to the U.S., I was the last person picked on the baseball team.

JP: What were you into before you directed that film in high school?

DV: Mostly music. But in high school, I wanted to register at the U.S. Naval Academy at Annapolis. I wanted to be a naval aviator fighter pilot. I wanted to be Maverick, Tom Cruise, *Top Gun*.

JP: So you came back to the States for college?

DV: I left Venezuela when I graduated high school. Back then I was fighting with my mom and just trying to be rebellious. My dad, who was still in the States, was like, "If you come live with me, I'll pay for college." So I moved from Caracas, which was a city of four million people, to a small town called Philadelphia, Mississippi, where I was pretty much the only Latino in the entire community college.

JP: When your dad brought you back to America, what did you envision your future as being?

DV: I honestly still thought I was going to enlist in the Navy. I was the only one among my friends who had dual U.S. citizenship, so I could do it. When I came to the States at 18, I walked into a recruiter's office, saw the basic training video that they have and I was, like, "Ummm, let me get back to you on that." I realized it was not going to work. Then I thought I would do music, so I went to community college and started to focus on drums. At community college, I had to take developmental English with all the football players because my English had stopped when I moved to Venezuela. At 18, my grammar and writing was at a fourth grade level. Luckily, the community college was in a very small town called Decatur, and they were super-supportive. A drama teacher allowed me to act in the plays, which I really liked. After my first play, I got a little plaque for best actor at the community college. There were only like 15 people in the whole department. But it was definitely a validation.

JP: So the English thing didn't end up being that big a deal?

DV: If anything, it ended up being my hall pass to fit in with all the different groups. Everybody kind of took me under their wing. I was different enough that I was not a threat, and people thought I was interesting.

JP: Was that when you got to hang out with all those diverse groups?

DV: Yeah.

JP: How did you transition from majoring in music to majoring in film?

DV: It was because my sister was majoring in film at the University of Southern Mississippi [USM], and because I had such a great experience making that film in high school. I would go visit her in the big college town and I liked what she was doing. I thought, "You know, I could totally do this." That first semester at community college, I was learning how to read music because I had been self-taught on the drums. But when you're 18 years old, and just learning how to read charts, and a 12-year-old kid comes in and whips your ass on the drums, you're like, "Hmmm. Maybe I started a little too late. What else can I do?" So I decided to do film. In community college, I was still getting my core stuff out of the way. But by the time I transferred to the USM as a film major, I was totally kicking ass, and I was super-focused. I was trying to make the most ambitious student films that had ever been done. They had heist scenes and police stuff. I was using the resources that my dad, as a doctor in a small town, allowed me to get access to. I remember never celebrating my birthday for 15 years because I was always working on a set. I was trying to get as good as I could.

Also, I would feel really self-conscious in these film theory classes when the other students would look at all this symbolism. To me, I wouldn't see the symbolism or motifs. I would just see a fucking white door and not a symbol for something else. I would feel like maybe I wasn't smart enough to do this. So I would compensate by learning about the gear and learning about techniques and getting a lot of practical experience. That's the reason I decided to work in the camera department. Because, if worse comes to worst, I could always turn on the camera myself. Later on I realized that people just have different circumstances, and different access to things. Perhaps they had access to all these literature books so they could throw all these references out. But that didn't necessarily translate to them being a good director. But at that time, I was just so intimidated that I thought, "Fuck, what am I doing here?"

JP: And this is at the University of Southern Mississippi?

DV: Right. Can you imagine if I was going to NYU? I would be terrified to go there because I always had very low self-esteem. I always felt like I could work hard, but I didn't think that I was that great at anything.

JP: Tell me about your decision to become a filmmaker.

DV: It felt like it was the only thing I could do. All my other cousins were engineers and lawyers and doctors. My mom was relieved that I didn't join the military. But I never had a back-up plan. I realized, "There's nothing else I know how to do." So becoming a filmmaker was out of necessity. Honestly, if I would have been good at something else, chances are I would have done *that*.

JP: When you finished the USM film program, what was your big plan for making it in Hollywood?

DV: I graduated from USM, and I was the first person in my class to get a job at a production company. It was based in Gulfport, Mississippi. Then, six months later, I was the first person in my class to get laid off. The company went bankrupt. It's impossible to have a production company in Gulfport, Mississippi.

I knew I could either go to Los Angeles or New Orleans. I had a dog then, a golden retriever. When I found an apartment that would take my dog in New Orleans, I moved there. I knew people there so it was easier to get experience than it would have been in L.A. where I didn't know anybody. While I was in Mississippi, I worked for free as an AC on a short film that this New Orleans DP did. He was really nice and he introduced me to everybody in the film community in New Orleans. When I got to New Orleans, I started researching the top production companies. There was a company called Morrison Productions and a director called Kenny Morrison, who is an amazing director. I would walk in and be like, "Hey, I'm here to drop off my AC résumé." And they would say that they weren't hiring. But I would drop it off anyway. Every week at the same time, I would go back and I would say, "Hey, I'm here to drop off my résumé again!" By the sixth time, they realized I wasn't going anywhere and they gave me a shot. Once I got in with them, they started booking me as a second AC on all their commercials. Little by little, I stepped up to first AC. I eventually joined the union and started working as an AC on TV pilots.

JP: What was your intention at that point? Did you want to be a DP?

DV: No. I knew I wanted to be a director eventually, but I felt like I needed to learn more. I would DP things for other people, and I was scraping up dimes and nickels and calling in favors just to make other directors' stuff look great. But I realized that if the director didn't do his job, it didn't matter how great it looks. Nobody says, "Oh, did you see that crappy movie with amazing cinematography?" That's when I decided to become a director. And if I failed, it would be my own fault. I decided to save up some money and go back to Venezuela and make a short film called *Cedula Ciudadano*. I wrote a script that had all my friends from high school. Then I got lucky and I got a grant from the Venezuelan government. I called all my crew member buddies in New Orleans and flew them to Venezuela. I shot on 35mm and it was the first time anyone had ever used a Steadicam in Venezuela. Even though I didn't know how to direct actors, I would just rehearse a bunch and do different things. I did all these one-take shots and I quickly realized what a difference it is to have a great actor.

Cedula Ciudadano gave me confidence as a director. It won all these different awards. It won the Los Angeles Latino Film Festival, and it got shortlisted for the Academy Awards. After its success, I thought agents would be knocking my door down, or that Spielberg would be like, "I have this great project that I can't direct. Will you direct it for me?" I was very naive.

I was in debt from the movie because the producer didn't do a good job. I ended up pawning my computer. I had to come back to New Orleans and pay a lot of credit card debt. Luckily, I was working regularly as an AC. But the short did get me into the Fox Searchlight Program. I did a short for Fox Searchlight called *Day Shift*, but it didn't do that great. Then they closed that department, so I never got a chance to even premiere it. But ultimately *Cedula Ciudadano* got me a gig directing a sitcom in Venezuela called *Planeta de 6*.

JP: How did you get to direct a Venezuelan sitcom?

DV: Because the actor from my short created the sitcom. He was one of the leads and also the executive producer. We had such a great time working together on my short that he wanted me to direct *Planeta de 6*. At first I was just going to DP it. Then the director took a different job, and I stepped up to direct.

JP: But you weren't even really a DP at that point.

DV: I wasn't really a DP. I was just bluffing my way through. And then they canceled the sitcom and I had to come back to New Orleans.

After the show got cancelled, I went from being the director of a sitcom with a 65-person crew to becoming an AC again. I was also still paying off the debt from my short film, so I didn't have any savings when I came back to New Orleans. I got my ass kicked, and I'm glad that I did. Because now everything I do, I can fully enjoy without any reservations or holding back. When I got back to New Orleans, it was nice to be able to take a step back as a crew member and not worry about overtime, or making your day, or the actor's ego, or the studio's notes. I actually welcomed the break.

I knew that once I got back on my feet, I had an idea to make a feature film that takes place in real time. It was about four girls who go to Mardi Gras. Two of the sisters get separated and they spend all day trying to find each other. Because I knew so many actors and crew, I could call in all these favors to make it. I shot it in a documentary, improv style in the middle of Mardi Gras. It was called *Looking for Charity*. I had two different units shooting in tandem. I had kind of done a story outline so that it would all work out in the end, and I would throw things out at the actors. It sounded so great. But it turned out to be boring as hell. There was not really a story to follow. Nothing really happened. If you're improvising something, you have to work all these things out. I had to learn that. Nobody has ever seen it.

JP: We all make mistakes, and it's about how we recover from them that matters. In essence, it sounds like the mistake you made was not having a script.

DV: Or not having learned enough about how to really direct the actors. I hadn't studied the craft of really directing. I was just too empirical. And I still didn't understand the essence of story. I mean, I took a screenwriting class in college, and I wrote a screenplay, but I didn't really understand the three-act structure. I would recognize it because I was told to recognize it, but it wasn't in my gut yet. My gut would tell me that something looked cool, or felt great. But I didn't correlate the two things. I learned that making *Looking for Charity*.

JP: There are projects I've done and not been happy with, and it takes me quite a while to get over it. How was that process for you after making *Looking for Charity*?

DV: I feel really guilty that all those people put in a lot of work and had nothing to show for it. The interesting thing is that parallel to making *Looking for Charity,* I started dating my future wife, Carolina. I had met her on a blind date right before I went to Venezuela to direct *Planeta de 6*. I met her on a Wednesday, and then that Saturday I moved to Venezuela. When I came back to New Orleans and had worked through all my shit, I ran into her again. We were dating for a while and then the Los Angeles Latino Film Festival invited me to apply to a writers' lab. I said to Carolina, who was also a writer, "Why don't we both apply, and I'll teach you how to format a screenplay? Then if we both get accepted, we can go." We both applied and she got accepted, and I didn't. So we came to L.A. and she was having an amazing time at the writers' lab. One day Carolina said, "I could get used to this place. Why don't we move here?" Fifteen days later we packed up the U-Haul in New Orleans and moved to L.A.

After we moved to L.A., I had to fly right back to New Orleans to work as an AC because I couldn't get work in Hollywood. Everyone I knew here already had a list of ACs they liked. So I was maybe the sixth guy on their list. That was a bit of a wake-up call. I had to start over from the bottom and work for free on people's short films so that when they got a real job, they would hire me. I was reaching out to everybody. But I never got a paycheck as an AC in Los Angeles. I only worked for free. It was really hard because I would have to fly to New Orleans to work for money. Then finally this one gaffer I knew got a job as a DP on a reality show shooting in Chicago, and he brought me on as a camera operator. That got me in with the L.A. reality operator guys. Once I was in with that crew, I started getting reality operating jobs all over the place. This was around 2003.

That first operating job was on a show called *My Big Fat Obnoxious Boss*. When you do those shows for 35 days, you get to be good friends with your fellow crew. Once I was friends with other operators, I was in the clique and they would bring me on more jobs. It was great. Then I started DP'ing reality shows. I was DP'ing a makeover show called *Ten Years Younger* and Carolina got a writing job on *Grey's Anatomy*. She said to me, "Dude, if you're serious about becoming a director, you need to quit your job on the reality show and go make your movie." She was really cool. Up to that point, I always had the excuse of having to make money. And it was a humbling experience that I had busted my ass doing everything I could and when Carolina was just 27 years old, the first job she got in the industry was as a staff writer on the number one show. She's just that talented. It's amazing that this person wants to be with me because she's way smarter than I am. But she was super-supportive so I quit my reality DP job.

Everybody thought I was crazy, but I was like, "Sorry. I have to go." And so for five years, I wrote like crazy and prepared to go back to Venezuela and apply for a grant to do a feature film. In 2006, I got a grant to make *Zero Hour*. Carolina kept getting more writing jobs, and then the writers' strike happened in 2009. We had gotten the grant in Venezuela, which gave us seed money, and we were both like, "It's now or never." That's what I tell everybody. Nobody hires you to be the director. You have to hire yourself to direct. And when you show what you can do, then people will want you.

JP: Where did the rest of the money for *Zero Hour* come from?

DV: In addition to the national grant, we had private investors. Luckily, the movie did really well. It became the highest grossing movie in Venezuelan box office history. Almost a million people saw it in theaters. In that movie, I used every trick that I learned with my short films and from anybody I had ever watched work. What ended up happening was, I tried to do so much that I wasn't able to do something in depth. The movie did really well in Venezuela, but it wasn't like a super-artistic movie from Latin America that gets shortlisted for the Academy Awards. So that taught me that I needed to trust myself and commit 100 percent to what I really wanted to say, and take a risk, instead of trying to cover my ass. I learned that if you just cover your ass, it won't be bad, but it won't be great either.

JP: Are you talking about the idea that the social message you had in mind got diluted by making a popcorn movie?

DV: Yeah. I mean that's the safe way to say it. But the reality is that I was scared about committing to taking a risk. Instead of trusting the material, I was falling in love with chase sequences and motorcycle jumps. What happened is that the people who like foreign movies with subtitles don't like action, and the people who like action don't like subtitles. So I was in this weird place where I didn't commit.

JP: How different is being a TV director from directing an independent feature?

DV: I just got back from directing *Orange Is the New Black*, and it was a total pleasure. Every time I'd directed before, I felt like what Coppola described on *Apocalypse Now*. He said that he felt like every day, he had to take out his guts and show them to everybody, and then put them back in. That's what it felt like to direct my feature because every single thing was on my back, from the checks, to the coffee, to the permits, to the locations, to post, to the fucking memory cards. Everything! So to be able to go in on *Orange* and just do the shot list and direct performances was like, "Oh, this is what directing is!"

Before I directed *Orange Is the New Black*, I used to hear directors say they loved directing, and I would think, "I clearly have never been on the same set as you have because I hate directing. It's so stressful." On all the other stuff I directed, the pressure was on. When it comes to directing TV, I welcome the fact that I don't have to reinvent the wheel. I just have to be efficient and get the best performances I can. And I'm okay with that. I don't care about winning awards. I am there to serve the script, the writer, the showrunner and the crew, so everyone can go home to see their kids. I still want to be proud of my work but at the same time, I understand it's not my movie.

JP: Even on your feature *Zero Hour*, you were handling all that producing stuff?

DV: Nobody had ever made an action movie like that in Venezuela before. So it was Carolina and me against the world. We had to really teach them a lot of things that they had never done. Nobody in Venezuela had ever done call sheets. I was the first one to explain what a call sheet was. By the time we finished the movie, the crew was like, "Now I understand what you're doing." Then we came back to Los Angeles and I had to do all the post-producing myself. I poured so much work into it.

We got the film with a sales company called HSI Films that had a big office in Beverly Hills. But it all turned out to be a front that later went bankrupt. I got some money but never got the contracts from any of the sales they did. Then I sold it to a distributor called Maya Entertainment. It was the first subtitled movie to ever be distributed on Redbox. They sold 15,000 copies. Amazon, Walmart and Target carried it. Then that fucking company went bankrupt, and I never saw a penny of it.

That's why I'm so happy to work in TV, because in independent films, I don't know how people make money. It's impossible to make a living being an independent feature film director. Basically, you are making the indie movie hoping to get a Marvel movie out of it.

JP: Despite not making money on the movie, and almost killing yourself doing it, you did get some recognition. And it also got you a directing job on the web series *Cybergeddon*, which was basically a TV show. How did you get that job?

DV: My agents were sending me out on a bunch of generals.

JP: Sorry to interrupt, but how did you get an agent, by the way?

DV: One of the actors in *Zero Hour* invited the producers of *The Fighter* to see the movie at the Los Angeles Latino Film Festival, and they loved the movie. They were like, "Dude, we want to work with you. Do you have an agent?" I said, "No, I don't have an agent." And they said, "Well, let me recommend you to my agent." Then once one agent hears that you're the new thing, everybody reaches out. I interviewed with all of them at the same time, and I just played them against each other. I ended up going with the guy I have today, who is amazing. The agency is called Verve.

JP: And they helped you get *Cybergeddon*?

DV: Anthony Zuiker, the creator of *CSI*, was launching an association with Yahoo. At the time, Yahoo was planning to launch a streaming video channel. *Cybergeddon* was supposed to be their big thing. And I was promised that this was going to change everything for me. It was this crazy schedule. I got hired in March and we had to shoot right away. By the end of July, it had to be delivered in ten different languages. It was 17 days of prep, and we shot it in 17 days as well. It was fucking crazy. It was the fastest thing ever. The interesting thing was that it had double the budget my feature had. But what it taught me is that there's only so much I can do as a director if the script is not great. And because he was Anthony Zuiker, the creator of *CSI*, who was I to tell him that some things were kind of cheesy? I was trying to do the best I could with the material, but in the end there was only so much I could do. It didn't do that great, and the CEO of Yahoo changed the branding for what they wanted to do, and I kind of got lost. It premiered, but nobody really saw it. It was huge in China, but that doesn't really mean much. To this day, what gets me in the door is *Zero Hour*, and not *Cybergeddon*. I realized that I basically have one more mediocre film before I start losing credibility in the market.

JP: What do you mean?

DV: People look at your first feature and say, "That was good. Let's look at the second one." Then they look at the second project and say, "Well, it's not as good, but we can blame that on the circumstances. Let's see how the third one is." And if the third project doesn't do better, it's going to get harder and harder to land a directing job. So I started to be way more selective with the jobs I was trying to get. At the same time, I was starting to have a family. And at the same time, my wife's writing career was doing amazing.

In the meantime, my agent was getting me attached to other movies as a director. But every time I would get attached to something, it would go into developmental hell. Or I would get attached to a movie and the person who was championing me would get fired, and then I would have to start from scratch at a different place. And so cut to, like, five years later and I haven't been on a set as a director in all that time. It's almost happened a lot of times. I've been attached to a movie with Halle Berry that was about to get green-lit. But to be on an actual set talking to an actor, I haven't been there for, like, five years. That's when I decided I'm done with features for now. I'm going to do everything I can to be a TV director. Because seeing the people who are directing my wife's episodes, I'm like, "How does this guy get this job? He's a fucking hack." And they're all, like, '80s bad actors turned TV directors. I'm sure you saw a lot of them. I was like. "I can do this way better." So I came up with a plan that I would apply to the diversity programs, and I was going to reach out to everybody.

JP: You applied to the studio diversity programs?

DV: I applied to the Sony one and I made it to the short list. But I didn't get in, even with all the credits and everything I had. And then, simultaneously, all the people my wife knew who were writers for different shows were slowly starting to become executive producers. So I'm starting to know them, and that's how I met the director Bill Purple. A friend of ours, who was the creator of the show, asked Bill if I could shadow him on an episode. Of course Bill wants to work for her again, so he was like, "Yeah, of course you can shadow me."

JP: How did you end up going from shadowing Bill Purple on *American Princess* to landing a directing gig on *Orange Is the New Black*?

DV: At the end of the day, it's about being prepared for when you get an opportunity. How it happened was that my wife had been writing on *Orange Is the New Black*, and because of that connection, she and I were able to develop a project with the show's creator, Jenji Kohan. The show we developed almost got sold to Amazon. They loved it, but then Jeff Bezos decided they wanted to look for the next *Game of Thrones* and our show was too small. Jenji saw that I handled it really well. I wasn't bitter or anything because I understand how the business works. I think that some people take it the wrong way, and I never asked her for anything in return. Then *Orange Is the New Black* just happened to have an episode coming up with a ton of immigration stories in it, and they were looking for somebody who spoke Spanish and could really direct it. Jenji suggested my name and they gave me a shot. The rest is history.

JP: Was that the first on-set directing you've done in five years?

DV: Yeah. The first directing that I was getting paid for.

JP: That's a long time to stick it out.

DV: I was always setting up projects during that time, and everything was always about to go. I could show you folders upon folders of pitches that I would go in with and get the job. Huge fucking contracts with these crazy astronomical numbers, and everything was about to go. But then it didn't. And then the same thing happens again.

JP: These were all features that you were developing?

DV: Yes, and they were all ready to go. But until you have the actors in place, the funding doesn't get secured. You always feel like everything's about to kick in, but it doesn't. When people move here, I tell them this: The great thing about L.A. is that success is always around the corner. The bad thing about L.A. is that success is always around the corner. It always seems like it's just right in front of you … and sometimes it never fucking arrives. Then all of a sudden, you're a 15-year overnight success.

After all this time, I directed an episode of *Orange Is the New Black* and everyone was surprised that I did a good job. I made all my days, I wrapped early, I got all these performances, and everyone was like, "Wow, this was your first TV gig?" I'm like, "I've been doing this for 20 years! It's just that now is when I got the opportunity." I've done every job you can imagine, from caterer to executive producer. I don't resent that it took so long. It's not because it's the white man club, or anything. It's a lot of fucking money to risk to hiring a "new" director. I get it. If I had a show, I would go with the people that I already know are good. So you have to prove yourself. The interesting thing with TV is that they are hesitant to hire feature directors. Nothing you do on a feature applies to TV. With feature directors, the buck stops with them. TV is different. In TV, the producer is the one in control. The TV director is a guest in the producer's house. "This is your room. We'll let you know when you can use the kitchen. Don't make a mess." Right now, I'm thinking about talking to my agents about applying to the Warner Brothers diversity program for directors. My agent said, "If you do the diversity thing, then you become like a box that they can check. Yes, the studio will pay your salary, but people want to hire the guy that just finished directing *Orange Is the New Black* because he's talented, not because he checks a box." But at the same time, I want to work. The other thing I was talking to my agents about is what route I want to pursue. I'm in a position where if I go the network route, I can make a great paycheck. You know, $45,000 per episode. And then you get residuals, another $45,000. So if you do a *Chicago Fire*, that's basically a hundred grand per episode. That's a lot of money. My agent has clients who do eight episodes a year, and they're living very comfortably. But then the guys who do those network shows don't get called for the cool HBO or Showtime shows, like *Ozark*.

So now we're planning my career. I'm going to try to just do gritty cable and streaming premium stuff, which means I have to start at the bottom again. I can use my episode of *Orange Is the New Black* as a calling card that shows I'm partway in the club. But I'm still starting over again. Now I have to go do more generals, and get them to give me a chance. It's a lot of fucking work. And there is no such thing as, "I'm set."

Geeta Patel

For a director who is challenging the long history of a Hollywood dominated by white males, Geeta Patel is nevertheless someone who honors tradition. Her first priority when I arrive at her Long Beach home is to make sure I have enough to eat and drink. It's how she was raised: Guests are important.

We settle into the backyard lawn furniture and I am quickly aware of how deeply Geeta honors her parents. She has brought them along on the journey with her. She lives simultaneously in a world of the past and future, and has found a way to use her connection to her family's traditions to propel herself into a new era. In the deepest sense, she is an agent of change.

. . . .

GEETA PATEL: I was the first person in my family to be born in America. My father came from a small village in India. The village pooled their money to send him here. He immigrated to Chicago, and I was born in Evanston, right outside of Chicago.

JACOB PINGER: What was the name of the village?

GP: Utaraj is where my dad is from. My mom is from Aandi. They're small, middle-of-nowhere villages. In my parents' villages, there is singing and dancing and oral storytelling everywhere. It's the most amazing thing I've ever experienced. My brother Ravi and I have always cherished the fact that we grew up around two very different cultures and went back to India so regularly. I'm from a culture that has arranged marriages, semi-arranged marriages, and some inequalities in how women and people of different castes are treated. So India was both beautiful and frustrating. The complexity left me curious about the many different ways of life and the stories and traditions.

I started writing about this. I wrote my first little book when I was eight or nine. Growing up, I started leaning towards the arts. My parents went through so much to give me my education. I was

Geeta Patel dedicated years as an independent documentary filmmaker before landing her first opportunity to direct television (Sean Reed).

always encouraged to go into science and math and all those typical things that you hear of with Asian-Americans. "Be a doctor. Be a scientist. Be a lawyer." That was always a battle with my parents. I wanted to go to art school and do theater. It was always, "No, no, no, Geeta. That's a hobby." I couldn't argue with my parents because I understood their point of view.

JP: What were your parents' lives like in India?

GP: First my dad came to the U.S. by himself because my grandfather had always heard of America. There were college programs to send engineers to study. My father has the kind of personality where he never looks back. Never regrets. He wasn't scared. He got off the plane and just looked forward. My grandfather sent my dad for the opportunity and excitement of it. It was like sending a man to the moon.

When my father came here, he was expected to make do with the eight dollars in his pocket and start in the engineering program. He also had to work and send money back to the family in India. My dad shared an apartment with seven or eight other guys. They would work around the clock while they were not studying. They were all vegetarians and sometimes worked in the meat industry. They started eating meat eventually and they adapted to the American diet, went to McDonald's and everything. My dad sent money home, and everybody in India was so excited that the plan was working. They almost forgot that it was time for my father to get married. We have arranged marriages, and my dad was like, "Hey! I want to come back. I need to get married." They were like, "No, no! Keep making money." He eventually came back and interviewed 12 girls. My mom was the twelfth. Mom was so young. She was 18. In her village, it was very prestigious to marry someone from America. Her father said, "Look, I believe this is a good thing for you." And my mom was like, "I don't want to get married. I am having fun." But we have this thing in our culture where you respect your elders to that extent. So when my grandfather said, "I really do believe this is the right thing for you," my mom said okay. Next thing you know, she was on a plane for the first time in her life. She had no idea how a toilet works. She got off the plane and there was snow in Chicago. She had never seen snow. She had a photograph of my dad that she held in her hand because she didn't even remember what he looked like. He had only come to India for two weeks to get married during his vacation. He had two weeks to find a bride, get married and return to the U.S.

JP: What was your dad doing for work in America?

GP: He was an engineer, but it took him a while to get that job. So at first he was working in restaurants and things like that. When my mom came, she took English classes. Eventually she was a secretary. She did data entry. She is self-made. She had gone to two years of local college in India and that was it. She would sell Avon and Tupperware without understanding English very well. Both my parents are very ambitious. They eventually started a company together called CP Resumes where they would write résumés for people. They moved to North Carolina because of the growing economy there. Eventually, computers got popular and they had to close it down. My dad became a financial planner and my mom became a realtor in Charlotte.

JP: How old were you when they moved the family to North Carolina?

GP: Fourteen.

JP: Were your parents part of an Indian community in Illinois or North Carolina?

GP: When my brother and I were younger, there weren't that many Indians, so we had less of a community. But by the time we got to Charlotte, there were many Indians in the U.S. It just kept growing.

JP: What was it like to grow up as the child of immigrants?

GP: I had a hard time with it. I was bullied when I was younger. I was told I was ugly by other kids at school.

JP: White kids?

GP: All the kids were white. There were no Indians where I went to school back then. I remember being called an ugly Indian bitch. That was one of the ones that stuck. It was tough. I never really felt like I fit in. I was embarrassed by the smell of Indian food. I felt very hairy compared to all the other girls because we have a lot of hair. I remember bleaching my hair blonde once. It didn't work at all. My hair was still black. I definitely had a tougher time accepting who I was. Then in Charlotte, I met more Indians at the temple. The other Indian kids and I called ourselves the Loser Club. We had to be at the temple while everybody else got to go out. Our parents were very strict. We weren't allowed to have boyfriends or go out to parties, not even slumber parties with other American girls. Our parents were worried that we would lose our Indian values.

JP: How did your parents deal with it when racist stuff would happen to you?

GP: My dad subscribed to the philosophy of detachment: "It doesn't touch you. Let it bounce off you." My mom was pretty tough. She's just like, "Don't worry about it." They are very tough but also very warm. They would give me a hug and say "I'm sorry" and all that. But they believed in the idea of "We move forward. We battle through this." My parents are so inspiring. They are less than five feet tall, but my dad will never tell you he's short. They're both so proud.

When I was in junior high in North Carolina, my father was going to drop me off with the temple kids for a vacation. On the way, we stopped at Denny's to eat. We went in and they wouldn't serve us. We just stood there and they just would not serve us. I got in the car and I was like, "I can't believe they wouldn't serve us. Dad, this is ridiculous." And he got mad at me. He said, "Geeta, do not let this touch you. We move forward." That was probably the formation of my interests in conflict resolution. You know, when do you act? When do you *not* act? How do you act? When I went to college, I studied conflict resolution, war, international relations and the partition of India. My first film was about conflict. Even the films I'm doing now. I think all of that took root from this.

JP: Was the racism any worse in the South vs. the North?

GP: I don't know. It was everywhere. I feel like North Carolina was pretty bad though. After 9/11, my mom and I were at the mall and some guy said, "Don't you try to bomb us." And I cussed for the first time in front of my mom. I can't remember what I said to this guy, but it was a kneejerk thing as I was going down the escalator. I said something like, "You motherfucker!" I was so angry that people would talk that way. My mom and I just moved forward and never talked about it. There was an understanding between us.

JP: Did you feel a connection to India growing up?

GP: I always felt a connection to India. When I was in college, I studied the history of India. Everything I wrote was about India. Both documentaries I did were shot in India. I was the first one born in America of our whole clan. As my cousins and everyone came to America, there were more Indians and they all had each other. They were more able to raise their children as if they were still in India. So a lot of my younger cousins married within our system. My last name is Patel, and we have a system in which Patels marry Patels. When I was growing up, we would go to Patel conventions where you meet other people with your last name from the same area of India.

JP: When you were growing up, did you feel like you were American or did you feel like there was a culture that you were not being allowed into?

GP: I never felt like I fit in when I was younger. I am not one of those people who say that college was the best. It was the worst for me. Part of that came from the fact that I was expected to marry an Indian guy. In our culture, you start looking for a marriage partner at that age. I was in a predominantly white sorority and the pressure that I would have to pick the race of my partner was a constant cloud over my head. That pressure forced me to look at myself as different. My friends were all talking about dating and having boyfriends and I wasn't allowed to date. There were great moments in college, but I think I was troubled and it came from my fear of not fitting in.

And that's what I wrote about. I wrote a screenplay in college that was all about that choice of who to be with and running between your Indian and American cultures, trying to figure out which one you are. The other thing that was hard for me in college was that I was a closeted artist. I was writing constantly. I didn't know it at the time but I really wanted to go into the arts. That was not something my family understood or supported. I wasn't a rebel and I understood my parents' fear. They had worked so hard to raise me in America and I felt the responsibility of that. When I graduated, I didn't go into the arts even though that's all I wanted to do. After college, I went to New York and worked in the first job I got, which was in financial management in a high-level MBA program with General Electric. It was a fast track program to CFO, which was hilarious. I didn't even understand finance. I did that for two years. After two years, my dad came to me and said, "I just want to see you smile." And he said, "Go."

JP: Go where?

GP: Go to Los Angeles.

JP: How did you navigate the expectation to go into an arranged marriage in college?

GP: I wrote about it. I wrote stories of escape. I internalized it. When I got out of college, I went to New York and they were setting me up with meetings with men. In my case, it was with other Patels. I went into the deepest depression because I wasn't feeling anything. So I wrote and wrote. That was my escape. I would write letters to writers that I was fascinated with. I became the uber-fan of storytellers. I wrote a letter to Aaron Sorkin, David E. Kelley and all these people. Then I would fly out to L.A. and I would meet some of them, just whoever would meet with me. I didn't want anything out of it. I would just ask questions. I wrote around 200 letters and faxed or mailed them. I was working in this finance job that I hated and wasn't good at. I was in my twenties and had never had a boyfriend. I was so confused. I was a mess. There was a lot of fighting with my parents at that time because that's when you're supposed to be picking a mate. They were like, "Come on. It's not that difficult." Where they come from, you just meet a few people and decide. But I wasn't ready, and I didn't like any of the Indian guys I was meeting.

JP: It sounds like a period of professional and personal angst was coalescing at the same time and creating a lot of turmoil. One of the ways you processed that was by writing letters to writers and showrunners in Los Angeles?

GP: Yeah.

JP: When did these people even get on your radar?

GP: College is when I started writing scripts. And as I was writing, I was watching and analyzing shows and movies. I couldn't help it. I sat down one night in a computer lab and just wrote my first script. I stayed up all night. Then I found Erin Cressida Wilson, who was a visiting professor at Duke. I said, "Look, I'm not in your class but can you please read this? I'm trying to understand myself." I must have looked pretty desperate because she took my script. Two weeks later, she called me to her office and said, "This is a beautiful script. And

I want you to go to NYU. I'm going to make some calls and get you in." I barely remember everything, but I said something like, "No, thank you," almost automatically because that's not what I do. That's not my family. I went to my car and I started crying. This thing that I had an instinct for but wasn't sure about was finally confirmed. And that's all I needed. I was just so happy that I wasn't crazy. That was a big moment.

JP: What was that script about?

GP: It was about an Indian-American girl who meets this white guy while she is visiting her family in India. They fall in love and there's conflict with her parents. It was absolutely a metaphor for me to work out my fears.

JP: How did you get this idea that you could communicate directly with these Hollywood writers and showrunners?

GP: I'm just that kind of person. It was this incredible desire to connect with the mystery of storytelling. I started writing all these letters in college. When I was in New York it went up a notch. I would come home from work and analyze the story structure of *Party of Five*. Then I would write a spec script. I remember literally sneaking into an event where David E. Kelley was being honored. It was this $500 per seat dinner and I talked my way into a seat at a table with all these CEO kind of people and their wives. I was in this sorority dress from college and they realized I didn't belong there. I had some drinks so I could be less nervous and just walked up to David E. Kelley and Michelle Pfeiffer. I said to David E. Kelley, "I came here just to meet you. I really need to talk to you. Can you talk to me?" He was like, "I'm flying out in the morning but here's my email address." I contacted his office and he got on the phone and I said, "I have this idea. It's a show called *The Hill*." He talked to me for 15 or 20 minutes, and he said, "Put together a treatment and send it to me." I didn't know what a treatment was. So while I was still working, I did this treatment. It took me three months and was about 50 pages. And I sent it to him. I was absolutely crazy. I was so desperate because I really thought I was going to get an arranged marriage and this was my way of escaping.

After I sent the treatment, I didn't hear back for a long time. Then I heard that Aaron Sorkin was in New York for the Upfronts. I called every hotel in town looking for him. I got Aaron Sorkin on the phone and talked to him about my treatment. He told me to drop it off at his hotel. I dropped it off. Then *West Wing* came out and Aaron Sorkin became Aaron Sorkin in a bigger way than he already was. After that, I couldn't get hold of him. Then I went to L.A. to meet David E. Kelley.

JP: He agreed to meet you based on your treatment for *The Hill*?

GP: Yes. Based on what I sent him, I guess. I met him in his office and we talked about my treatment. *The Hill* was about similar subject matter as *West Wing*. So David E. Kelley said, "I really want to do this but I want to see how *West Wing* does first." I remember being such a brat about it. I thought that if *West Wing* was good, then the idea had already been done and we shouldn't copy it. So I never got back to him. I think he even told me to write the pilot, but I never did because I didn't want to copy *West Wing*. And that was it. I went back to New York and kept doing my job. But I actually made several trips to L.A. to meet with other people that I had written letters to, just to listen to them talk about their lives. I met Les Moonves. I met Warren Littlefield, who was the head of NBC at the time.

JP: What was your success rate with these letters?

GP: Very low. I wrote about 200. I think I met 20 people. But it was my ticket because after those two years of working in New York, I was just so miserable. This love of the arts was not going away. And my dad knew it, and he told me to go to L.A. Can you imagine as a dad who doesn't understand this and is so scared for your kid? It was so weird for him. But he said go. At that point, I'd written all these letters and one of them got me a meeting with Kario Salem at ABC and he told me he needed an assistant to work with him on a new show that he had created. I got a call from one of the producers, Alan Poul. He told me that Kario wanted to bring me on but the producer seemed skeptical about me. He asked me if I knew how to use screenwriting software, and I told him yes, even though I had no idea … yet. He was still skeptical, but he said, "Okay, you'll start next week." I quit my job in New York and within a week I was in L.A. I called all the other assistants from all those meetings I had done and I asked them to teach me how to use this screenwriting program, which they graciously did. I worked as Kario's assistant for two years.

JP: It's so hard to meet powerful people in Hollywood even when you have connections. And you were somebody with no connections. But just on the strength of writing letters and fan mail, you were able to get face-to-face meetings. Those letters must have been pretty compelling.

GP: I think I used to bake them all cookies. I would never do that now.

JP: Those must have been good cookies.

GP: Some time after all that, during one of the million times I lost my way and lost my confidence, my dad would say, "Where is my daughter who made those cookies for David E. Kelley?" As in, "Where is that warrior princess who doesn't give a shit?"

Kario had this new show called *The Beast* starring Frank Mangella. I was kind of double-titled as the showrunner's assistant and writer's assistant. I was doing all these custodial things. Taking notes at meetings, getting coffee for him, getting things for his girlfriend. I was his right hand and he was a great boss to me. We did the pilot for *The Beast*, and then because of studio issues we had to do the pilot a second time. So we went into our second year with the show. By that point, Kario and I were the only two people still there from the beginning, all the producers changed. So I was really empowered. I ended up with an associate producer credit. At that point, I had my hands in it on so many levels. I was the go-between for Kario and the writers and as I saw people working on the script, I decided that I didn't want to be in a writers' room.

JP: When you first took the job, what did you think you were going to end up doing?

GP: I had no idea. I just wanted to learn. I mean, writing was the only thing I knew. So I definitely thought I was going to be a writer one day. But I didn't feel confident in my ability. So all I wanted to do was learn. I'm one of those slow movers in that way. I never wrote anything while I was there.

JP: And those were two years during which you should have been getting married?

GP: Yeah, exactly.

JP: When your dad said, "I just want to see you smile again. Go to L.A.," he was obviously giving you his blessing to leave the finance job and make a go at Hollywood. But was it also him saying on some level that they were no longer going to push you into an arranged marriage?

GP: No. That arranged marriage stuff was still aggressively going on while I was working on *The Beast*. I worked there for two years and when it was over, Kario went on to be a big production re-writer and he asked me to come with him as his assistant. At a certain point, I felt that I just wasn't being taken seriously. I started wearing full suits in order to change that perception of me. I just didn't want to be "that Indian girl." I wanted to be considered "the person who's writing with Kario." And I asked Kario, "Can we do something about this?" So he changed my title from assistant to associate screenwriter. He just made up a title that nobody else had. He was so good to me. I was very timid, very shy and very insecure. I kept thinking, "All these people are so talented. I'm not talented. I can't do what they do." I remember sitting next to him in the car and he said something to the effect of, "You're going to do great things one day." I never forgot it. He was a wonderful mentor. I just lucked out.

JP: When you were working for Kario and started wearing suits, what did you mean by you wanted to stop being treated like the little Indian girl?

GP: The whole #MeToo movement kind of stuff. I felt like, and I'm not saying it happened, but I just felt like I was this girl in the room.

JP: Were the rooms very male?

GP: Totally male. I was working in action movies. I was in meetings with all these very big, powerful executives. They happened to all be men. And there were comments that were made, like Kama Sutra comments. And, you know, "Honey, get me a coffee." Stuff like that. I just felt that it was time for me to be taken seriously. I waited a long time to be taken seriously. It wasn't like I just showed up in my early twenties thinking that I was entitled to anything. It had been years at that point. I talked to my dad a lot throughout all this. He is my best friend. If I couldn't tell my dad something, it meant that there was a problem. And there were times when I would be talking to my father and I wouldn't be able to tell him about my day because I was embarrassed that I was maybe being treated disrespectfully. Kario never treated me like that. Kario was great. It was just the environment. And so I started wearing long sleeved shirts and full suits. Kario used to laugh that I looked like an agent every time we walked into a room. He was like, "We are the creatives. Why are you dressed in a full suit?" But I just didn't want anyone to look at me that way. And here I was in my twenties, long black hair. I mean, you can only do so much. I'm a chick. Kario really fought to protect me and get people to treat me with respect and equality. At the time, a friend of mine was working for a pretty high-level person at Imagine Entertainment. She took a note from me and went and did the same thing, she said, "Please stop treating me like this." And she got fired. So I know I was lucky to have Kario as a boss.

JP: Do you think things have gotten better?

GP: I definitely do. I think there's been a lot of change. I've also learned how to create the change in my own environment. I'm not the timid person I used to be. I've learned how to assert myself.

I kept working with Kario on big action movies that he was rewriting. After four years of doing that, he said to me, "You're an associate screenwriter, but I can't make you a writer." I was scared, and I thought, "Well, I can't be a writer. I'm just going to work in the studio," and I took meetings as an executive. After a few meetings, I thought, "This isn't what I want to do. I want to take the plunge. I want to take the risk." So I told Kario that I was going to take some time and start writing and find my voice.

I've always been all or nothing, so I started writing a novel. It was based in a war zone because I had studied wars. I picked Kashmir, which is between India and Pakistan. I started running out of money so I moved in with my parents in North Carolina and kept re-writing the novel over and over again. I kept getting rejected by publishers. I remember Tom Werner told me that the key to writing is to just keep writing, and I remember thinking that. Just keep writing, just keep writing. You're going to learn, you're going to get better. I wasn't this insta-writer. Years went by and I thought, "Well, I need to go research this novel. Maybe that's what's missing." I was writing a love story set in a war zone so I went to Kashmir. When I got there, I saw that these people were dying in a vacuum. No one understood what was really happening. The news was wrong. I was in my twenties. I wasn't good at anything. I had no real profession. I think in that moment, you are just following your bliss, and in that moment I wanted to document this war.

JP: Moving back in with your parents when you worked on the novel—what was that like for you?

GP: It was scary being in my parents' house and not being married. It was scary because I didn't know what I was doing with my life. I was in my later twenties at that point and I was just following something.

JP: Did you feel like you had failed?

GP: Actually, no. I felt inspired. I was obsessed with the story I was writing. It was another version of what I had written in college. It was about a female war journalist who's Indian and falls in love with a white guy. I mean, seriously, it's screaming therapy.

JP: So you decided to research your novel by going to one of the most dangerous places in the world? That says a lot about your sense of adventure and independence.

GP: I was definitely a scaredy-cat back then. Still am. I wasn't really one of those adrenaline junkies. But I was so obsessed with this project. All the themes of my life were somehow embedded in this story. It was conflict between countries, conflict between people. Love. Choices. Politics. I think I needed to go because once you start taking steps, at some point you're running. So I found myself in Kashmir and was completely absorbed by the things that I saw. I decided to document it. That was where my head went. It wasn't like I wanted to be a filmmaker. It wasn't like I wanted to document Kashmir so I could be a director. None of that. It was literally about doing the work. I came back to the U.S. and I talked to [documentary filmmaker] Senain Kashgi, who I knew from a South Asian cultural program in Los Angeles. I asked her to show me how to use a camera. I said, "I'm going to go to Kashmir." And Senain said, "Why don't I go with you because Kashmir is Hindus and Muslims. Indian and Pakistan are fighting over it. I'm Pakistani Muslim and you're Indian Hindu. Let's create something that people can watch without feeling like it's biased." So we went to Kashmir and started shooting. Senain and I put that first trip on our credit cards. Then in order to apply for grants to finish the film, we sent a work-in-progress to Sundance. We got rejected. We sent it to PBS. We got rejected. Tribeca rejected us. We got rejected by everybody. So we applied again. And this time, we got the grants. We got into the Sundance Labs. Somehow the film was turning into a documentary and along the way I was the director. I didn't really understand what that meant. It was something that I never dared to aspire to be. At that point, the novel was on hold. We were going back and forth to Kashmir and the film took us about seven or eight years to make. It's because it was all undercover in a war zone where they were looking for us. We eventually had to leave because it was too dangerous. We had to go into hiding.

JP: What was the response to *Project Kashmir*?

GP: It's hard to really say. The film was very niche. We made it for the people of Kashmir and for our communities that hated each other so much. I believe that it served that purpose. We felt successful when the Muslims said that it was pro–India and the Hindus were saying it was pro–Pakistan. We thought, "Okay. We have done what we set out to do. We humanized everybody." It was a wonderful experience. I grew up during that film.

By the time I came back from Kashmir, I had my balls. I knew who I was. I had my confidence. I was no longer a timid, shy person. I was strong. I had been in the middle of bullets. I knew what I wanted to do and I knew how to go get it. At that point, it was very clear to me that I wanted to be a director in the narrative space. I wanted to do large, epic stories. I wanted to do action. I just was not afraid any more. I decided I wanted to write an action movie that had something to say. It was called *Mouse*.

As I decided to do this, I was broke. I had sold my car to finish *Project Kashmir*. So I was riding a bike around L.A. I was living with my brother Ravi, who was basically taking care of me. I was just a mess. Even though I said I wanted to do all this stuff, I had no means to do it. So I worked as a secretary. I was working in a temp agency just trying to keep myself above water. I wrote the script for *Mouse*. It was this weird, crazy action film. I wrote a letter to Grant Hill, the producer of *The Matrix* and Terrence Malick's films. We got together and I gave him the script. He read it and he came on as the producer. I created a martial art for the film and started working with Jeff Imada, the fight coordinator of *Fight Club* and *Bourne Identity*, and also with Sidi Larbi Cherkaoui, who is this beautiful choreographer. This all took years and years. I went through four or five different choreographers.

JP: During this period, were you still temping?

GP: Yeah. I'm a positive person. I get that from my parents. I remember, when I was temping, thinking that all of this was going to be a romantic story one day. I'm so glad that it's sort of true now because back then I think it was just a coping mechanism. I just kept reaching out to people to help me make *Mouse* because that's what I knew how to do. Write a letter, be respectful, and see if someone gives you five minutes. When they give you five minutes, maybe they'll offer ten. My rule of thumb was, I never asked people for things. I put it out there that I was looking and I left it to them to offer.

Years went by and I really had no intention of making another documentary. I was still living with Ravi in West Hollywood working on *Mouse* and just trying to figure out what I was going to do with my life. Ravi is a comedian, so the way he deals with things is through humor. I deal with pain like a normal person. I cry. He had just broken up with his white girlfriend of two years who my parents didn't know anything about because, you know, Patels marry Patels. We were all on vacation in India and Ravi was cracking me up. He was like, "We are so messed up. Look at us. I just broke up with Audrey and mom and dad still think I'm a virgin." The whole thing was so funny. So while we were on vacation, I had a camera and I started filming the family trip. Ravi was so funny, I couldn't stop filming him. We came back and Ravi was pushing me, "We have to make a documentary about this. It's so hilarious." I said, "Hell, no. I'm never making a documentary again." The last one was eight years of my life that I was never going to get back. I was single, exhausted and broke. So he said, "Well, I'm going to do it," and I was like, "Well, you're not going to do it without me." So I called PBS and sent them the footage. They were, like, "Oh, yeah. This is rad. You're taking something that is a very sad situation and it's really funny the way you guys are dealing with it." So we got funding from PBS and I put *Mouse* on hold.

We started making *Meet the Patels*, which documented how Ravi let my parents set him up to find a mate. That took another seven years or so. I was doing the odd jobs on the side. Ravi was acting and doing fine. I was the one who was always struggling. We ended up teaching ourselves how to edit because it was so important for it to be our voice. We edited for about two years and next thing you know, I'm directing another documentary. I loved every moment of it. When we finished it in 2014, nobody wanted it. It didn't get into Sundance. It didn't even get into Tribeca despite the fact that Tribeca helped to fund it. It didn't get into South by Southwest. Ravi and I were so depressed thinking, "Wow. This movie must suck."

At that point, we had finally gotten into a documentary festival called Hot Docs in Toronto. My dad had this great idea of taking the whole family up to Toronto and doing things our way. We hit the ground running and got the whole community involved. We got the word out to all the Indian temples in Toronto. My dad went through the phone book, literally looked up all the Patels and started calling them all. We went door to door to different businesses with our flyers. We went crazy trying to get people to come see our film at Hot Docs, and we filled the theater. It was packed the first night and all those people must have gone and told their friends about it because the next night it was packed again. There were lines around the building. From then on, it started going to all these small film festivals and people were lining up to see it.

But we were not getting a theatrical release or anything. I was home broke after it all and I couldn't get arrested in the film business. I thought, "Okay, it's over. My time is done." I was meditating a lot and trying to find an answer to what to do next. And within that dark time, I got a call from Grant Hill, my producer on *Mouse*. He said, "I'm working with the Wachowskis on a show called *Sense8* and we need a favor from you. Can you come to Chicago to meet them?" I think I had five or six hundred dollars left in my account at that point. I was broke. And he sat me in front of the Wachowskis and we talked for five minutes. We didn't really have much to say. They left and Grant said, "Did you get the job?" I asked, "What job?" I had no idea what he was talking about. And he said, "Let me talk to them. They have something that they want to shoot in India. They didn't talk to you about that?" I was like, "You told me not to ask questions, so I didn't ask any questions!"

I went back to L.A. and Grant called me later and said, "They want you go to India and shoot second unit on a scene that needs to be shot immediately because it's an actual event that's happening. They want a neorealism style where three actors are actually coming down in this million-person parade in the middle of Bombay." And he asked, "Can you leave tomorrow morning?" So I got on the plane for India and had a complete meltdown because all my friends and family were like, "How did you get this job? Are you sure you're the second unit director? You're not even in the DGA." And I agreed with them. I didn't know how or why this happened. I thought maybe I misunderstood. So I got off the plane at one a.m. and the crew was waiting for me in the hotel. It was an Indian crew and they're like, "Hello, madam. We told them not to send you." I asked, "Why did you tell them not to send me?" and they were like, "Because we don't have permits to shoot this." At that moment, I realized why I was there. The only thing I really knew how to do professionally was shoot undercover, guerrilla-style in India, so that's what they wanted me to do. Get this scene, somehow, without permits and with cops everywhere. And India is no joke. You can get put in jail. But I was excited. There was not a moment where I was scared. I was like, "Wow! This opportunity was created for me."

We pulled out the map of the city and next thing you know, it was like *Ocean's Eleven*. You've got this motley crew of young camera guys in India who had no idea what the style of the show is. We were a six-camera, roving shoot, and they had to avoid getting caught. We were practicing exercises of how to throw the camera to the other guy if the cops came at you. How to ditch the cops, where the trains are, where the tunnels are, all that kind of stuff. At the same time, I was teaching them the artistic things of how to frame shots, how to get the color. It was awesome. I had a shot list put together from what the Wachowskis wanted. They were going to come to India to shoot first unit with the main director, James McTeague, who had directed *V for Vendetta*. I was going to shoot second unit. I had three days to prep it. Then the Wachowskis called and said, "You know what? You and James seem to have a handle on this. We're not coming." Then James McTeague called a day before shooting and said, "I can't get my visa. I won't be able to make it. You're going to have to direct first and second unit." I was like, "Great." Then he gave me this little pep talk to the effect of, "You know, Geeta, please don't get arrested. Just so you know, we were never going to do this. We were never going to shoot it with the real event. We were just going to recreate it during principal photography. But Grant told us about you and we thought we'd sort of throw money at it and see what you could do. So please just don't get arrested and don't get shut down. We don't expect you to get that shot list." And I was like, "Okay, great. No expectations."

So we shot it the next day. We got everything, and came home. I edited it together and sent it to the Wachowskis. They called me and said they were happy with the footage, and they asked, "Would you like to finish first season with us?" So I was second unit director that first season of *Sense8*, doing whatever. The joke was that I was Special Projects Unit.

I never, ever in my wildest dreams would have thought that I would have the opportunity to learn like that, front row and never be questioned. The Wachowskis and James McTeague never once questioned my abilities, and they had every right to. They treated me like I was one of the crew. After I came back from that, the next thing you know, *Meet the Patels* had gone viral. Everybody was watching it, and we had a Netflix deal. Ravi and I had a deal with Searchlight to adapt the documentary into a feature screenplay and direct it. We signed with UTA, which was great. The first thing I told UTA was that I wanted to direct television. They said, "Okay. But you realize it's going to be really hard to get into TV. You're a documentary filmmaker and nothing you did was that big." It was a big fight.

JP: Even though you had already shot second unit on *Sense8* for the Wachowskis?

GP: So that's what's funny. Nobody seemed to care. It didn't amount to anything. I can't explain it. I could not get jobs off of *Sense8*.

JP: This is one of the mysteries of breaking into the scripted world of television, the opaque rules that seem to exist. In your case, going from *Meet the Patels* to second unit director on *Sense8* shows that you have a big range of directing skills. And yet, per your agent, that still wasn't enough to get you in to direct TV?

GP: You know, I get it from their point of view. They want to hire someone who they know has done exactly what they're doing. They want to see your résumé and see that you've done it before. It sucked for me because I needed an opportunity and they just wanted a safe bet. The thing that helps someone cross over is when there is someone doing the hiring who sees that you are talented, that you have something to bring that will enhance the show and that is worth the risk they are taking on a first timer.

My agents had a hard time sending me on meetings. So I was very aggressive. I was the biggest pain in their butts. I would call them every day. I would email them. I would be like, "Please send me to this person. Please send me to that person." So they started sending me out. I was meeting people but I wasn't getting anything. I kept doing that for about a year.

Then what happened is, I went for an interview on *Survivor's Remorse*. I found out that the executive producer, Victor Levin, was a guy I had met at a film festival. I emailed him and said, "Victor, I'm going in to interview for your show." Victor turned out to be another angel. He called me on the phone and said, "Geeta, I'm going to do everything I can to make this happen for you." I went in for my final interview with the showrunner, Mike O'Malley, and within one minute he just stood up and said, "You got the job because Victor loves you so much. So I'm not even going to interview you." Victor came up to me after Mike left the room and said, "Don't fuck up." That's how I got my first episode.

JP: How did you know how to direct a half-hour TV show?

GP: I didn't. I mean, the one thing I knew was my instincts as far as how things should be. But I didn't know how to talk to actors. I didn't know anything. So I called a bunch of directors and they all helped me with the diagrams of the cameras and stuff. But it was overwhelming. You really have to practice it. I read the books of how to talk to actors. But it was still hard. After the first day, I went to my car and I cried.

Before I directed, I had to shadow another director, Peter Segal, and that was really helpful. I watched every move he made. We spent hours and hours at dinner afterwards. We are now very close friends. Shadowing Pete was everything, and I appreciate that Starz created that opportunity for me. The only funny thing was that on my first day of directing, Mike O'Malley announced to everybody, "Okay, you guys this is Geeta. She's going to be directing her very first episode." I was like, "Oh, no! Shhhh!" The crew is very hard on first-time directors because they know that you don't know what you're doing. It's a very scary time where you have to pretend you know what you're doing even though you've never done it before. That's why I went to my car and cried after my first day of shooting. I called a very well-known, high-level director and I said, "Dude, I just cried in my car." He said, "I cried in my car the first day too."

JP: What was so scary about that first day?

GP: You take everything personally. If an actor was in a bad mood, I thought, "He thinks I'm a bad director." If someone's not listening you think, "It's because I'm not speaking to them correctly." I blamed myself for everything. Being a first-time director, I thought everyone could just see right through me. I've always been a very sensitive person. It's worked for me as a storyteller, but it also works against me in being so vulnerable. I think my greatest Achilles' heel as a director is that I hate to let people down. And when you're out there and things are not going the way they're supposed to go, I blame myself.

Your first episode can be tough. I was so happy when it was over. But I also got to take so many risks on that episode. I did a step-off crane shot that tried to mimic *Boogie Nights*. I just said I was going to do it and no one seemed to stop me. It was a really complicated shot. We had done four or five takes and I was crapping my pants because I didn't know what I was doing. So Mike O'Malley came up to me and asked, "You've done this before, right?" I was like, "No." But then we got it by the sixth or seventh take. It was a long day but we got it. I got in a lot of trouble with the producers for that because we went into overtime. I felt so bad about the whole thing.

We finished the episode and I had just worked my butt off. I felt really comfortable with the camera, and it was more the people side of things that was hard. In every job as an episodic director, you're the new kid. And on your first episode, you're especially the new kid. For me, not everyone was excited to have me there. There was some testing, or perhaps hazing, involved. There's a lot of support too. But I just needed to get through my initiation on that one. And you don't know until many months later if you've done well or not. I finally got the call afterwards that they were really happy with my episode. I was relieved. After that, I got *The Mindy Project*.

JP: Did it get easier to book jobs after that?

GP: Yes. Someone told me that once you've done two episodes, you're on your way, and once you've done seven or eight, you're *in*. By the end of that year, I finally felt comfortable, like, "Maybe I'm going to be okay."

JP: I have heard from a number of directors—women and/or people of color—that they had encounters with white male directors and were told, "I'm not working right now because of you. You guys are taking all the jobs."

GP: It's so funny because I keep running into the same situation. I met a director recently who had been around for a long time. Somebody from the DGA came to visit the set and asked the director what he was doing next. The director said, "I don't know what I'm doing next because all these minority females are taking my jobs." I was standing right there, and he didn't seem to put it together that this was really not appropriate. It was really intimidating because if I let it get to me, and sometimes I have, I go on to a set feeling like I don't deserve to be there.

I got yelled at by the DP on one of my first jobs. He just screamed and yelled and said, "You don't know what you're doing. You don't even deserve to be here." Then some other directors and I got together and he got fired. We all realized that he had yelled at all of us and we all happened to be female.

During my first episode, I wanted to quit directing. Halfway through, I called my father and said, "I'm out. I don't want to do this. This is too hard. There's too much pressure." I'm so glad I stuck with it, because what I've learned is to be assertive and confident and to understand that old quote by William Goldman, "No one knows anything." It's true. As soon as you think that you don't belong, it just starts spiraling. The most important thing is to be confident. So what I do is, I have a very strict process now. First, I'm very, very prepared for all my shoots. I have diagrams. I have shots. Not everybody does that, but I am so prepared for everything that there is never a question of me not knowing that I'm going to do my job to the best of my ability. Secondly, when I go on a set and I want something, I ask for it, and I ask for it again. I don't ever back down. But I do it with kindness. I never raise my voice, which is very hard.

There was a certain point where I kept complaining and my father said, "You are not a victim, Geeta, so stop acting like one or you will never be successful." That has been the best advice. There are so many different reasons you can come up with for why you didn't get an opportunity or why someone is not treating you well. However, once one starts thinking that way, the world shifts in that negative direction. It is career suicide. If I start thinking I'm not good enough for a job, or I didn't get that job because of some physical or other quality I have, then that means that I can see myself that way. The way I feel about myself is exactly how others will feel about me. So I stopped seeing myself through others' eyes, just like my dad who is under five feet has never seen himself as short. Instead, I have learned to see myself through my own eyes: as Geeta, someone who is hard-working, qualified and capable. This was the secret for me. Confidence. It's been the key to everything appearing in my life.

Ken Whittingham

Ken Whittingham cannot be on a studio lot for five minutes without someone shouting a greeting to him. Everyone knows Ken. I have worked more with Ken than with any other director, and as a crew member I have always loved it. We get out early and we invariably have fun. His openness to collaboration is legendary. He just wants to direct the funniest show possible, and he makes it clear through his actions that he wants everyone to be part of that process. He does not even have to say it. He just exudes the message of, "Come be part of this adventure with me!"

Directing television can be like sailing a choppy sea. But I have never seen Ken get angry or upset on set. And I have never seen him treat someone with disrespect. Ken rides the waves with the best of them.

· · · · · · · · · · · · · · · · · · · ·

KEN WHITTINGHAM: I was born at Queen of Angels Hospital in Los Angeles. It's no longer there. Growing up, it was just my mother and me. My parents separated when I was very young. My mother and I lived in a duplex in Los Angeles and the city started to get a little rough. This was the mid–60s. By the time I was seven or eight, my mother decided to buy a house in Altadena.

My mom worked for State Compensation Insurance Fund, she was a claims adjuster. She worked there for 42 years. She also had a catering business on the side. At a young age, I would go work with her. I would help clean up the kitchen and pass out hors d'oeuvres at parties in Los Angeles. She worked for well-to-do people in L.A. like the O'Malleys, who used to own the Dodgers. She'd work in Beverly Hills, West Hollywood, Hollywood, Bel Air. High-end parties.

JACOB PINGER: Working for people who were in the TV and film business?

KW: Yeah, I think so. There was a guy named Don Loper. He was a famous designer. You see his credits on Lucille Ball's show and stuff like that. I remember him and a few actors. But I really didn't know much about Hollywood. They were just rich people. There were music people as well. She worked with Quincy Jones.

JP: So now you're possibly working with people or the children of people that your mom was catering for back in the day.

KW: Right.

JP: Did your family have any industry connections?

KW: There was one guy in particular named Gene Patton. He was a prop guy on *The Tonight Show*. Gene was the first African-American in the prop union. His son and I were best friends. Gene would take us to see *The Tonight Show* every once in a while if someone we liked was going to be on, like Richard Pryor. But I never thought about entertainment as a career path.

JP: Did Gene tell you what the industry was like?

KW: He never talked about it. Later on, he became famous as Gene Gene the Dancing Machine on *The Gong Show*. That was the only person I knew in the business. My friends and I were athletes. We were also kind of the class clowns. We would hang out as people walked by in high school, and tease them to make people laugh. That's what we were kind of known for. But it wasn't to be mean. It was just to make people laugh. We loved comedy. And we were very strongly influenced by comics of that time. And when I say comics, really, it was Richard Pryor.

When my friend's dad went to work, we would sneak into his album collection and pull out Redd Fox, Richard Pryor and Bill Cosby records. We really connected to

After starting his scripted career in the CBS mailroom, Ken Whittingham worked his way up the ladder to become one of the most respected directors in the industry (Jacob Pinger).

Richard Pryor because he was more current and closer to our age. He was cutting edge. My friends and I were also big fans of *Benny Hill*. Then when *Saturday Night Live* was starting, we would get together on Saturday nights at 11:30 to watch it.

JP: Many of the comics you named were African-American. What was your awareness at the time as far as any sort of cultural division between black comedy and white comedy? Was that something you were conscious of?

KW: Not at all. There were just certain people we thought were funny. We loved the comedy of the '60s. *Gilligan's Island*, *The Addams Family*, *The Munsters* and *Gomer Pyle*. But the stand-up comics probably had more impact on us because they were a little bit more, you know, X-rated. A little more shocking. As a kid, you go, "Wow. That's really cutting edge." There was also Lenny Bruce and guys like that. But it was hard to get a chance to hear them. My friend's dad's albums were the only ones we had exposure to. You couldn't hear those comics anywhere else. It wasn't on the radio.

JP: So what did you want to be at that point?

KW: As a young person, I wanted to be a basketball player or football player. Then when I got to high school, I saw that football really wasn't going to happen. I said, "I'll play basketball." Midway through high school, I realized that I was probably never going to make it to the NBA. So I was kind of drifting and not really thinking about what I wanted to do. No one ever talked to me about college and what it had to offer, or about the difference between universities, state colleges and junior colleges. So I wasn't really thinking about college at all. I ended up going to Pasadena City College and when I got there I got this thirst to be successful. I literally looked in a book and asked, "What are the most promising careers for the next decade?" The book said public relations. The book also said, "First you should take some journalism classes." So I did, and I became more interested in that. I still liked sports a lot, so I started taking pictures of sports and doing photojournalism. I was on the newspaper at Pasadena City College, which was fun. Then I transferred to California State Northridge and was on the newspaper and radio there. I won a Golden Mike Award for a radio show I produced.

After I graduated, I started working for CBS News. I had a friend who worked for a community outreach program in Pasadena who helped corporations find people to interview for jobs. I was majoring in journalism as a sophomore and I was looking for a job. My friend said, "There's going to be this job opening at CBS in the mailroom. You want to interview for it?" I drove to CBS to interview, and I got the job. But it was going to be temporary for that summer. It was a very short-term thing where they took people from different communities and put them in this program. So at the end of the summer, I was going to go back to college for my junior year. But before I did, I went into the guest relations department at CBS and said that I wanted to be a page. A page was someone who worked on various live shows. They would stand around in their red polyester jackets and black polyester pants, pass out tickets and help seat the audience. That's how I got my start. I started in the mailroom and then worked as a CBS page during my junior and senior years. After I graduated, I talked to a couple of people there and I transferred from being a page to being a production assistant in the news department.

JP: Did you ever have a sense that there was any racism in the industry, that there was any sort of stumbling blocks for someone who wasn't white?

KW: No, it was something I really didn't have to contend with. I wasn't really aware of it because of growing up the way I did. The topic was all around in the '60s. There was the civil rights movement. There was rioting in Los Angeles in 1965. There were things going on all around the country. But in this little microcosm of Pasadena where we had busing integration early on, I had exposure to different cultures starting in the sixth grade. So going into the world of television, I was kind of used to being in that environment. There was a handful of African-Americans, a handful of Asian-Americans, a handful of Latin Americans. I was kind of used to those numbers. I really didn't give it too much thought.

JP: How did you fare in news?

KW: Doing live television was a very stressful environment for a PA. I was running around getting copy to the graphics department. They would make a graphic, and then I'd run it back up and put it on an easel. I would literally run to the airport to get a tape that just came in from Atlanta. I would drive the reporters to do their stories. I was doing anything that needed to be done. It was always high tension. Then I moved up and became a field producer. I would go out and interview people in the field and use their responses on air. I had various different jobs.

JP: How old were you when you became a field producer?

KW: I was 23. That was during a time when drugs were very prevalent, and a lot of the news producers would snort a bunch of cocaine, and go in for the news broadcast. Then they would come out and want to change everything. It was very frustrating and stressful. I developed an ulcer at the age of 23. Another major problem for me was seeing that we weren't really reporting the news fairly. We weren't fully reporting the news about all of L.A. That was the beginning of gangs in Los Angeles. I would call the police precincts and find out things, and then call my news desk. I would tell them there was a beheading down in Compton, or there were five people shot down there. They would ask, "Where was it?" I'd say down on Manchester or something. And they'd say, "Well, that's not news. That's something that happens somewhere else." So the news was very, very slanted, and it drove me crazy. That was a factor in me getting an ulcer. It was the anxiety about not reporting the news fairly. I decided at that point to do something else in my life because I wasn't really happy. So I got a job doing research, saved up $7000 and backpacked around Europe for six months. That was a very eye-opening experience. I think before I went, I was a very materialistic person. Living in L.A. was about what kind of clothes you had, and what kind of car you drove, and what you did for a living. In Europe, I realized that everybody wasn't materialistic, and everybody wasn't worried about what you did or how much money you had. It was about your character. That's probably one of the biggest things I learned. I also saw that there was this underlying racism in America, not just in the South or the East but also in L.A. In Europe, I saw a different acceptance of African-Americans. I didn't realize how differently we were treated in America until I went there. I think California is a little deceiving because there is racism here, but it's not in your face. In Europe, they didn't understand what this whole racism thing was about.

JP: Where did you go?

KW: I went everywhere from Sweden to the island of Crete. France, Spain, England, Italy, Germany, Holland, Belgium and Denmark.

JP: When you came back, did you have any immediate sense of change in your awareness about race in America, or did that grow gradually on you?

KW: That took a little time. As a young person, I wasn't really aware that there was a problem. In college is when it really hit me that racism is still a thing. It's not just in the South, or something you read about in books. When I came back from Europe, I had more of an awareness of it. But something about me is that I have always tried to transcend race.

JP: When you came back from Europe—is that when you got into working on multi-cam sets?

KW: Yes. I got back from Europe and a friend of mine called. She knew I didn't have a job, and she said, "Hey, we need a production assistant on this show *227*. Would you be interested in being a PA?" At first I said, no. But then I asked, "How much is it paying?" It was nine months work and made about $25,000 a year, which was actually about what I had been making as a CBS field producer. So I said, "What the heck." It was a very humbling experience because now I was back to running around getting people coffee, delivering scripts and even picking up laundry for the producers. I was 26 or 27 years old by this time, and it was humbling.

I still wasn't sure exactly what I wanted to do when I got that PA job. During my first year, I thought maybe I wanted to write. So Marla Gibbs' son and I wrote seven show ideas and pitched them. They bought one. So we got a show produced. Then I decided that I wanted to be a multi-cam director. But I didn't know anything about directing and I didn't know anything about acting or any of that kind of stuff. So I decided to become a stage manager, which would give me the opportunity to learn about acting and television comedy while making money. I took that opportunity as a stage manager and used it as my directing training ground. I did that for five or six years.

JP: Can you describe the stage manager's job on a multi-camera sitcom? Is that different than what an AD does in single-cam?

KW: Basically, on a multi-camera sitcom there is a first stage manager and a second stage manager. And they do the same things that the assistant directors do on a single-camera show. They organize schedules and get actors to set. I think the assistant director's job on a single-camera show is a little more intense than a first stage manager's job on a multi-cam show.

JP: Can you tell me about your first directing job?

KW: My first directing job was on a show called *Malcolm and Eddie*, a multi-camera show back in '97 I believe.

JP: How did you get that first opportunity?

KW: At that point, I started going to editing all the time and really watching the directors to see what they did on set, both the good ones and the bad ones. When I finally felt that I was ready, I let everybody know. Every time I got a job as a stage manager, I would try to negotiate getting a shot to direct, but it was very hard to do because no one wanted to give me that first opportunity. Around that time, I was the stage manager on *Malcolm and Eddie* with Malcolm-Jamal Warner and Eddie Griffin, who had a reputation for being a real handful. It turned out I was the only one who could really wrangle Eddie. I was like "the Eddie Griffin Whisperer." Then a friend of mine at another show asked me to come work for him as a stage manager, but he also said that he would give me a shot to direct. The studio found out that I might be leaving *Malcolm and Eddie* and they said, "You can't leave. You're the Eddie Griffin Whisperer. What can we give you to stay?" I said, "Give me a shot to direct."

When I directed my first episode of *Malcolm and Eddie*, I knew that I had to make a splash. I couldn't just do something average. So I ordered a crane, which was unusual for a multi-camera show at the time. And they were like, "Ummm, all right…" We were doing a '70s-themed episode, and I started the shot up on this disco ball and did a crane move down to reveal the scene. Everyone was like, "Wow! That was pretty cool." So that got me my second episode.

For the next two years on *Malcolm and Eddie*, I would direct a couple shows, and then go back to stage-managing. They ended up promoting me from stage manager to camera coordinator, which meant I would arrange all of the shots. When you're shooting on a multi-cam, you need to have someone there to get all the camera guys in position, and that's the camera coordinator. It's almost like doing a live event. So for instance, you would say, "Okay, B-camera, you have shot number 97 coming up. It's going to be a three-shot. So when the director snaps his fingers, you go to that shot."

JP: Becoming a camera coordinator was a bump up from being stage manager?

KW: Correct. But I wasn't very good at it.

JP: That's an honest answer.

KW: Yeah. But I tried. [*Laughs*] The next year was season three of *Malcolm and Eddie*, and they said, "You have to make a decision. Either you're going to direct or you're going to be a camera coordinator." So I said, "Okay. How many am I going to direct?" They said, "Five," and I said, "Great." Five was enough episodes to take care of my family. But then Malcolm-Jamal Warner decided that he wanted to direct as well. In fact, he decided that he wanted to direct almost all the episodes. So my five went to zero. I was out there with no job, but then another show called me. It was *Moesha*, which was a show that I had actually directed on when I was working on *Malcolm and Eddie*. So *Moesha* called me and asked if I knew any available stage managers. Because I didn't have a job, I said, "Me. I'll take it." It was a very humbling experience to be their stage manager because I had already been a director on the show. And then my directing agent dropped me because I didn't really have anything going on. I was just kind of out there, and it was all about trying to re-invent myself again.

JP: That's a tough position to be in. And your personal response to that probably makes a big difference in terms of how it all turns out. How did you deal with it?

KW: I knew I was going to have to reinvent myself again. Fortunately, the writer-producers on *Moesha* created another show called *The Parkers* and they promised me an episode to direct on the new show while I was still a stage manager on *Moesha*. I came over to direct an episode of *The Parkers* and I knew I had to make a big splash again, just like with my first episode of *Malcolm and Eddie*. So I started adding all these single-camera elements to this multi-cam show to make it look a little special. I was doing all this really cool single-camera stuff. The episode came out so cool that it was kind of confusing to the producers because they didn't know what I was doing. Like, I had a scene where we did a montage with the camera. I just floated the camera from left to right, in and out of black to transition from one scene to the next. When it was edited together, it looked like one continuous piece. That was something that hadn't really been done on a multi-camera sitcom. But I knew I had to do something special to get another opportunity. After that, *The Parkers* offered me ten episodes.

At that point, I said, "I'm done with stage managing. I got ten episodes to direct for next year." But then, and it was kind of funny, the *Parkers* producer who had offered me the ten episodes got fired by the head of the studio, and I was kind of collateral damage. So I didn't get the ten episodes. I got maybe like two or three. But then I did my few episodes of *The Parkers*, and that led to something else, and then that also led to something else.

JP: So what's the lesson there? Is it perseverance?

KW: It's perseverance and believing in yourself. Remember that when one door closes, another one opens. Whatever you do, try to do the best you can, and know that will be your calling card for the next thing. Can you show it? Is it representative of what you do?

JP: When you look at someone's IMDb page, it's easy to think that their career was just a series of sequential events, and that each one led seamlessly to the next. You don't always think about the ups and downs.

KW: I remember the day my directing agent called and said, "I have some good news and some bad news. The good news is, I'm pregnant. The bad news is, I'm going to have to drop you as a client." And I had to laugh at it even though I was really bummed. I wasn't happy being a stage manager. My mom passed away during those years and left me the house I grew up in in West Altadena. So the way I thought about it was, "I have a roof over my head, and that supports me to take chances in this business." The house was virtually paid off, so I didn't have to worry about a mortgage or buying a house. I knew I could still make a good living as a stage manager, and so I could take more time and have more choices. When one door closes, you just say, "Well, I'll try this other thing." To me, every new thing I could achieve was gravy, because in a worst-case scenario I could still be a stage manager. I wouldn't necessarily be that happy because it wasn't creative enough, but it wasn't the end of the world. And I knew that since I had already directed some stuff, that I could probably direct something somewhere else. There were not a lot of networks at the time, and cable was still really new. So there wasn't a lot out there, but I knew that there would be something for me. I was very positive. I never really got down about it.

The year after I lost the episodes from *The Parkers,* I got maybe six or seven episodes of television. And then the next year, I probably got ten or twelve. Then it kind of took off. I started doing single-camera shows and it spiked to the point that I was doing almost 20 episodes a year. I would do like ten multi-cam and ten single cam shows. That's around the time I was doing *Bernie Mac* and *The Office* and *Scrubs* and stuff like that.

JP: A lot of the shows you did early on had mostly African-American casts. In your transition from multi-cam to single cam, did you also experience a line between working on "black" shows to working on "white" shows? Was that a thing?

KW: Yes. It was a big thing. Basically it was the line between non-network and network. So there was UPN and WB. And then there was ABC, CBS and NBC. My first show that didn't have a primarily African-American cast was *Becker,* which had Ted Danson from *Cheers.* It was a different level of comedy. And it was a definite thing. It was hard to break into that network world because I had done all those UPN shows and people didn't really take them that seriously. It was almost like doing a kids' show. You know, like a Nickelodeon- or Disney-type show.

JP: Other than there being more pressure on a network show, was there any real difference?

KW: It was a little bit more pressure because there was initially more at stake. I wanted to start doing network shows and this was my entrée in. Being on a network was a big thing, even if it would have been an African-American show.

JP: Did you ever have a sense that your personal career represented a bigger cultural issue?

KW: You mean as far as representing African-Americans? Yes, for sure. It was always there, even stage managing or being a PA. I always felt a responsibility to set an example, and that it wasn't about me. Because there were so few of me in the industry, I had to be the best I possibly could, and not reinforce any stereotypes that people might have, and not fuck up. And I still had to be me. Years ago, I set up a meeting with Harvey Weinstein about doing a movie. As the meeting approached, I didn't feel like I had my stuff together. I had too much on my plate at the time. So I canceled the meeting with him because I didn't want him to look at me like I didn't have my shit together. I didn't want him to yell at me for wasting his time. It's very important to me to represent because whatever you do might carry through in some guy's mind, as in, "That's just how African-Americans are. We tried to hire this one guy but he didn't do it. Well, we tried!" I'm not ever privy to those kinds of conversations, but I'm sure they do happen. You never know.

JP: Now you have a ton of directing credits. You are firmly established. When you get a job today, do you still go in with the sense of responsibility that you have to represent African-Americans?

KW: Yeah. Every day I step on a set.

JP: I've heard some pretty disturbing things from fellow crew members about this kind of stuff. And it's definitely been disheartening at times. Like, comments about how a novice, non-white director only got the job because of their skin color. But that crew member would never say anything like that about the shitty white male director we had the week before.

KW: It is disheartening. I hear it. There was this one guy I knew back in the day. We used to be friends. And he made a comment to me. He had directed a bunch of episodes and became very successful, and very rich. But he did something in his personal life that kind of derailed his career, he was kind of ostracized from the business. Later he was trying to get a break again, and he made this comment: He said, "I guess I got to be a woman or a black person to get a job." Sometimes people can't step back and look at themselves.

Racism is something that I've lived with for so long. I'm not surprised when it pops up or when people say certain things. I don't try to hate anybody. I know everybody is different, and has their different viewpoints. They may not have exposure or experiences with certain groups of people. And that forms their opinion. So I respect that even though I don't necessarily agree with everything they say or think. I have had conversations with many people about race, and a lot of people think, "Well, you don't really have to deal with it." And I'm like, "Sure I do. I deal with it almost daily, but it doesn't make me mad."

Not long ago, I was on a certain show. I came in, and everyone was very aloof and arrogant and weird. I was wondering, "Why is everybody not being nice to me?" I had to go in and ask them, "Am I a diversity hire? Is that what's going on here?" And they said, "Oh, no, no, no! That's not it." I said, "Are you sure? Because if that's the case, I'd rather not do the show." At this point in my career, I never want it to be that. I think that opportunity should go to somebody else, because I've been doing this for so long.

JP: When you come in to direct an episode, your energy and enthusiasm are very apparent, which is why I think a lot of people like working with you.

KW: I have to say that to this day, when people say they like to work with me … it's still almost unbelievable. It's a huge, huge compliment. But it's almost unbelievable because I'm not really aware. I'm so outside of myself. It really surprises me because I never really studied comedy. I wasn't one of those kids who was like, "I'm going to be a comedy director!" I just have a real funnybone. I think that drives me and excites me. I only really do comedy, and I'm always thinking, "How can I elevate it? How can I make people laugh? How can I take what's on the page and make it even funnier? What can I add to the process?" I've been blessed to work on these really great comedies. Sometimes I have to pinch myself because this really wasn't in the plans.

I came up as a stage manager doing multi-camera comedies. I would be the one talking to actors because, back then, the director was in the booth. He would have me tell the actor what to do. So I had to talk to the actors. And I had a tough set of actors back in the day. I used to work on *227* with Marla Gibbs, and as the stage manager I had to be clear, concise and convincing about what the director wanted them to do. That job gave me a strong sense of how to talk to actors. But I think what really drove me was my understanding of what was funny and what wasn't.

At some point, I got a chance to start directing multi-camera. Later, when I started directing single-camera, which is more like traditional filmmaking, I had never shadowed anybody. I had never been to film school. It was purely instinct on how I saw things. And I have gone with my instincts throughout my career. Where the camera should be, how it should be played, what's the funniest image, what's the best reveal? I take it through a process to find what is going to be the funniest way to shoot it. Where is the comedy? And that's what keeps me excited about doing what I do.

JP: When you first got hired on *Becker*, did that feel like a big step in your career?

KW: It was a huge step, and it taught me something. I don't think I really did a great job on that episode. It was hard for me to navigate. There were layers to the script, and it was very nuanced. I wasn't used to directing very nuanced shows. I would just read the words and say, "Okay, here's what they're supposed to say. They'll do it." But I wasn't experienced enough to say, "Say it like this. Now say it like this. Now do this other line like this," and that's what it really had to be. I think the actors were getting a little lost, and I really couldn't help navigate them to where they needed to be. So they would go past me and call over to the producers to ask for help. I wasn't used to that. I should have been more dialed in. So *Becker* really helped me to understand that you can't depend on the actor to deliver a line in the way you think they should already know. Back then, you didn't really have tone meetings in multi-cam, so you might assume some lines in the script mean a certain thing and they're like, "No, it means this other thing." In single-camera, you have tone meetings to make sure that everybody is on the same page about the meaning of the script.

JP: Was it a big deal when you jumped from multi-cam to single-cam?

KW: It was a huge deal. I was doing a multi-cam show and I heard they were looking for an African-American director to do an episode of *The Bernie Mac Show*. It was a very sensitive episode because they were using the N-word. So somebody said, "We should have an African-American director do it because it's such a sensitive episode." There weren't very many African-American single-camera comedy directors at the time. There were film guys but not comedy guys. So I was called in because I was already pretty big in multi-cam. I was dying to do a single-cam show, and had been bugging my agents about it. The *Bernie Mac* people somehow got in touch with me and I went in to meet. They asked, "Why do you think you could direct a single-camera show as opposed to a multi-cam?" I said, "Because it's about storytelling. If I can tell a story with four cameras and a couple of hours on a stage, I can surely tell it with one camera over a week's time." And they bought it. They said, "All right, let's try it." But for my first episode of single-camera comedy, they gave me only four days instead of the usual five because the other director needed six days for his episode. I did that *Bernie Mac* episode in *three and a half days* because I was so prepared and full of adrenalin.

JP: What do you think about the state of the industry right now for somebody who is just starting out?

KW: I think we are at a really good place right now. I've never seen it so diverse. And I think that even though there's more content, the competition is stiffer. Back when I was coming up, they would sometimes just throw anybody in there to direct. And it was more about favors and nepotism. But now, if you don't deliver, even if you're related to somebody, you're going to get called out on it. Be it by an actor, the studio, or whoever. There's more on the line right now. There were bad shows in the '80s, and I worked with people who should not have been directing. They were just relatives of someone, and they didn't care. I mean, literally, you could hear them on the phone ordering cars while the scene was going on. It was like, "Wow!" It was a money train for a while there and there was a real disrespect for it. The author Hunter S. Thompson had a quote back then that the TV industry was filled with hustlers and pimps who were doing a lot of crap. I think it's gotten a lot better. There are still some people that try to get a break and are not cut out for it. But the ones that aren't serious about it don't last long. They get exposed.

JP: What advice would you give somebody who is trying to get into directing?

KW: One thing you really have to understand as a director in television is that it's not a director's medium. It's a writer's medium, and you're not going to be the boss. You can be a boss to a certain extent, but at the end of the day, it's a producer who hires you. And it's a producer who is going to have the final cut. I was very passionate when I was starting out. The producers would say, "Hey, why don't you do *this*, why don't you do *that*?" And I would be like, "No." I was kind of crazy back then. And I didn't get asked back to some shows because you have to do what they want you to do. It's their show. A movie is different. You can do your thing. But in television, you have to be collaborative. It's not all about you if you want to get asked back. I know this one director who was on a show last year and at one point the producers asked her to do a two-shot. She said. "No," because she didn't think it would ever make the cut. The producer said, "Yeah, but I want you to do it." And she said, "No. I'm not gonna do it." And she didn't do it. And she wasn't asked back.

You have to know that either you do it their way, or you can get your own show. Because at the end of the day, the network might come along and say, "You know what? We need a two-shot there. Can you re-shoot it?" You have to answer to somebody at some point even if it is your own show. So I guess my answer is this: Be collaborative.

JP: Sometimes it can be hard to define a good vs. a bad director. I've noticed there are times when a really good director's episode doesn't turn out that funny. But a not-so-good director can have a really good episode. How do you define the difference between a really good vs. a mediocre director?

KW: You know, it's almost like catching lightning in a bottle sometimes to have a really good episode. Sometimes it can be great on paper and then it's just not good visually. And it could be the fault of the director or the concept is wrong. What seems like it's going to be funny sometimes doesn't work. I did a show recently where the whole idea was about people obsessed with posting to social media. It seemed like a really funny idea. But then when you actually see it on air, everything is on small screens, and it's all tiny. You start to feel a little claustrophobic and the joke doesn't really come across because it's too insular. So there are different reasons why things are funny or not.

And there are different ways to cut things to make jokes funnier. The final edit is ultimately up to the producer. Sometimes directors will come in and shoot a bunch of stuff and say, "You guys figure it out because I don't know how it's supposed to cut," and sometimes directors will have a very clear vision. Sometimes their vision works, and sometimes it doesn't. It's really hit or miss. There are so many different ways to cut something. A producer might get a director's cut and hate the way it's done, and then re-do it. The director didn't write it, so maybe they missed something. For instance, Kenya Barris, the showrunner on *Black-ish*, has gone on record that he does not even look at the director's cut. He just looks at the editor's cut. And then there is also the network's influence, and the studio's influence.

I try to shoot things in a way that I want the show to be edited so you can't cut it too many other ways. I learned that early on. That's why I move a little faster than other directors, because I know exactly what I want. And sometimes I might not get asked back, but very rarely.

JP: In multi-cam, is the director physically on set?

KW: It used to be that the director would be in a booth. But now, the first two or three days you're on the set and you're staging it. You're putting it on its feet and getting the performances out. Then the producers and writers come down for a run-through. They watch it. They determine what's funny and what's not funny. Then they go back and re-write it. They come down again the next day. It's a very different process than single-cam. In multi-cam, you are basically putting on a 45-page play two or three times a week, and then tweaking it. Then there's the time factor. You will come in at ten in the morning and need to do a one o'clock run-through. So it's rushing through staging and trying to get performances worked out. And hopefully everybody remembers their lines when you're doing the run-through. It's really different than single-cam.

It's not my thing any more. I used to be into it. You can become very rich directing multi-cam shows because traditionally those are the shows that syndicate the best. Shows like *King of Queens*, *Seinfeld*, *Everybody Loves Raymond* and *Big Bang Theory*. Even the crappy multi-cam shows get syndication.

JP: Do you make shot lists?

KW: I don't always make traditional shot lists. When there's a big scene, and there's maybe 12 people around a table, that's when I'll make a shot list. It's so everybody is on the same page and we just kind of mark off the list. Or if it's a very complicated action sequence, or a fight or something like that, then I'll make a shot list. For the traditional two or three people in a room, I'm not going to make a shot list for that. But what I *will* do is take schematics or set plans and literally walk on the set to figure out where the camera should be. I will find the best angles with the most depth to make the prettiest pictures. I will also make little sketches and write down next to each scene what shots I need. Like, "I need a cross from John to Joan, and then I need a cross from Joan to John. And then I need a two-shot and then a single." I write down all that stuff. That helps me picture it in my head. By the time I get there on the day, I already know exactly where everybody is sitting and exactly what shots I need.

JP: I think there's a deep sense of confidence when a director is collaborative. An un-confident director might not take advice from the crew because they are afraid people will think they can't make a decision. But actually the opposite is true. People *like* working with a confident director because they sense the respect and open-mindedness. Some of the less experienced directors will actually shut those people down on set, and limit who they will listen to.

KW: Which is really bad. I will take a joke from anybody if it's funny and it makes sense to the story. I don't get intimidated by that. And I will give them credit because at the end of the day, it's going to make me look good.

JP: I've noticed that you're very clear in your direction. People are never confused.

KW: That's a big thing I learned early on. As a director, you need to be very, very clear about what you want. And know what you want to say before you go out there and say it. You can't hem and haw. If something's not working, you have to be clear about that as well. Like, "Okay, we need to try something else."

JP: Anything else you want to talk about?

KW: I saw one of your questions was about the difference between schmoozing and networking. I've never really been a good schmoozer. I'm still not. I'm not the kind that really goes to parties and wants to meet people. It was hard for me, you know? I do try to get along with everybody, but if there's somebody who clearly is not into me and doesn't want to be around me, I stay away. I don't deal with those people. It's one of my pet peeves when I think that people are arrogant or mean and dismissive. I won't even want to meet them. I think about when I'm an old man and I still want to have the respect of my kids. I want to know that I never let anybody belittle me or make me do something just for money, or compromise myself in any way.

Zoe Lister-Jones

I spent four seasons filming Zoe Lister-Jones on *Life in Pieces*. Her talent as an actress during that time was obvious. She could take an otherwise ho-hum scene and breathe life into it with ease. When she finished her excellent feature film *Band Aid*, I thought, "How did she manage to write, produce and direct an indie film while simultaneously working full-time on a network series?" The answer, of course, was with ease.

• • • • • • • • • • • • • • • • • • • •

ZOE LISTER-JONES: I grew up in Brooklyn, New York. Both of my parents are visual artists. My mom is a video artist and my dad is a conceptual photographer who has also done video art later in his career. I was raised very much a part of the New York art world in the '80s and '90s. I was exposed to really incredible artists, which I feel very grateful for. My mom and dad are both feminists. My mom taught me to look at media through the lens of gender equity and inequity. That was a really big part of my upbringing. I was raised in a kosher Jewish household. We went to synagogue every weekend. It was a conservative egalitarian synagogue that had a female rabbi. When I was five, we got a new rabbi who was a man and I cried to my mom because I didn't realize men could be rabbis. Judaism and Jewish renewal were a big part of my upbringing. I think that's informed a lot of my work.

JACOB PINGER: Were your parents together throughout your childhood?

ZLJ: No. They split up when I was nine.

JP: Did they both stay in New York?

ZLJ: They did, in Brooklyn.

JP: When did you decide you wanted to be an artist? And did you go for music first?

ZLJ: No. I was always drawing. I really loved drawing. I loved writing too. I started to write short stories in elementary school. I wrote poetry when I was getting into adolescence. I didn't get into playwriting until college. But when I was about ten, my mom put me in acting classes at this place called HB Studios in

Zoe Lister-Jones came to directing through writing, producing and acting in her own micro-budget feature films (Daryl Wein).

121

the West Village. I think she did it mostly because I was a really shy kid. She saw that I would light up as a performer in the privacy of our home, but I was an only child and I felt much more comfortable around adults. Being in a class with kids was scary to me, and I overcame some fears there. I loved those classes.

My high school was a public school in Brooklyn called Edward R. Murrow, and they had a really amazing theater department. I auditioned for the musicals. I wasn't confident as a singer, but I was in the chorus for a number of musicals. I was sort of on a journey that was really about confidence. During my senior year, I was the star of two black box plays, and that was the year I started to understand that I wanted to pursue acting in college. But I was afraid of putting all my eggs in that basket. I think it was mostly because my parents were both artists and I saw the struggle that it was for them to pursue that life—the pain and the financial uncertainty. There was no part of me that was naively just throwing myself into the arts. Part of me wanted to have a backup plan. Pursuing acting was a really heavy decision for me to make.

I got a scholarship to go to Tisch School of the Arts at NYU and my mom said that I should pursue it. It was kind of the opposite experience of most kids who pursue acting where I was the one saying, "Shouldn't I do pre-med?" And my mom was the one saying, "No. You should pursue acting." So I went to Tisch. When I was there, I took a class where I started writing sketch comedy. I loved writing roles for my friends and myself. I was going to the Atlantic Theater Company acting school and David Mamet would occasionally drop in unannounced. Whenever he did that, everyone would have to drop whatever they were doing and throw up whatever scene they were working on for him to watch. Mamet was notoriously cruel to students and just very direct. One time I decided to put up a scene that I had written. He usually stopped most students in the middle of their scene just to tell them why it was garbage. But Mamet let me get through my whole scene. When it was finished, he asked me who wrote it. I said that I had written it. He told me that I should write a feature. That was like a huge vote of confidence.

Then I had a teacher named Siobhan Fallon, an amazing character actress who had done a one-woman show. She was teaching a solo performance class and she really encouraged me to create my own one-woman show. So upon graduating, I put up a one-woman show that I had written called *Co-dependence Is a Four Letter Word* in which I played 11 different characters grappling with heartbreak. That was how I got my first agent and manager. Then the trajectory continued in terms of me starting to get acting work in theater, indie films and TV. I also continued to write. Then my husband, Daryl Wein, and I wrote our first feature, *Breaking Upwards*. We shot it in 2008. It was a true labor of love that he directed and that we both produced and starred in. It premiered at South by Southwest and got us a full-page feature in *The New York Times* because we made it for $15,000. That film opened a ton of doors for us in the feature world as writers and producers, and for Daryl as a director. We then co-wrote and produced a movie for Fox Searchlight, *Lola Versus*, which was a dream of ours. I acted in it and Daryl directed. Then we made two more features together. We worked so closely in all facets of making those indies. I had been acting more and more in television over the years and eventually I wanted to try my hand at directing. So I wrote and directed a feature called *Band Aid*. That was also a true labor of love. But our history in the indie filmmaking world had taught me so much about how to make a film on a shoestring budget and still create something that was meaningful and personal. With *Band Aid*, I tried to really focus on the process over the product because I think I had started to feel a little lost in the intersection of art and business. I really wanted to just focus on the art-making of it. We shot *Band-Aid* in 12 days with an entirely female crew, which was an important incentive for me. It premiered in competition at Sundance, which had been a lifelong dream. I am now making my second feature, which I'm about to go shoot. It's the reboot of *The Craft*.

JP: Did you ever feel like your parents put pressure on you to go into the arts?

ZLJ: I don't think there was pressure. They were exposing me to art, but not for any other purpose than that was just their life and I was hanging out with them a lot. I had a lot of options to do any number of things. But I was a deeply feeling young person, and so art seemed to be a place that I was gravitating towards.

JP: When you talked about the hardships of growing up with artists as parents, was that mostly financial hardship or a lifestyle of insecurity?

ZLJ: Definitely financial. Both of my parents are brilliant artists but they were never able to make a living from their art. My mother was a professor of video art at Rutgers University and I saw that that position made it so much more difficult for her to focus on her own work. My dad did a number of different jobs. He worked at art magazines. It made me aware of the sacrifices that a person makes in order to earn a living, and the impact it has on your time to make art and also the energy you have to put towards your art. Financially, I saw that it was always a struggle.

JP: With your parents' background in the fine arts, did you ever feel any conflict over the artistic status of working in TV?

ZLJ: I've always been so grateful to make a living from my art that I never looked down upon the medium of television. When I started acting in multi-cam sitcoms, which are definitely not considered cool in the art world, I felt like the people that I wanted to like the shows were not going to. And that's never the nicest feeling. It's always nice to be working on something that is shiny and zeitgeisty. But again, I've always just been so happy for the security and the community of my work in television. And my parents have never been judgmental about it either. I think they're just proud that I'm making a living from what I like to do. It's something that I have never taken for granted.

JP: You've pursued multiple career tracks simultaneously. You've had a full-fledged career as an actor as well as a filmmaker. Did you always see yourself as an actor first and a filmmaker second?

ZLJ: I always loved writing. And actually, I thought that I might be a writer before I was an actor. That's part of why I was apprehensive about going to acting conservatory. I didn't know that I wanted to write scripts at that point, but I got a big award for a short story I wrote in high school. Writing was something that I was being recognized for and that felt good. In acting school, I got the bug writing comedy sketches. Then I wrote my one-woman show. It was a thrilling intersection of my two passions where I could create my own work as an actor and not be dependent on anyone else to do so. I could write the roles that I wanted to play and create the worlds that I felt were important. So I think it happened organically. As I started getting more acting gigs, Daryl and I collaborated on writing *Breaking Upwards*, a script that was based on the early part of our relationship. As we made that film, Daryl was able to teach me a lot about guerrilla filmmaking because he had been making films since high school. I quickly learned all these tools about how to produce a feature. Things were all happening simultaneously in my early twenties in a way that was really exciting.

JP: Talk about deciding you wanted to be a director.

ZLJ: I considered myself a filmmaker for a really long time because of how many films we made. By the time I wrote *Band Aid,* we already had four features under our belts. I felt like directing was the natural next step for me. I think I wanted to create a world entirely on my own. It was a thrilling prospect even though it was also really scary. But I was also ready for it. I was excited to take that leap.

JP: What setbacks have you had and how did you overcome them?

ZLJ: I recently wrote and directed a pilot for ABC called *Woman Up*. It was a huge victory to be given that opportunity and a rarity for a woman to wear the hats of both writer and director in the world of network pilots. I felt so excited to try to shift the paradigm and also tell a story that felt important in terms of the broken-ness of our world while still being funny. *Woman Up* was a comedy with seven female leads, all of which were inter-generational and very diverse. It was sort of the first time that was going to be on network television. I am so deeply proud of the show we made. Getting the news that the pilot wasn't picked up was just devastating. So much about being a filmmaker and an artist is contending with the deepest heartbreak, much more so than celebrating the victories. But that heartbreak on *Woman Up* was hard. It's one thing when you look at a project you did and it's clear why it isn't right, and all the things you could have done better. But *Woman Up* was something that I, and a lot of other people, just loved so much. In that situation, it's really confusing as an artist to think, "What lesson am I supposed to be taking from this?"

But I don't think of it as a setback in terms of my career. In fact, because the opportunity to make *Woman Up* was so big and the product is something I am really proud of, it has only helped open other doors for me. The other thing I take away from that experience is that it was going to be really hard for me to simultaneously do both *Woman Up* as a series and direct *The Craft*. But I was willing to take on the challenge. I guess the thing that I always try to come back to when dealing with those heartbreaks is that the universe has a plan and that it happened for a reason in the way that it did. I just focus on the gift that it was and then try and move on to the next thing, or to take a break. I think the thing about being an artist is that there's such a primal need to create, and out of heartbreak comes some of the best art. So it sort of fuels the fire in a way that can give you an ass-kicking, but it will sometimes kick your ass in a good way.

JP: Talk about the changes you have seen over the last few years for women working in film and TV.

ZLJ: It's a very exciting time for women in film and TV because there are a lot more opportunities. I'm grateful that there's been a welcome sort of paradigm shift. That said, I still think we have a really long way to go. Women are still challenged, questioned and con-descended to in a way that is deeply part of the patriarchal consciousness that people are unaware of. Even though a lot of women are being given opportunities, I still think there can be a certain amount of cynicism about those opportunities from the people around them. It's this idea that women are getting the opportunity because it's trendy, but are they actually talented or know what they're doing? It's that kind of questioning that has been happening for centuries when it comes to women's capabilities as leaders. That is the deeper and more stubborn shift to address.

I have very supportive people around me, which is awesome. But as a first-time female director, part of the reason why I made *Band-Aid* with an all-female crew was because I had witnessed that kind of questioning and condescension around female directors much more than I had witnessed it around male directors. I wanted to set myself up for success by being supported in the deepest way by the people around me. That's not to say that there aren't many men who are deeply supportive of women on sets. But there always tends to be one or two people who will say something undermining or create a double standard that they're not even aware of. I actually don't think any of it is malicious. I think it's just such a deep part of the way that we all have been raised in a patriarchal society.

JP: What role does Judaism now play in your life?

ZLJ: Judaism has played a big role in the content of my work. In *Breaking Upwards,* the big climactic scene takes place at a Passover Seder. In *Lola Versus,* we were the first film to ever shoot in Russ and Daughters, which is a true badge of honor as a Jew. And in *Band Aid,* the characters are dealing with being the children of Holocaust survivors. It's such a part of who I am that it comes up a lot in the characters I write. Judaism isn't even something that I consciously or overtly put into my writing. It's just part of the fabric of who the characters are.

I was also raised to be aware of the omission of Judaism in so much of popular culture. In my experience growing up, we wouldn't get Rosh Hashanah or Yom Kippur off from school. The teachers were so unaware of how sacred those holidays were that they would schedule exams on days when I would have to be absent. I've encountered a number of times where someone would say that the Jews run Hollywood or that someone "Jewed" them out of money. Even growing up in Brooklyn, I would see swastikas and anti–Semitic graffiti. Because of the way I was raised, I have always been a person who would use my voice to try to change that. In my career, I've battled a lot for trying to make it okay that Judaism is present.

As an actor, I have always tried to push for some parity on the holiday episodes because it's like, why can't there be an acknowledgment of anything but Christmas? I will often see on a Christmas episode that there's no room for even a menorah on set. There's also never been much space to take Jewish holidays off. I never felt that I could even ask for it because I didn't want to miss a day of shooting or put the production out. But no one would ever think of working on Christmas. That's unimaginable. In that way, there is a sense of invisibility for Judaism, which is unfortunate. I think there's a sort of latent anti–Semitism that's not aggressive, but it comes out as not really honoring those who are Jewish.

That's something that my mom really influenced in me because she's always felt that too. It ultimately boils down to representation, which a lot of people are talking about now. It's nice to see yourself onscreen. That's something that we all should be fighting for—all of the people that have not been represented for so long. In terms of my personal journey as an artist, having the spiritual outlet of Judaism is really an aid when you're dealing with such deep heartbreak all the time. Returning to rituals that are nostalgic and nourishing can be really helpful.

JP: After you direct *The Craft,* will you still be interested in directing television?

ZLJ: I am really interested in directing TV. Directing a pilot is like the Holy Grail in TV. So the fact that I was given that opportunity without ever having directed an episode of episodic television was really amazing. Doing a pilot is such a fun way to direct TV because you really get to create a world. You're not just getting plugged into something that already exists, like on a long-standing show. That's fun too, but it's a really different set of muscles. I got offered an episode to direct this fall but I couldn't take it because I will be shooting *The Craft.* I'm especially interested in the cable streaming space because there's so much incredible content right now and so many people that I'm dying to work with.

Jaffar Mahmood

An avid student of human nature, Jaffar Mahmood has told me that airports make the best classrooms. He loves people-watching: the way people behave when they think no one is watching, how a few gestures convey so much information to the careful observer. You can learn a lot from just sitting quietly in a terminal. In fact, it is a vital weapon in Jaffar's directing arsenal.

When I sat down at the long wooden dining room table in his Highland Park home, I felt as if I was being watched. Sure enough, when I turned around, his two cats were staring me down, analyzing my behavior and figuring me out. Perhaps Jaffar taught them. After all, in an earlier life, he was a professor.

. . . .

JAFFAR MAHMOOD: I was born and raised in New Jersey in a small town called Tom's River. Back then, it was very white, very much like *The Sopranos*. It was all Italians and Jewish people. And then there was my family and me. I have a white mom from New Hampshire, and my father is from Pakistan. All my friends were white. So I just ignored the fact that I was half–Pakistani for a really long time, pretty much all through high school. I didn't even see myself as "ethnic." I just identified as a white guy with a weird name. That is how I needed to view myself for survival, because high school and middle school are tough when you're different. I went to a public high school of 2000 kids and there were maybe ten minorities.

JACOB PINGER: It's amazing that you got through high school living in a stereotypically white area in New Jersey, and you never had a sense of the world as a racist place.

JM: Well, that's not entirely true. I can give you a really early example. It's fifth grade and Mustafa, a fully Pakistani kid who is my best friend to this day, is in the same class with me. It's the first day of the school year and the teacher is reading the attendance sheet. Again, it's Soprano-land, all Italians and Jews. The teacher is reading the attendance sheet, and she's like "Tony, Sue, Jacob," whatever it is. And then she gets to Mustafa's name, and she's like, "Okay, I can't pronounce that." She said those exact words. Then she keeps on going, and gets to my name, and it's like, "Yeah, I can't pronounce that." She gets to the end and says, "So did I call everybody?" And Mustafa, who goes by Moose, looks at me and we're like, "Ummm, you never called on us." And she goes, "Oh right, the really complicated names." I'm not making this up. And so she says, "For the rest of the year, you're gonna be 'Hey,' and you're gonna be 'You.'" That's a fact. I'm 11 years old, and I'm like, "*Okay…*" She's my teacher. She's like a parent figure, right? I never even told my parents this.

Fast-forward to a week later and we have our first pop quiz. Up at the top where it says "Name," I wrote my name and handed it in. And she's like, "No, no, no, sweetie. You have

126

to write 'You.' Or otherwise I won't know who that is."

JP: That was straight up racist.

JM: Yep.

JP: How did you end up pursuing a career in the entertainment industry?

JM: My dad's a doctor. He came to the United States from Pakistan in the late '60s. He did his internship and residency in the States. And that's where he met my mom, in a New York hospital. So my dad was a doctor and his dad was a doctor. I should have been a doctor too. That pressure was definitely there.

One day when I was eight, my dad sat me down and said, "Jaffar, it's so important to do what you love in life. I'd rather you get by paycheck to paycheck doing something you love as opposed to making a shit ton of money doing something you hate." For an ethnic dad to tell his only son this was a big deal. The stereotypical ethnic dad will say, "You're going to be a doctor, a lawyer or an engineer. Pick one!"

Jaffar Mahmood worked as a film professor while never giving up on achieving his dream of becoming a network television director (Jaffar Mahmood).

But my dad told me that you have to really love what you're doing. Of course, there was a code in there of, "I hope what you really love doing is being a doctor."

I was always a good student with good grades in science. So I thought I would be a doctor. I got into Tufts University for undergrad and did pre-med for about a week. I quickly learned that it wasn't for me. I was also taking a class in econ and kind of enjoyed that. I decided that if I were an econ major, it would give me options. It was the hardest phone call I had to make, calling my dad and telling him I wasn't going to be a doctor. But he said, "Jaffar it's your life. Just know I could have handed you my practice. It could have been very easy for you. You decided to go a harder route and I have to respect what you want to do as long as you're passionate about it."

So I went down the econ path, and was doing investment-banking internships in Manhattan for a couple of summers while I was in college. But I had no passion for economics. Everything changed when I spent my junior year in London. I took a lot of fun classes there and one of them was an art history class that dealt with film. As a kid, I had this weird obsession for film and TV. I was that geek who just consumed everything. I was the human IMDb. I would remember who directed what, and who acted in what, but only on current stuff, never anything from before I was born. I loved film and TV, but as a kid from Jersey I had zero connections to Hollywood so it was never a conceivable career path.

So I was in London taking my very first film class, and I had to write a midterm paper on Hitchcock's *The Birds*. I was 21 years old, and I had never seen a movie that was made before I was born. When I watched *The Birds*, I was like "What the fuck is this?" My brain began to explode in the best possible way. Suddenly I didn't care if I got lower grades on my other papers. I just wanted to read about Hitchcock. So I went to the library in London, checked out 12 books, and I wrote this awesome paper on the Oedipus complex in *The Birds*. It was the first time I decided to put my personal self-interests ahead of a grade. My father's whole talk was always, "I will pay for your college, but your job in return is A's. No B's." That was my job. Now for the first time, I said, "Screw the grade, I want to do this for me." That's when a light bulb went off. I knew that I had to go back to the U.S. for my senior year and start interviewing for investment banking jobs. But the idea of going back to Boston and interviewing for those jobs actually gave me shivers. That year in London was the first time I was developing myself in relation to the arts, going to museums, and movie festivals. I had become obsessed with Hitchcock. And even though I had no idea how to get to Hollywood, I started thinking about going to film school. Maybe that would give me the connections to somehow have a career in film. So I ran down to the computer lab and typed in the only two film schools I knew, which were NYU and USC.

I applied and got into the Peter Stark Producing Program at USC in 2000 and I had never made a single thing. I thought I was going to be the next Jerry Bruckheimer. At USC, I learned the fundamentals of how to shoot things, and how story structure works. I made a little short film, and all of a sudden I was like, "Oh wait, this is directing?" Before that, it was just theoretical. I didn't actually know what directing was. And once I tried it, all the hairs on the back of my neck were tingling. It was so cool. You're manipulating feelings, pulling the strings on people's hearts and emotions. It's like a little orchestra. I was freaking out. I realized that producing is cool, but it's *not* directing. So two weeks after starting the producing program at USC, I knew that I wanted to direct. I started to take every opportunity I could to direct more. I even won a grant to do a second thesis on top of the thesis I was required to do. With this grant, I made a short called *The Eastern Son*.

When I graduated from USC, I wanted to be an indie filmmaker. I had my short film and I wanted to jump right into my first feature. The short didn't get into the massive film festivals, but it went to a number of decent ones. Unfortunately, no one ever told me that going into the industry with just one short film is futile unless you also have a feature script that is similar to or in the same tone as your short. Any interest you're going to get off that short film is useless unless you can back it up with a feature script. And I didn't have one.

The problem was that I didn't really enjoy writing. I didn't even write the scripts for my short films at USC. I loved directing, and I respected producing. But writing wasn't for me. It didn't come easy. It felt like a book report. But you can't monetize a short film, and this industry is all about making money. So the short film can get you meetings but the very next question is going to be, "What's your next thing?" And your next thing better be a feature that they can sell, because if an agent or manager can't make money off you, then why are they talking to you?

I had about six meetings with managers and producers off my short film, which was pretty good. Every single one of them asked, "What do you got next?" and I was literally like, "You tell me!" They would say, "What are you talking about?" and I would say, "I was hoping that the reason you're meeting with me is that you have a project that you think I'd be good for." And they were all, like, "No. We want you to generate something that you're going to give us." And I would think, "Well, no one told me this in film school!" I didn't know that in the indie film world, you have to write your first film yourself. No one hands it to you. And it was this horrible lesson because I hated writing. I ended up squandering all of those meetings. So that's what I always told my students: Don't even go out with your short film until you've got a polished screenplay. When the short opens the door, and you get a meeting and they ask, "What do you got?" you say, "I already have a feature script written, and it's a feature version of the short," or, "It's in the same tone. Would you like to read it?" You don't want to be like, "Well, I have this idea for a movie…" No. You have to strike immediately. No one gave me this info when I was in school, and so I squandered years.

JP: You graduated from USC in 2002. In 2006, you started shooting your feature film, *Shades of Ray*. What were you doing during that time?

JM: After USC, I got a job working as a research coordinator for a production company that made documentary films even though I had zero interest in docs. It was the perfect gig for two reasons. The first was that I was working in the industry and not as a waiter or at The Gap. Because the minute you start to take your foot out of the industry, things happen. All of a sudden, you get promoted to manager at The Gap, and now you're making good money and advancing in their system. At some point, do you really want to come back into film and start over? I notice that a lot of times when someone leaves the industry, they never return. The second reason it was the perfect gig, and something that was vastly important to me at the time, was that the job was completely stress-free. I was making minimum wage and living paycheck to paycheck, just like my father told me to do. But I was happy doing it. The job allowed me to come home and write. There was a two-year period where I was just writing a bunch of crap scripts before I got to *Shades of Ray*, which took me another year to write. At the end of 2005, I started to raise money to make it, and I started shooting in the fall of 2006.

JP: Did you ever get discouraged during that period?

JM: Hell, yeah, because I wrote three terrible scripts! What really got me discouraged is that because I didn't have the courage to write on my own, I partnered with someone. He was one of my friends from grad school. But his day job was as an assistant to two writer-producers. So he worked long hours and they would need him at different times. We wrote two scripts together, but when we started getting into the second script, he got promoted to creative executive, and his priorities just weren't in writing with me any more. When I would be jazzed to write all weekend, he would say, "Sorry, dude, I can't write this weekend." It wasn't his fault, but I started to resent him because I wasn't in control of my own destiny. And that's a dangerous place to be. The benefit was that I learned from him because he was a very good writer. I wrote with him for about a year, and it was enough that I gained the confidence to write on my own. I didn't need the crutch anymore and I finally went off to write on my own. I was the master of my own fate.

JP: How did you turn writing from a chore into something you could spend that much time doing?

JM: The lesson I learned was to write a story that only you can tell. Something that is unique to you and that no other director can come in and steal. If you sell it to a major studio, they can't hire a different director. So I turned inward and asked myself, "What is really specific and special about me? What is my unique story that no else can tell?" Once I figured that out, writing was not a chore any more.

JP: Describe how you got the film made. Did your USC connections help?

JM: A major benefit of the USC Peter Stark Producing Program was the access it gave me to the program's successful alumni, known as Starkies. There is an unspoken code that when a fellow Starkie reaches out, you have to respond. So of the five Starkie alumni that I reached out to, three read the script and one was actually interested. It was a small company but they had their own equity, and they were making character-driven ethnic films like *Shades of Ray*. My script went up the chain to different people at the company and I got a meeting. I was sitting with the president of production, and he said, "We love this script. It checks every box. We want to make this movie and a million dollars feels like the right budget point." I was freaking out, thinking, "Holy shit, this is happening! I'm gonna make my first feature!" Then the president said, "There's just one thing. We love the writing. Everything should stay the same. Same storyline, same structure, same script. But we're just not comfortable with the fact that the main character is half–Pakistani. Can we make him half–Latino?"

This was 2005. It was post 9/11 but still pre–*Slumdog Millionaire*, which allowed South Asian culture to be a little more embraced by Hollywood. So it was this weird limbo time when pretty much every South Asian in a movie was a terrorist, a cab driver, or a 7 Eleven owner. Even so, it was hard for me to get mad, because I was also a producer. I understood the economics of things, and he had a valid point. He said, "Listen, we have a really good relationship with George Lopez. We know if we get him the script, he'll play the dad. And Latinos are a proven demo. They go out and see movies. Whereas South Asians don't." Of course you could argue they don't because no one is making movies for them in America. They only go to Bollywood movies because that's all that comes to them here. The businessman in me respected his decision. But the artist in me was like, "What the hell do I know about being half–Latino?" It's not that I couldn't direct a half–Latino guy, but I birthed this script. It was super-personal, and to all of a sudden just change the ethnicity? All the nuances would go out the window. I was like, "Can I think about it for a couple of days?"

I called my parents and all the people who are important in my life. Everything in my gut felt wrong. I felt dirty. It was the hardest call I ever made. I had to call the president of production and say, "Respectfully, I really appreciate the offer but I have to decline." And that was it. That was the only nibble. Now it's early 2006. Pre-Kickstarter. And I'm back to square one. This is where I utilized the fact that my father is a doctor from New Jersey and knows a ton of wealthy Pakistani professionals. I flew home and he opened up his Rolodex for me. I went door to door to all of his friends with a pitch of my business plan and a copy of my short film. My angle to all of them was this: Here is a chance for you to help change the cultural landscape and invest in a movie that stars a half–Pakistani guy who is not a terrorist or a cab driver. He's just an everyday guy trying to figure out love and make his parents happy. Here is a chance for you to be socially responsible to your community.

In 2005, there was still a lot of backlash to 9/11. And I got this groundswell of people saying, "Shit, yeah!" I raised just over half a million bucks from 38 individual investors. It was old-fashioned indie filmmaking.

JP: *Shades of Ray* was a huge tentpole in your career.

JM: Absolutely. I wouldn't be where I am today without that movie, even though it was an absolute failure when it came to launching my film career. I made it hoping it would launch me as a film director. It did nothing for that. The sad part is when you make your movie with no ties to distribution; you have to find a distributor later. And timing is everything. When all was said and done, my film came out in the fall of 2008, the start of the economic downturn and also a writers' strike. Everything bad was happening at once, and it was a disaster. When my movie came out, all the indie labels were shuttering. No one was going to buy a tiny movie with no famous people in it. The indie distribution companies were going out of business. Companies that would buy movies like this literally didn't exist any more. That's when my movie happened to come out, so it just sunk. My movie was literally a blip. It was five years of my life from writing it to seeing it on a screen, and I couldn't even get an agent or a manager. Because of the writers' strike, every agency said, "We don't know how we are going to get gigs for our current clients. How can we take on new clients?" And the problem is that when you don't get an agent right on the heels of your movie coming out, it's like a house that doesn't sell on the market. People ask, "What's wrong with that house?" No one wants to buy that house. So no one wanted to rep me. It was a disaster. I learned so much making the film, but I had nothing to show for it in terms of advancing my career.

JP: What were your next few years like?

JM: I had quit the research job to shoot *Shades of Ray*. Once the movie came out, I started to segue into teaching film school part-time. The feature helped me do that. Even if it wasn't a huge success, the fact that I had made a feature that played at some respectable festivals allowed me to get a teaching job. And teaching film school pays pretty good money. I have a Masters from USC, and no one cares. That's never gotten me a job in the business. But it gives me the benefit of being able to teach. So I taught for years. I love the idea of imparting wisdom about all the shit I had to go through and the mistakes I had to make. I'd like to impart that to others so they don't make the same mistakes.

JP: When did you stop teaching and became a full-time director?

JM: Teaching was from 2008 to the fall of 2016. So it was over eight years.

JP: How did you not get discouraged during this time?

JM: I did get discouraged. But what was great was that I was teaching filmmaking classes. I wasn't teaching theoretical stuff. I was in the trenches with my students. And it kept me fresh. My directing brain was working even when I wasn't making my own stuff.

JP: So you've never had a job completely outside TV or film?

JM: Nope. I was a teacher, but still teaching film. I never took my foot out of the door. I'm a huge believer in that. I would say that to anybody going forward. Don't work outside of the industry. That's really important if you want to become a director. It's different if you're an actor. There was a point a few years ago when things were really tight for me and I almost became an Uber driver. I was literally at the point where I put the application in, I met the guy, and I was a day away from being an Uber driver. It was my father who told me not to do it. Perception is everything in this town, and that's the truth. If I were to somehow pick up a showrunner in my Uber, is he really going to hire me to direct one of his shows? It's the sad reality. That's why teaching was the best thing for me. I felt like it was an honorable thing. That mattered more once I was getting my face out there as a director and really networking with people. I was trying to pitch myself as a feature director trying to segue into TV. That's what I would say when I was shadowing. I wouldn't say that I wanted to be a director, but that I *am* a director. I'm a feature director trying to transition into this new world. It was all about selling myself. It's very important to introduce yourself as a director because people make judgments right away.

JP: What was your first step back into the TV directing world?

JM: During the teaching years, I was able to get into the network directing programs. So even though my feature sunk like a stone, it was the perfect sample for a single-camera half-hour comedy director.

JP: How so?

JM: Studios don't want a single-camera half-hour show to be super-cinematic. They want to tell a great story with great performances, and move it along. So without me knowing it, *Shades of Ray* was this awesome sample for something I didn't even know I wanted to be yet: a single-camera half-hour comedy director.

The seed was planted by Jake Kasdan, who executive produced my feature. Jake saw me directing and he was like, "Jaffar, you should think about directing for TV. You shoot quickly, you don't over-think things, and you're really comfortable talking with actors. Those are the most important qualities of being a successful TV director. Also, you're just likable." That's another important thing.

But what I quickly learned is there's a massive difference between trying to break into being a film director and trying to be a TV director. In the case of film directing, it's the wild west. An accountant from Idaho can write a screenplay that happens to be awesome, and somehow if he knows a family friend who is a Hollywood producer and that producer options the script, the accountant can direct it. And all of a sudden, he can be nominated for an Academy Award. Crazy shit like that can happen. TV directing is the exact opposite. You find out that it's a white-walled country club and you have to be invited in. There's no back door. You literally have to wait in line to be asked in. So I was like, "How do I get into that line?"

I started to do my research. The DGA had released a really comprehensive study about hiring practices for TV directors. At that point, 86 percent of everything on TV was directed by a white male. That's when the DGA said, "We need to change this." They basically shamed everyone, and the studios started the diversity directing programs. I got into the ABC program because I submitted *Shades of Ray*. It was a two-year program, and the way it worked was that you shadowed established directors. One of the early questions when I got into the program was, "So do you want to be a one-hour or a half-hour director?" You have to make a choice early on. One piece of advice I give to up-and-coming television directors is to pick one or the other. Don't say you want to do both because then they don't think you're passionate about either. In my opinion, you want to be an absolute king of one thing for a while. Once you have made a name for yourself, then you can branch out and do whatever the hell you want. But in the beginning, you should specialize. Everyone wants to put you in a box, so go ahead and put yourself in the best box that represents what you can do.

What led to my decision to do half-hour comedy was shadowing on my first show in 2010. It was *Grey's Anatomy*. Watching a director have to direct a surgery scene, I was like, "Ewww!" No offense to anyone who likes to direct surgery scenes, but for me it was really clinical and boring. Then I shadowed through post, and I talked to the editor who had been there for a couple of years. I told her my whole story and said that I was still kind of hedging between one-hour and half-hour. She very simply asked me, "How important is quality of life to you?" I said, "Very." And she said, "Then be a half-hour director." I asked her, "Why do you say that?" and she said, "I can tell you from my perspective being a one-hour editor. Every director that comes into my suite and sits on that sofa that you're sitting on right now is exhausted and dead. And not happy!" I asked, "Why?"

She said, "Seventy-five percent of one-hour dramas don't shoot in L.A. They are in Vancouver, or Toronto, or Atlanta or Albuquerque. They are all over the place. The directors are very rarely home. They are constantly traveling. They're never with their families, and they are just beat up. It's exhausting. In half-hour comedy, it's the exact reverse. Ninety-five percent of comedies shoot in L.A. You're always home. If you don't know what to do, go to half-hour." I thought, "That's pretty good advice."

So I specifically asked the ABC program if I could please shadow on a half-hour comedy. I ended up getting to shadow on *Happy Endings*. I walked onto that set and they were laughing and having fun. I thought, "This is my vibe."

JP: How many directing programs did you do between 2010 and 2015?

JM: I did three programs: ABC, NBC and then the WB program. Meanwhile, that whole time I was teaching. I took time off to shadow if I could find a sub. I had so many "almost" opportunities during those years. Probably a sane person might have finally said, "Screw this," and walked away. But I looked at it like this: At the end of each calendar year when I was teaching, I would always ask myself, "Did I have some kind of forward progression? Did something happen this year that didn't happen last year that got me this much closer to actually directing for TV?" And as long as there was at least a baby step forward, I could justify giving it one more year of staying as a teacher, and just making it work.

But it was tough. In 2012, I lost a number of opportunities to possibly direct on NBC's *Community* where I had been shadowing. There were so many ups and downs in those directing programs, and I got close but things were not clicking for me. My movie was finished in 2008, and in those four years, nothing had come of anything. For the first time ever, I was like, "You know what? I'm a good teacher. I enjoy teaching. Let me just see what the universe does." And I applied for my very first full-time teaching job. It was at Rutgers University in New Jersey. The job was to start and run a new film program. Tenure track, an amazing salary. It was kind of a cool gig, close to my family in Jersey. I applied for the job and it came down to me and one other guy. It was really close. And I'll tell you what, if they had offered me the job, I would have gone and I would not be here right now. But they went with the other guy. It was just one of those things where fate decided for me. That was the closest I ever came to finally ejecting.

JP: You've suffered a lot of slings and arrows. How does one deal with rejection in this business?

JM: You can't take rejection personally. Everyone is going to protect his own ass, right? It's not that they don't like me. It's just that they don't like the idea of someone new, because if I fuck up, it's on them. So I just never looked at it like I'm not good enough. I just needed to find the right show at the right time with the right producer. I just had to keep chipping away. I just had to keep meeting new people, keep networking and get into the next program. That's how I looked at it to stay sane.

JP: Tell me about finally getting that first job.

JM: It takes a perfect storm for your first gig on a network series. It can't be the first season of a show. They will never under any circumstances let a first-time director do any episode of the first season of a show. Even if you're the son of the creative of the show, you're not getting it. When you look at the résumés of anybody directing during the first season, you will see that they already have a large number of episodes under their belts, before they are even going to be considered for the first season. The other thing you're never going to get as a new director is an episode on the last season of a show. The final season, they are going to give it to all the veterans, all the people who have already directed for the show, and it's goodbye. They're not going to give it to some brand new random person. So you have to find a show that's in the middle of its run. And then you also have to find a show that is not a mid-season replacement where they are only doing 13 episodes. That's even harder, even if it's their second season but it's just 13 episodes, you're not getting any. So the first season, the last season and a mid-season replacement, you're never getting it. There are just so many caveats. Trust me, I've learned.

My perfect storm finally came in early 2015 at NBC. I had been bouncing around the network for three years. All the NBC execs knew me from my shadowing and just going around to meet everybody. They all hoped good things for me. When *About a Boy* got a second season with the help of my mentor, Todd Holland, I was offered an episode.

By the way, and this is important, when you make a connection with somebody in a mentor-mentee relationship, you have to stay in touch with them, and don't just squander that relationship. But also don't bombard them with a million things. I was very smart about how I stayed in touch with people. With directors, the smartest thing to do is any time I watched an episode they directed, I would be like, "Oh my God, I saw your episode. It was awesome. I loved that moment, I loved this moment." Make it about them. And then maybe put in one little update at the end about what you're doing.

So I did my first gig in January of 2015, and I crushed it. But then, before my episode aired, the show got cancelled. Even though they shot 20 episodes, NBC pulled the series after maybe episode 16. My very first episode of TV never saw the light of day on NBC. The problem is that on your very first episode, your worth as an up-and-coming director depends on this question: Did the show ask you back? That's the number one question that any producer who will hire you for your second episode is going to ask. That's the proof in the pudding. If the show invited you back, then you're good. But when the show gets cancelled, they can't ask you back. So no one knows for sure. It gets tricky. At the same time, you also have to move quickly because if there's too long of a gap between your very first and second episodes, it's like, "How come you didn't get hired again earlier?" If you give anybody any reason not to hire you, they are not going to hire you.

So this is where going through all the directing programs became so helpful to me. In the spring of 2015, the NBC sitcom slate basically went belly up. They scrapped all their older single-camera comedies. Everything coming was a new show. *About a Boy* was gone, *The Office* and *Parks and Recreation* were gone. It was going to be all first season shows in the coming season. So I was screwed there, because they were not going to take a chance hiring me on a first season show when I only had one episode under my belt. Again, it's all about timing, right? So NBC became a dead end to me at that time.

Thank God I went through the Warner Brothers program as well. The head of that program was a guy named Chris Mack. We just bonded. He saw my episode of *About a Boy* and he loved it. Then he went to bat for me and called the producer over at the Warner Brothers show *The Middle*, which had a full seventh season order. That phone call got me a meeting with the line producer over at *The Middle* who is basically in charge of finding possible directors for the showrunners. I take this meeting with Werner Walian, an amazing guy. By now it's May of 2015 and the first director program I did was back in 2010. In that time, I had shadowed on countless shows and met all over the place for countless general meetings.

JP: How many meetings did you take between finishing your feature in 2008 to this point when you met with Werner Walian for *The Middle* in 2015?

JM: I would say in the neighborhood of 40 meetings over about seven years. It was a lot. But this was such a life-changing meeting. So Werner was like, "I'm an apples-to-apples guy. You did a single-cam comedy. We are a single-cam comedy. And I base a lot on personality. Something just tells me you're going to be a good fit for this show." And he was like, "You know what Jaffar? I'm gonna take a chance on you. You got the job." Recommendations are everything. He booked me for the end of January 2016, which meant that I had an entire calendar year between my first and second gig. So guess what? I continued teaching almost full-time. What else was I going to do? I wrapped my episode of *The Middle* in February of 2016. That was my second directing job. Then the huge thing that changed my career was that in March 2016, *The Middle* got an early renewal for an eighth season. So luck finally happened where I got into a show that had a future. It wasn't the last season, and it wasn't the first season. It was in the middle of a successful run. After they got renewed, I got a text from my agent saying they wanted me back and were offering me two episodes during the eighth season. I just prayed that it would continue.

JP: What have you found to be the biggest difference between directing TV and features?

JM: In the feature world, the director is king, whereas in TV the writer is king. You have to know your place as a TV director. It's technically your set, but you have to know that if the showrunner comes in and says you need to shoot twice as fast, then you have to figure out a way to do it. It's just that simple. That's the biggest thing, knowing the politics of how to navigate, because there's tons of politics in TV directing.

Another difference is that when you direct actors on a TV show, like Minnie Driver on *About a Boy*, she already knows her character backwards and forwards. You're not going to come in and tell her motivational stuff about her character. You're just there to give her direction within the moment. For instance, "In this moment, I feel like you could punish him a little more." Or, "In that moment, I feel like you let them off the hook a little bit." You can just talk moments with her. You can't get into backstory or motivation. As a TV director, it's not your place to talk to the leads in that way. The actors knows their character better than you are ever going to know them. All you can do is nudge them.

JP: What roles in the current environment do race, age, gender, etc., have in getting work as a director?

JM: The sad reality is that I know it cuts both ways. Part of what's happening in terms of why I'm getting some momentum is that there is an element of, "Last season we hired all white guys, and one white woman." I think there is a conversation that happens behind the scenes within the networks and studios where they say, "It's great that we hired a woman, but we can't just hire white women. Let's get an ethnic woman if we can, or an ethnic guy." That's immediately creating an opportunity for me. And it just so happens that I'm good, and my name is Jaffar Mahmood. That's why I think I'm getting more gigs than I would have maybe three years ago. Now they might be getting forced by the network and studio to have more ethnic people due to public perception. It's a huge advantage for me. But on the flip side, when I walk onto a set that is predominantly white actors, and predominantly white crew, and I'm coming in with my hard-as-fuck name, which is always a thing, I will still have crew members on day five pronouncing my name wrong. It's not that hard. We've already gone over this. It's Jaffar. During my struggling times, maybe back around 2010, I very seriously considered legally changing my name. I almost went to "J. Mood." I was *that close* because it was driving me insane and I was thinking that my name was possibly holding me back.

Sometimes when I walk onto an all-white set, I feel like I'm probably being privately judged and looked at as different. So I feel like I have to be that much more prepared. I have to be that much more personable, that much more affable, and that much more on top of it. I need to know the script inside and out. There's no winging anything.

JP: When you work, do you feel like you are representing all of your ethnic group?

JM: I don't think that way. But I know that it does happen. I hear it from my agent. Say a show brings in a diverse person and that diverse person screws it up. The show is probably hesitant to bring *another* diverse person in. They'll just say, "Well, we tried. And look what happened." That exists.

JP: Everyone thinks the TV industry is so liberal. What may surprise them is that the industry has this current of reactionary conservatism. Does that surprise you at all?

JM: No. At the end of the day, Hollywood is very corporate. And its corporate backbone is going to be conservative. Because of my business background, I came in with eyes pretty open. You just look around and you see that almost every producer and writer is white, and they're mostly male.

JP: What do you tell an 18-year-old kid living in Jersey who is thinking about getting into the industry?

JM: Only attempt it if it's genuinely something you *love*. You can't be casual about it. Don't try to work in film and TV just because you kind of like it. It's way too hard and competitive to attempt if it's not part of your DNA. There shouldn't even be a question for you. Once I had the idea of going to film school, there was just nothing that was going to stop me. Then once you decide to have a career in film or TV, you need to specialize. You need to know what it is that you want to do. The sooner you can decide that, the better. You can PA on set. It's a great way to explore and see what everyone does. But the sooner you have a specific idea of what you want to do, the sooner you can start to build a career path.

Whatever the case, make sure that you don't blow your shots. Every shot is critical. There's no half-assing anything. Every gig is full focus, full attention, always killing it. And I'm not taking my foot off the gas at any point in time.

Anya Adams

The walls of Anya Adams' house are literally filled with artwork—the spoils of a lifetime spent around her artist father. It is like walking into a homey art gallery. Visiting Anya involves a lot of playing with her rambunctious little dog Jack. As we sit down to begin the interview, Jack has nestled up next to me for a good long cuddle.

Full disclosure: I have known Anya my entire life. She is my cousin, so I can state with full authority that her powers of group motivation are off the charts. Her smile is embracing and her energy is like an ocean swell that carries you along. But don't think for a moment that her good vibes aren't backed up by passion and intensity. She can call upon that power as needed to get a listing ship sailing straight again.

· · · · · · · · · · · · · · · · · · · ·

ANYA ADAMS: I was born in Vancouver, Canada, to Jim Adams and Betty Kleiman, who later changed her name to Chrystal. My dad still lives there, but my mother has passed. I went to Waldorf School until grade six. We later moved to Victoria where I went to a private high school called Glenlyon Norfolk.

My parents got divorced when I was five. It wasn't combative, but they didn't have a great relationship. They had different ideas about how you should be in the world. My mom was more of an activist. She cared about the folks who were forgotten and wanted to make social change. She was a pediatrician. My father is an artist.

When my parents divorced, my brother and I stayed with her. We would visit my dad once a week. Incidentally, my mom did not have a television. She believed in reading. So visiting my dad was the only time I got to watch TV. *The Wonderful World of Disney*, *The Beach Combers* and *M*A*S*H*. That's what we got to watch. I loved *I Dream of Jeannie*. But I wasn't really aware of a lot of television programs. I was more aware of movies. My dad would take us to the movies. I

Beginning as a trainee in the DGA Training Program, Anya Adams spent years earning her stripes working longer days than anyone else on set (Jacob Pinger).

137

loved going to movies. *Xanadu* was my first favorite movie. My mom eventually got a TV when I was about 16. It got one channel, which was the Canadian Broadcasting Channel, so it was news and PBS-type stuff.

JACOB PINGER: What arts were part of your life growing up?

AA: I did a lot of theater and reading. I loved to read. I also liked to be in plays, and I did ballet for a couple of years. I stopped ballet because I was the tallest ballerina, and so I always had to play the boy. When we were little, my mom tried to inspire art in me and my brother. One of the ways she did that was, she had us write stories. We would make them up and she would write them down.

JP: What was it like growing up as a mixed-race person in Vancouver?

AA: It wasn't great. When you grow up and you don't look like either of your parents, it's not the best. It was difficult in school because my brother and I were always the only mixed race kids. If somebody else in the class was black or another race, they were usually 100 percent that race.

JP: Was the school predominantly white?

AA: Every school I went to was predominantly white.

JP: Was that something you were aware of as a young person?

AA: I was very aware of it. I have an Afro so even though I'm light-skinned, I was very aware that I looked different than all my friends. Most often it was a struggle with my hair. Like, how do I try to make myself look more like everybody else? I think as a young girl, you want to fall in with a crowd and feel like you're one of those people. That never happened to me. I had a group of four friends and we were kind of like the outcasts. The other three girls were white, but they felt like outcasts for different reasons. It taught me how to code switch really well. My brother and I were often looked at to represent the "Black Opinion" just because of how we looked, even though we were so white in our upbringing. It was a weird thing. One of the things I really wanted when I was a child was to get to the United States as quickly as possible so I could live with other people of color and learn about the culture I was missing out on.

JP: Can you define code switching?

AA: It's the ability to traverse different cultures and assimilate or fit in. That's how I see it. It's like, can I go and speak to five white men and feel comfortable and have them feel comfortable with me? And then can I go speak to five black men or, you know, two white women or whatever? Am I able to traverse cultural boundaries in a way where I can kind of fit in?

JP: How do you think the skill of code switching comes into play in a Hollywood career?

AA: Oh my God, I think it's very necessary. Being a television director and going around to different shows, you have to be able to figure out the culture, assimilate and execute what's needed.

JP: So code switching is a skill that comes into play based on the gypsy nature of being a TV director?

AA: I think so. A lot of people use code switching as protection.

JP: How does this come up in terms of getting a job and dealing with a Hollywood power structure that is still predominantly white and male?

AA: I suppose it does. I think there's a course correction going on right now to get more women and people of color into the industry. The industry is so vocal about so many things but they haven't been great with diversity. People are shining a light on that now, and there is this "Holy shit" moment in the industry about needing to change. For me, it's been so much easier than for other female directors who were coming up before me and had to battle against this bullshit of not being judged solely on the merit of their work.

JP: Where did you go to college?

AA: University of Victoria. I studied psychology with a minor in sociology.

JP: Up with People came along and changed your life.

AA: Up With People was an international student program that would do a two-hour professional stage show. You would travel around and perform the show in every community you visited. You stayed with host families and did community service. The idea was to show that young people from around the world could work together and have a positive influence everywhere they went.

JP: What drew you to Up with People?

AA: The energy and the excitement and the idea that we would travel. It was also the performance aspect. I wanted to perform. I got accepted into Up with People, but then I had to raise money to go on the road with them. I basically raised it by asking my family. We traveled through the States. We traveled all through Denmark, Germany, Belgium, Luxembourg and Liechtenstein. In later years, I went to Hong Kong, Australia, Canada. I traveled so many places, and I got a lot of stage experience. I learned that I'm not a great singer and I'm an okay dancer. What I excelled at was speaking. My biggest skill was being able to connect with the crowd and just go out there and have fun as the front man.

JP: Did you ever get a leadership role within Up with People?

AA: Yes. I was a production manager for two years and then ascended to cast manager. I was with them for seven and a half years.

JP: When did you first realize you had leadership skills?

AA: I've always been a leader. And depending on my environment, I'm not afraid to speak my mind or speak the thoughts of other folks.

JP: Does that quality help you as a director?

AA: I think so. As a director, I think you have to be powerful, depending on the situation. With children, you have to be powerful in a loud, "Everybody pay attention to me" way. And in other situations, you have to be powerful in a quiet way. You also have to be very sure about what you want. Learning how to be powerful is something I definitely learned from my mother.

I was still in Up with People when I realized, "I don't think I want to be a psychologist." As Up with People was coming to an end, I was trying to figure out how I could get into the movies. I didn't know much about it, but I was just enamored with the lifestyle. I wasn't going to be an actor, but I thought I could be a casting director. I was searching for stuff on the Internet, trying to figure out how to become a casting director, and I stumbled upon the Directors Guild of America [DGA] training program. I looked at the website and was like, "Oh, I'm doing this." They had this VHS video called "Autographs and Sunglasses" that you could send away for. The video had this guy explaining, "When you're a trainee, you have to carry a bag of quarters so you can call the office from a pay phone when they page you." It was way back when there were no cell phones. It was crazy but I knew I wanted to do it.

I was living in Denver at the time and I applied for both the New York and the L.A. program. It was a really rigorous process because the applications were incredibly detailed. You had to take a two-hour IQ test. In the end, I didn't get into the New York program. But I did get into L.A. I was then about 30. I moved to L.A. and they gave us three weeks of initial training. I had never been on a TV set. Then they put you on a show and you were expected to just learn the job.

JP: What job did you do as a trainee?

AA: It depended on the production you went to. The first show I did was *Malcolm in the Middle*. My job was to run base camp. I had to make sure the actors got breakfast in the morning. I signed them in, made sure they got to hair and makeup, made sure they got to set, made sure they got signed out, made sure they had their lunches, made sure they knew about script changes. All that kind of stuff. I was also responsible for the production report, which is basically a compilation of everything that's happened throughout the day. So if somebody fell down at lunch, I needed to note that on the production report. If we were waiting for an actor to come to set and it held up the shoot, I had to write that in the report. At that point we were shooting film, so how many feet of film did we shoot? What were the in and out times for every crew member? You had to write all that in the report. It was a lot.

JP: What were your impressions of the TV industry, jumping into it like that?

AA: It felt right to be behind the scenes. I was learning how to deal with stress, although initially I wasn't the best at it. As somebody low on the totem pole, you're often asked to carry the mantle of stress for those higher up. I was always tired. The trainee is typically the first one to arrive and the last one to leave set. I was often in at five a.m. and out at ten p.m. On *CSI Miami*, I might even come in at four a.m. because an actor was getting prosthetic makeup. It was really hard. One time I woke up and panicked. It was 5:30 in the morning and I was supposed to be on set in Long Beach at 6:00, which meant that I was going to be very late. I threw on my clothes and ran out of the house. I was driving down the street and I realized that it was Sunday and we weren't shooting. My life was a constant panic because in this industry, if you arrive on time, you're actually considered late.

JP: How long did the program go?

AA: I was a trainee for a year and nine months. I worked consistently my entire time. Some trainees now take two to three years.

JP: What were some of the things that you had to do on a daily basis?

AA: You had to know how all the actors liked their breakfast burritos. You had to know if they wanted you to knock on their trailer door five times or two. You learn that if you are stepping into a makeup trailer, you always have to knock on the door first and then say, "Stepping," because if you step on the stairs before you say anything, you might jolt the makeup artist and mess up the actor's makeup. There were lots of crazy different details to learn.

JP: What was your first official job after the program?

AA: I worked on *CSI Miami*. I was a second-second AD.

JP: What was your goal at that time?

AA: When I joined the trainee program, my goal was to become a first AD. My situation was very unique in that I started on *CSI Miami* and I went from second-second AD to second AD to first AD. I was there for seven years. I had supporters who helped me advance. I could express an interest to my bosses and when the second AD moved on, I would jump up. I always tried to be more than just my job title. One time when I was a trainee on *CSI*, we were out shooting and the cameras split up to shoot two different things. So two cameras went one way and the third camera stayed behind. All of a sudden, all the production staff walked away from that third camera. So I just went up to stand by that camera because I knew there always had to be an AD with each camera. I said on the walkie, "Hey, C-camera is getting ready to roll." Somebody came up to me afterwards and was like, "Dude that was so great of you to do that. Thank you for stepping up." It was just paying attention. I've always been that person.

As a trainee, you need to recognize where you should be. And you take care of your director. If you're a trainee and they are doing a big set-up and there's nobody standing by the director, then go stand by the director. You're part of the director's team.

The trainee is such an important position. Think about it. You're standing by the director. You're hearing everything that's being said. You can help your first AD by communicating to them what the director is saying. You know what's coming up because you're hearing it straight from the horse's mouth. This is extremely important. You can help move things forward. I loved being a trainee.

JP: By the time you left *CSI Miami*, you were a first AD, and you continued to work as a first AD for some years. At what point did you decide you wanted to be a director?

AA: It was when I got to work on *The Mindy Project* as a first AD. I was so excited to work on a show that was written and run by a woman of color. I think seeing Mindy Kaling execute her show made me think, "Why can't I do this?" Up until that point, I hadn't seen myself doing anything like that. I never saw myself doing those creative jobs like directing until I saw Mindy Kaling running a show. And then I was like, "Wait a minute. I can do this."

JP: Are you saying you never saw yourself doing those kinds of higher-level jobs meaning that you never saw a woman of color in those positions? How do you mean that?

AA: I had almost never worked with a woman of color director or even a woman of color first AD. I was just navigating the environment thinking about what I could do rather than what I want to do. Seeing Mindy Kaling run her own show was definitely inspirational. It gave me the balls to be able to go up to her and tell her that I wanted to direct. I had heard of other first ADs directing before, and I felt like I could say something to her. She was an inspiration for me, even though she didn't give me an opportunity to direct. But she gave me the wake-up call that I needed.

It's a big deal to say you want it. A lot of people have a hard time articulating that. I thought I was in a good position on *The Mindy Project*. People liked me and I thought that if I said I wanted to direct, maybe I would get the opportunity. When I finally asked her, Mindy said, "Show me some of the stuff you have done." I said, "Great," even though I hadn't done anything yet. That made me realize it wasn't going to be handed to me, I was going to have to find a way to show I was capable and committed.

JP: What is the importance of a young woman of color seeing a successful woman of color in the role of director or producer?

AA: It's important because it can pull back the gauze from your eyes. If you're not seeing it, it takes you longer to come to the conclusion that you can make it. Had I started researching this industry earlier and known all of these black female directors and that it was a possibility for me, maybe I would have just gone right into directing. But I didn't have any of that. When I went into AD'ing, there were only four other people of color in my DGA trainee class. One dropped out. The other three are still AD'ing.

JP: So there's almost this limiting factor that some people may not be aware of?

AA: I think so. I think you put restrictions on yourself. I put restrictions on myself, like, "I can't do that," or "I'm not going to do it because I don't see myself in that place."

After *The Mindy Project*, I wanted to see if I could direct. I was approached to be a first AD on *Black-ish* and I told the producer and the UPM that I was interested in directing, and would they consider it? They said, "Yeah." I was excited to be on a show that was about an African-American family, written by black writers and run by a black showrunner. I was hungry for that. It was exciting to be part of what they were creating in film and television history.

JP: Talk about the political process of getting somebody to give you a chance to be a director.

AA: It depends where you're coming from. If you're coming up through television, you need to get the support of the studio, the network and the showrunner. Everyone has to have faith in you. You build that by being on the show in some capacity and showing your desire to direct. If you're coming up through the ranks, you have to be in a specific position such as DP, AD, editor or script supervisor. I think it's harder if you're in makeup or hair, for instance, although it's happened. But I think you have to be in a position where people look at you as someone who can lead, who is clear and understands shots. And who can deal with actors. And you have to be good at your current job.

On *Black-ish*, I made it clear that I wanted to sit in the edit room and just learn things so that I could be prepared to direct. Then I got the support of the studio. This is the thing I tell other people who want to direct TV. I ask them, "Do you know the people from the studio? Do you go to the table reads and introduce yourself?" You have to go out and get yourself in front of them. One of the most memorable pieces of advice I ever got was from one of my mentors, Sam Hill. He said, "You have to act like there's a party going on and you weren't invited. And just get in there. You can't wait for the party to come to you." When I was on *Black-ish*, I made it a point to know all the producers, the writers, the studio people. I went and found out what execs I needed to talk to at the studio. When we wrapped season two, I made an appointment with Sydnee Rimes, an ABC exec for the show. You have to go out and tell people, but you have to be responsible about it too. You can't be like how I was with Mindy Kaling, where I was like, "I want to direct, so I get to direct, right?" You have to fucking put in the work. I think the smart way to do it if you're coming up is, you have a job and you work that job. You work that job and all the people around you, and do it in a non-annoying, proactive way. There are some people who just don't figure out what the right time is, which is important. It's not always about starting off with, "Let me talk to you about my directing." It's just you connecting with them. It's such a huge part of this industry. Who do you connect with? How comfortable are they with you?

JP: Let's look at how you got to direct your first episode. You were on *Black-ish* as a first AD. Then you made a short film called *Lemonade Mafia*. You expressed to Kenya Barris that you wanted to direct. How did you make that first episode happen?

AA: I sent Kenya the short. I don't even know if he watched it. But he knew that I wanted to direct. Everybody around me knew that I wanted to direct and felt like I could. You have to get people around you to support you moving into another position. And there was support for me to do it. It's about having people champion you. On *Black-ish*, I had people supporting me and offering my name up when opportunities to direct might appear. Kenya just had to say, "Yes. I'll trust you with an episode."

Part of that is just being comfortable talking about it with other people. When you're on set, it's being able to talk to the producers, talk to the writers, talk to the script supervisor, talk to anyone about the fact that you want to direct and what you're doing to achieve it. Talk to people, but not in an annoying way. A good way to do it is to ask people questions. Get to know the DPs and ask what they like or dislike about directors. If you want to learn about shots, ask those questions too. I think it's a big part of getting people on your side. I wasn't able to go to UCLA film school and come out as a director. I had to really win people's hearts and minds over to me. It's a slow process. You can't expect it to happen quickly. You just have to put your head down and go for it. You have to want it to happen and try to make it happen for yourself, but also not be totally devastated when it doesn't happen right away. It takes time.

JP: I imagine that by the time Kenya Barris even considered you, he was surrounded by confidants who were championing you.

AA: Right. I think if Kenya brought up to somebody that he was thinking about maybe giving Anya an opportunity, they would say, "Oh, yeah, I think she'd be great." That's how you want people to feel. So it is a little bit of a campaign. I don't think I was necessarily thinking about it in those terms, but that was the way I felt I needed to do it. I wanted to get everyone to support me so that if I wasn't given the opportunity, they would be disappointed.

JP: How did it feel to finally get an episode of *Black-ish* to direct?

JP: I was on set AD'ing and Kenya called and said, "We want to give you an episode." I actually fell on my knees. I was like, "Oh my God. Thank you." I had been working towards the goal, but I didn't expect it to happen because we were already halfway through the season. I was so scared.

JP: What was it like as a first-time director?

AA: I felt a lot of pressure because I wanted to do right. I was super-nervous, and the biggest nervousness I had was about post because I'd never been through editing. My short was edited by one of the *Black-ish* editors and she just did it so fast. So I didn't have to slog through the post process. I really felt like that was where I was lacking. I did sit in the editing room watching other directors' footage, but it's different if you haven't shot the footage yourself and are not actively creating the story. I was very nervous about getting into the editing room and not having what I needed. On set, I would ask, "Did I get everything? Is this what we want?" It wasn't necessarily about if I was talking to the actors right or anything like that. It was more like, "Am I getting the footage I'm supposed to get?"

JP: How did you know in the end that you got what they needed?

AA: The DP, the script supervisor and the writer, they are always on set. I knew that if I got what the writer wanted, then I was covered. TV lesson: Get what the show wants. If the creator wants this, you fucking give it to him. A great example of that is, I just directed *Glow*. In pre-production, the creators had me watch this one director's cut because they felt like it best represented the show. In that cut, I noticed that the scenes always started with the actors in some way. Somehow the ladies were always in the opening shot. So when I was directing my episode, whether they were dynamic starting shots or not, I always wanted to be on the girls right away and not be finding them.

On a show like *Speechless*, they like to have singles of everyone so they can cut around things. It's such a fast-cut show and they want to be able to cut, cut, cut. So if you do all these connective shots, sometimes they don't use them because they're too long. I've learned that you need to get singles to help speed up the episode even if it's not necessarily what you want for coverage. That's stuff you have to learn as you start working. You don't come in as a film school grad knowing that.

On my first episode, I was very unsure about stuff, but I was lucky because the crew was supportive. I could go to the camera operator and say, "Would this be kind of cool?" He would say, "That would be great. Let's do that." You're collaborating as opposed to coming in and slamming your idea through. And the crew people know what to do because they're shooting every day. As a first AD stepping into the directing role, I was like, "I can do this, no problem." But when you actually step into the role, you realize that it is a completely different platform that you're standing on.

JP: How did you learn to direct?

AA: I'm still learning to direct. One of the things I'm discovering as I watch different television shows is that things either resonate with me or not. I can feel in my gut if something is not working. I try to activate that intuition on set in terms of gauging performances and how to use the camera. The thing to remember about television directing is that you're stepping into a world that's already made, so you're just learning their language and trying to infuse a little bit of yourself into that. Figure out how each show works and then put something of yourself into that—a little something cool that you thought of.

I learned to direct by standing behind many different directors and seeing how they did things. Being an AD is a great way to learn that. There are so many directors, and all of them have different strengths and weaknesses. It would be fantastic if all directors were amazing at everything, but that's not the case. Also, directors' personalities are different. Some people are so detail-oriented and specific and just want to get these very specific things, which might be their Achilles heel. There are others who are so unprepared, they don't even read the script. They come in and are just like, "Oh shit. It would have been great if we had a crane for this, but I didn't think about it."

There are other people creating the scene with you. The camera operator, the actors, the sound people. You have to collaborate with those people. For myself as a director, I'm not as adept at cameras and lenses, so I lean on the DP a lot more in terms of that. I might say, "Hey, I'd like it to feel like this." I don't go to the DP and say, "We need a 15-foot techno crane with a zoom lens." I'm not that person. I think as you move into this job, you have to give yourself a break and just accept that you're still learning things. You learn as much as you need to in order to facilitate what you want.

There's such a myriad of directors with different skill sets. I don't think that whoever's reading this should have to think, "When I become a director, I have to have all these skills on lock, 100 percent." But you have to have a baseline to be able to function. I didn't take acting. But I did take psychology, so I know how to talk to people and get their ideas. As you start directing, you become more confident in your interpretation of things. That's basically what people are hiring you for. How do you interpret the material, and is it in line with their thoughts and feelings? They will hire you if you understand what they are trying to do and your interpretation embellishes but also represents that. I think that's all instinct and experience. It's not anything you can learn in a class.

JP: Our industry is still pretty racist in many ways. When you step on a set, do you ever have a feeling that you're representing more than just Anya Adams? Do you ever feel pressure that part of what you're doing is representing all black women, and that your success or failure reflects on that broader issue?

AA: I absolutely identify as a black woman. However, I don't go into meetings or jobs with that in the forefront of my mind. I go into my job as Anya and do the best I can. Yes, there is racism in this industry for sure. But I try not to think about racism when I'm at work. I just try to come in and do my best as a director.

JP: Have you ever personally experienced racism or sexism on set?

AA: Yes I have. I just don't use that as a default.

JP: I think I understand what you are saying. If you witness negative behavior on set, you have to interpret the reasons behind that behavior in some way. Maybe they said something because they had a bad day. But you don't have to fall into a trap of negativity about it. You can push past it with positivity, regardless of the reason they said that thing.

AA: One hundred percent. So when you asked me if I ever experienced sexism or racism, I have, I just try to avoid being triggered and focus on the work and the positive people around me. Thinking about sexism and racism is just not my go-to. I think that's both good and bad. The bad part is: If I'm not seeing it, I can't address it. The thing about not acknowledging it and just moving forward is that the micro-aggressions you experience start to build up and people who perpetrate them think they can continue to do so. By not acknowledging sexism and racism, it's not like I'm not experiencing it. It's just that I'm trying not to let it hold me back.

JP: It's an interesting place to explore because it's where the societal and the personal interact. There are all these societal issues at play, but then there's the day-to-day way it affects the individual. I've heard about instances where a white male director comes up to a fellow director who is female and/or non-white at a DGA event and says, "I can't work now because of you."

AA: Oh, that's fucking bullshit. That happens to me all the time. All the time. But I don't look at that as racism. A lot of the women and men coming up now that are people of color are really fucking good because they have to be, to break through the thick ice of white men directing. So the fact that some people are complaining about really good directors getting jobs is bullshit. It's just them being used to living in this small select world of mediocrity. But that's not what it is any more. Now the trend is toward really good directors whether they are black, white, green or whatever. It's a ridiculous statement to tell someone you can't get work because of them. It is perpetuated by managers and agents who can no longer get their white, male clients work, and use this paradigm shift as an excuse for their failings. The bottom line is: A lot of white guys are working, so what are they talking about?

JP: As a white guy, I can't imagine what it would be like to have somebody come up to me and imply that they're not working because of my race or gender. That's just incomprehensible.

AA: But that is what's happening. Unfortunately, it is a sad excuse. At the DGA awards, somebody said to me as a joke, "You're taking my jobs." Really? I took your job on that show that did 25 other episodes this year? And that one episode that I got was "your" episode? Are you saying this to the other white guys on that same show? And why are those white guys working and not you? It's fucked up. That happens a lot, though.

JP: How do you respond to that in the moment?

AA: You just laugh and play it off. I'm not going to get into it with them.

JP: Are people doing it as a sort of teasing thing? Or is it combative?

AA: No. It's total joking. You know, like, "Ha, ha, ha. I can't get work because you're taking all my jobs, ha, ha, ha." It's totally passive aggressive behavior. Some of the directors that have done that to me are people that I know. I AD'd for them. I don't know if they're saying it to other up-and-coming white directors.

JP: I've talked to some white, male directors about this. They said that their agents and managers tell them that they can't get them hired on certain things because the network wants to do diversity hires. And some of them see it as the managers and agents just finding an easy way to say, "I didn't try to get you a job this month." Maybe the showrunners are telling the managers, "I can't hire your guy because I've got to bring in a diversity hire." It's a really convenient excuse. And that is racism. How does that get dealt with?

AA: It's not all managers and agents, obviously. But I think it is a comforting idea for a white male director that used to work 15 episodes a season who is now only working seven to tell himself that he is working less not because of skill but because of race. He is still working though; he is just not sharing the number of finite shows with a few others. The pool is growing and as the pool grows it becomes talent that is rewarded, not race.

Steven Tsuchida

Steven Tsuchida is a laser. He's one of those remarkable people who looks at the world, decides what he wants, and just goes about getting it. Point A to point B. It's that simple. Steven fully understands the power of personality and salesmanship. It is no surprise to hear about the number of times he has talked himself into jobs and opportunities.

My conversation with Steven was so absorbing that I hardly noticed the traveling shadows across the wall that indicated a setting Santa Monica sun. We went way over the time I asked him for, and were eventually stopped only by the fact that I had to return Steven to his patient family.

· ·

STEVEN TSUCHIDA: I was born in Honolulu and grew up in a very typical middle-class home. My grandparents came from Japan around 1890. My family has been in Hawaii for over a hundred years, which is quite typical for a lot of Japanese-Americans. My parents were born in Hawaii and I am Japanese-American. I grew up very entrenched in Hawaiian, Japanese and American culture. I spent my first 18 years in Honolulu and didn't see much of the world. To put it bluntly, I just spent 18 years in Hawaii. Therefore, I saw the world on television. I have older brothers and sisters who all left for college and I had a father who was very encouraging about us seeing the world. He would say, "Hawaii will always be here. You can always come back." So I made a point after graduating high school that I would not go to college in Hawaii.

JACOB PINGER: You never left Hawaii until you graduated high school?

ST: I went to other islands. But that's still Hawaii.

JP: What did your parents do?

ST: My father was an accountant for a property title company. My mother worked at the perfume counter in a department store. My father grew up when Pearl Harbor was bombed. He was drafted into the war. That's when the G.I. Bill was created, and after the war, he decided to stay in the continental U.S. to get an education. He went to school in California. During that time, he worked as one of those guys you would see in old movies who worked in a big house wearing a white suit. He was like a houseboy for a family in the Hancock Park neighborhood of Los Angeles. The college was free because of the G.I. Bill. But he got room and board for being this houseboy in Hancock Park.

For people who lived in Hancock Park, it was like in the old movies. You would see some Asian man serving you drinks or something. My dad said it was actually quite a good experience, meaning it wasn't horrible in a racist or demeaning way. That was just his job, to do stuff around the house. He lived in Los Angeles after the war. Unfortunately, he could not find a job as an accountant. Finally, someone said to him, "Kenneth, let's be honest. No one's going to hire a Japanese accountant because there's always going to be an equally qualified white person." My dad said it wasn't an overtly racist statement. But it was just like that. He said it was much more racist if you were black.

JP: Was he an accountant while he was working as a houseboy?

ST: No. During the houseboy time, he was going to school to become an accountant.

JP: But he was a veteran?

ST: Yeah. Luckily, he didn't have to fight in the front lines. He worked in Seattle as a Japanese translator picking up the transmissions.

JP: He was in Hawaii when Pearl Harbor was bombed.

ST: He was a high school senior in Honolulu on December 7, 1941. And literally, in the next two days they were like, "Well, school is over. You guys are graduated be-

Steven Tsuchida parlayed his extensive experience directing commercials into a career as a television director (Jacob Pinger).

cause the draft is coming." He didn't get drafted in the first wave. It took almost a year. So he and these other 17-year-old guys built an airfield by hand. It took ten months. It's still there.

JP: What was your parents' community like then? Were his friends white or of Japanese descent?

ST: They were all Japanese. It was during a time when Hawaii was not a state. My father was raised very Japanese. He spoke Japanese to his siblings and parents. I suppose there was not official segregation in Hawaii, but my father and others who were not white and did not speak perfect English could not go to the same schools as white people. The terminology they used back then was that you could not go to the English standard school if your English was "pidgin" or "broken." For his elementary school, my dad went to a Japanese-run school. And for high school, he went to … I guess it was the school for not-white people.

I grew up on the same land that my father grew up on. My family has lived in the same place for the past 125 years. I went to all the public schools for white people that my parents couldn't go to. After the bombs dropped on Pearl Harbor, my dad said that everyone stopped talking Japanese and became American pretty fast, which is why I did not learn to speak Japanese. Everyone just stopped.

JP: Did your dad decide to go back to Hawaii because he felt he wouldn't be able to get work in California?

ST: Yes. The war had been over for three years. He couldn't get work and then someone just point blank told him he wasn't ever going to be hired because he was Japanese.

JP: What did your grandparents do?

ST: My grandfather on my dad's side came to Hawaii from Japan with his brother. Most people came to Hawaii during that time for field work in the agricultural business, primarily sugar cane. My grandfather had many jobs. Handyman, raising chickens, delivering milk. He cooked food in the house and then delivered it. He was like an ancient Uber Eats, or an old-fashioned version of a roach coach. He was delivering food to construction sites and fields to sell to the workers. Luckily, it was so long ago that my family was able to buy this chunk of land in Hawaii. It's still in my family.

My father was the only one of the kids who went to college. Back then, they were all so poor that the siblings would have to go work in the pineapple fields or go be a tailor and make money for the family. It was such a different time. My father's story is something I always tell with pride because it really instilled a great sense of adventure and determination in me, and a sense of not letting failure be something negative. Rather, failure is a learning lesson or just another step in the path. The things my parents have done, it was tough. I'm lucky that they paved that road for me and then let me start at a different level. I asked my father, "Did you live in a really Japanese house?" He would say, "Oh, yeah. We had a fire in the middle where we cooked the food. And we had a furo outside." The Japanese-style bath is called a "furo." You scrub yourself outside and soak yourself in a big concrete tub. They heated it up with a fire. It sounds like ancient times. When you think about that, it's like, "Well, at least I got running water, and I don't have a fire in the middle of my house." It sounds crazy, right?

I love telling these stories. As an adult, these are the things that give me strength to do things that are difficult, like trying to break into Hollywood. For anyone who wants to try to do anything that requires many "no"s before getting a "yes," I think how you were raised plays a big part. Successful people have different stories of how they made it, but they share the same theme of resilience. I remember reading about Quentin Tarantino, and the idea that behind every overnight success is ten or more years of hard work. It only seems like it happened overnight.

JP: Do you remember anything specific that your father said to you?

ST: Yes. But there is not a direct correlation to my job as a director. It has a correlation to being happy and working hard. Being happy may seem unconnected, but I think you need to find joy in this painful path we all take. My father did two things with me. Number one was, he said, "We're going to send you to college anywhere you want to go, but you should go away from Hawaii." And second he said, "We are only going to give you money for four years. So you better graduate in four years because you're not going to come home." And he always said this: "It doesn't matter what you do. You can be a garbage man. If you're happy at that, then you have succeeded."

During high school, I wanted to pursue the arts but I wasn't sure what that meant. It was clear that I was not going to be an artist like Van Gogh or Warhol. But I wasn't sure what kind of job you could get in the visual arts. Painting, drawing, photography? My mother said, "Are you really sure you want to get a degree having to do with art?" And my dad would say, "You know what? We told him he's only getting money for four years. So whatever." And he kept bringing up this garbage man idea, I don't know why. He said, "You got to be happy in what you do, and you got to make it happen for yourself."

So I was instilled with the idea that I was only going to get money for four years. Actually, in my senior year of college, I was already working full-time, so I stopped taking my parents' money. I only took it for three years. I paid my own way through school in the last year. I went to Long Beach State, which was very economical at the time. When I graduated, it was only $700 a semester. I worked full-time at a Japanese restaurant and went to school. My parents kept saying, "You're not coming back, by the way. And you're not getting money after this year." So I knew that I needed to do it on my own. I learned about defeat and failure. When you succeed, you go, "Wow. So that's how it works. Those five no's turned into a yes." I think it was a really good character-builder for me. So my father's lessons are not pertaining to filmmaking or Hollywood, but they pertain to the hard path that it takes to get through any career.

JP: How did you choose Long Beach State?

ST: I went to Long Beach State because they had a very good program for graphic design and advertising. The career I chose was advertising. After college, I worked as an art director for almost six years in New York City.

JP: You talked about being a high school student and thinking you wanted to go into the arts. What in your young life connected you to the arts?

ST: It's hard to pinpoint the exact thing. My personality has always been one of imagination. I think that's very common for most children. One of the best things about having children now is that they give me a constant reminder of this unbridled imagination that's not hampered by the realities of life, like paying your mortgage. What was great for me was that my parents never held my imagination back. I think if I were to stereotype Asians, it's that they can be raised in a way where they think that success is based on academic merit. That's no joke. That's how Asians think. Like, you should be a doctor, or whatever. My parents didn't think that way, particularly my father. His thinking was, "You have to make your life your own. And if you're going to be poor, so be it. As long as you're happy and you did it on your own." So I had a very vivid imagination. And it was never curtailed. I was really into comic books. I had a huge collection. By the time I graduated high school, it was in the thousands.

JP: What were your favorites?

ST: Daredevil. Avengers. X-Men. I was ordering my comics from a place in Texas, and they would already come pre-packaged. Then I would go to a comics store and read them there so that I didn't have to actually touch my own comic books. I would buy two of each comic knowing that I could maybe sell one in a year. Towards my senior year, I was going to these very small gatherings in Hawaii where people trade and sell and I would sell comics there. I was learning about value and how to make money. I think comics are a fantastic foundation for visual storytelling and have such a natural connection to filmmaking. They are lacking many things, but they have a lot in terms of character building, emotions, editing and color. It's fascinating how they can tell a story with just individual frames. I was really into it.

When I was majoring in advertising in college, I didn't even think about filmmaking until my senior year. I was talking to a friend named Mark who was a real film-head. One day we were talking about *The Godfather* and I told Mark I had never seen it. Mark said, "Wait, what? Are you fucking serious?" But I had never taken any film classes and *The Godfather* just seemed like some old film to me. I wasn't into that stuff. Mark gave me the VHS tapes of *Godfather* and *Godfather 2*. I put them in and just sat there watching four hours of *Godfather*, back to back. That was the first filmic experience for me where I was literally blown away at a deeper level. I was more mature then, about 20, and I had the ability to absorb how much of an artistic achievement it was. It was a breathtaking piece of art. That's when I began to think of film as art. But it seemed to me like movies were being manufactured in this distant, gilded silver dome called Hollywood. It was a place without an entryway. I was at Long Beach State, for God's sake. The farthest you could get.

JP: It wasn't the physical distance to Hollywood, because Long Beach is only 30 miles away. It was something else. It was more of a metaphysical distance, right?

ST: Yes. Remember, this is a time when there were no small video recorders. There were no smartphones or Internet. Everything was shot on 35mm film. The physical barrier to making a film as a young person was huge because of the equipment you needed. Back then, you were essentially shooting film with fire and chemicals. It just seemed really hard. Where would I get lights or a camera like that? It just seemed like a mystical thing.

JP: As a kid in Hawaii, did you ever have a sense that your horizons were limited as a non-white person?

ST: Actually, no. My theory is this: First of all, I grew up in Hawaii, which is predominantly Polynesian and Asian. For the most part, I don't know anyone whose parents were not born in Hawaii. Everyone is third, fourth and fifth generation. In the continental U.S., most Asian people you meet have parents who were born in another country, so they are just first or second generation. Secondly, I lived in a place where I'm the majority. I have a strong sense of being an American. I wasn't raised with these stereotypical Asian expectations of having to become a doctor and focus on grades, or playing the violin and having to translate things for my parents, and blah blah blah. I just grew up as an American. My racial identity as an Asian is not the same as for other Asian people who were born and raised on the mainland and whose parents are from China or Korea. I'm Japanese-American. And the Japanese-Americans have been in America for a long, long time.

I had the confidence of never experiencing racism. Zero. I didn't even have the mentality of being a minority. It's only when I came to the mainland that I realized, "Hold on. Something is different here." But even though I started to understand that the world could categorize you based on how you look, for the first 18 years of my life, nothing bad happened to me from a racial standpoint. I think that strengthened my sense of who I am and what I can do. As the years went by, my outward personality was, some would say, closer to what a typical Asian would be in terms of being a little quieter and hard-working and aiming to please. I had a very clean-cut image when I graduated college and went to New York. I had never been east of Las Vegas or even seen snow, and I got a job in New York as an art director. I worked at a big advertising agency called Deutsch.

JP: Did you have any contact with the film or TV world in college?

ST: In my senior year, people were working these internships. They would intern at an ad agency or a design studio. One day I was reading an issue of *Details* magazine, and there was an article about this up-and-coming young director named Michael Bay and the company he worked for, Propaganda Films. The article talked about things the company was doing, like a pilot called *Twin Peaks*. I thought, "What's a pilot?" At that time, Propaganda was the biggest commercial and music video production company in the world. And I was heavily influenced by commercials. Propaganda Films sounded like a fascinating place. The company was in Hollywood, but I didn't have their phone number. This was before the Internet. I thought, "Well, I should just go there." So I drove up from Long Beach and I remember being really impressed. They had this cool building with a guy washing cars, a valet guy, a café in the lobby and three receptionists. That seemed pretty heavy. Three receptionists! I went in and said, "Who do I talk to about the internship thing?" They were all standing there like, "What? Who are you? Do you have an appointment?" I said, "No. But I would love to talk to someone about interning." They let me talk to the office manager, and I said, "Hey. I would love to just hang out here." He explained what a PA was, and asked, "Do you want to be a PA?" I said, "No. I want to be in a position where I can come here once a week and just hang out and learn about commercials and music videos. I want to be near the powerful people." They said, "That sounds okay, I guess." So I did things like errands, and sometimes I would ask to sit and watch them take a meeting. I would sit 40 feet away just watching them. Sometimes I would go to set.

They asked, "Are you sure you don't want to work?" I said, "No. I have a job in a restaurant." I couldn't waste my time being a PA. I wanted to be able to talk to editors and producers and directors and just find out what this whole production company thing was about. I would go around and ask people what they did. And people were very open to this kid asking all these questions. I worked there for three months in the vault making dubs, which was copying video tapes and FedExing them to ad agencies, record labels and studios. It was really interesting to see all these heavy hitters there. Here was Michael Bay, and here's a guy named David Fincher, and a guy named Spike Jones, and Antoine Fuqua. David Lynch was doing the pilot for *Twin Peaks*. It was really dazzling. The company eventually became Anonymous Content.

When I graduated college, I was still determined to get a job in my degree. Three months after I graduated, I went to New York to become an art director. I was an art director for six years. About a year into my job, my boss came to talk to me. I was the only Asian person, and maybe the only person of color out of the 75 people in the entire agency. There were definitely no other Asians or African-Americans. My boss, the creative director, a really cool guy, sat me down for a one-year review. He said, "Hey, Steven. What do you want to be?" I said, "I think it would be really cool to be in your position. A creative director." He said, "Oh, that's what you want to be? Well, not to sound racist or anything, but people look at you and they don't think that about you. They don't think you're going to be the boss. They look at you and they see a hard-working guy who is falling into this stereotype of doing your job, doing what we ask you to do, and not voicing your opinion. This is advertising, Steven. If you don't agree with us, you should speak up. We may not agree with you. We may get into a fight. It doesn't matter. The point is, you have to practice that. That's how it works in advertising, for your voice to shine. You have to get your voice out there. You've got to change people's perception of you. They're not looking at you in a racist way, as in, 'That guy will never be my boss.' They're just thinking of you as the worker." It wasn't like he was trying to be an asshole. He was just being blunt about it. He said, "This is going to sound like a compliment but it's not. You're too much of a gentleman. It's okay to make enemies."

I thought that was pretty good advice. I think it was a way to get me out of my shell. I had only been in the advertising business for one year. And during that time, certain things would happen, like I would be standing at a corner to cross the street. There were a lot of Korean-owned delis in the area. And two different times, someone came up to me with some melons or a bunch of flowers and asked, "How much are these?" Or I would go to one of our vendors, like a post-production house or a printing place. I was about 22 and clean-cut. I would walk up to reception and they would say, "Are you making a delivery? Dropping off or picking up?" I would say, "I'm not a delivery boy. I have an edit session today." Then they would go, "Oh! Sorry. What was your name?" These were like micro-aggressions of some sort. It wasn't to be mean. It's just their perception, and I understand how people perceive things. People see me walking in, maybe I'm not dressed nice enough so they think I'm the messenger. So I try to flip it, and not think of everyone as evil. I can't change them. I can only change myself. I started thinking that the perception of me was not right. And from then on, I grew my hair out long, had a goatee and started dressing cooler. It changed everything. People started thinking of me as the artsy Asian guy. It was a fascinating lesson in branding, presentation, stereotypes, expectations and either fitting into them, breaking them, or using them. It's something I have thought about from that point even until now. It's just human nature to take visual cues and plop people into little categories.

I began to understand that in the creative fields, there are a lot of people who are just as good as you. The thing that we are all buying into is that we want to work with the person and not the portfolio. There are exceptions, such as those filmmakers like Godard, or Lucas or Coppola, who are on another level. But for the other 10,000 of us, there are lots of people who could do our jobs. At the end of the day, we're buying into the people and not their portfolios, you know? Back then, it was something I was thinking a lot about. I changed my look and people thought I was somehow cooler because I guess I looked cooler. If you look strange, then you must be artistic. I was just trying to break the stereotypes. I'm not saying you have to change your look, but something about you has to stand out. My thing is that it's much easier to change yourself than other people. People don't change. It's you. When you change, you change the world.

Around my fourth year at Deutsch, my boss, Craig Gillespie, told me he was going to quit and become a commercial director. When Craig said he was going to direct commercials, it seemed like a cool trajectory and it made me think, "I'm single now. I'm already making tons of money, but in two years I won't be able to walk away from this job. Now is the time." That's when I decided to quit my job, apply to ArtCenter in L.A. and put together a commercial reel. So I took out an $80,000 loan and moved in with a friend in L.A. who was only charging me $100 a month for rent. I was 28. I graduated from ArtCenter when I was 30.

JP: You must have had a lot of confidence compared to the other ArtCenter students. You had already been out there making a living as an art director.

ST: I did. But then I got knocked back down two years later. The school was a great experience. I went there to make a commercial reel because I knew that commercial directors had graduated from ArtCenter. The process was that you put together your reel of four or five fake commercials and then you looked for a production company to sign you on. Commercial production companies have sales agents in each sector, West, Midwest and East. The sales agents are basically your agents as well as the executive producers in the company. That's the only way it works. You needed to be signed to a company. You couldn't just be this freelance dude floating around. I already knew about the business coming in because I was from an ad agency. I could walk the walk and I had seen so many directors' reels. I fashioned my reel with that in mind. I got a tremendous amount of meetings with all these very large companies. But not a single one said that they would sign me. A year goes by and nothing happens. I began to wonder, "Wow. I thought I was cool. I'm really not that cool." By then I knew I could not keep trying to get signed by a company with this year-old reel. Advertising is all about new. So I was like, "I think I need to make a couple more fake commercials. Ugh." So I spent six more months re-doing my reel and I added two more things. I took my reel back to three or four companies that had shown the most interest, and one of them, Oil Factory, signed me. I did commercials for almost ten years. I wanted to do music videos because of their artistic merit. But that never really took off. However, I started doing commercials very quickly and that did take off. It was during a time when there was a lot more fruit on the commercial tree, meaning a lot of money and fewer directors. Things changed after the dot com bust.

JP: What got you signed? I'm sure you went to school with a lot of people who never made it.

ST: I did. I would say that only about one out ten people make it. In our business, you have to understand selling yourself. That's actually true in any business, could be the oil business, the health business, could be selling crackers to a person who doesn't want crackers. I really understood about selling myself. I think your work gets you in the door. You could write a screenplay. You could do photography. Whatever. But you're going to meet other writers and photographers, and eventually it's the one you just click with. I understood that. I walked into Oil Factory knowing that I needed to sell myself. I wanted to show them that when the company needed to pitch itself, they would know that Steven Tsuchida was going to be great on that conference call with the agency. I knew how things worked.

People ask me what they should do to get there. Look, I'm not going to lie. You need to do good work. But there are a lot of people doing good work. You also need to be a fucking cool guy or cool girl. A movie producer is going to look at you and say, "Can I have a beer with this guy? Can we have a friendly kind of argument vs. a bad argument? Is he inspiring yet flexible?" Everyone is looking for inspiring yet flexible. Now these are just bullet points. It's going to be different for every meeting. I'm just saying that I was very cognizant of the power of personality. There's a common theme for many of the people who do well. There's something about them that makes people like to work with them. That's the thing that I started learning during my time in advertising. It's the power of persuasion, because that's what advertising is. The cult of personality is important. I started to use these terms like "perception" and "branding." It sounds so terrible to dehumanize us in that kind of way, but it's the perception of who we think we are.

I have another story about perception. Back when I started as an art director, people thought I was a delivery guy. Because of that, I grew my hair out. But in film school, I thought I didn't need to have this look anymore, so I cut my hair short again. When I started directing episodic, I still had a clean-cut look. And then something happened to me both at Fox and at Paramount: I would be on set at the craft services table or something, and someone would come up and say, "Hey, are you the accountant?" One of those times, strangely enough, they asked me, "Are you the accountant's brother?" Now it's irritating to think that I had to change my look again, but whatever. It was time to grow my hair out for a second time. People were insanely embarrassed when I told them that I wasn't the accountant, but that I was actually directing the TV show. Even to this day, you're not going to find a lot of Asian-American directors. I also get asked if I am the AC because there are a lot of Japanese ACs out there. That's why my hair is long again.

JP: When you were directing commercials, did you have in mind that one day you were going to break out of commercials and make TV?

ST: Yes. I went to ArtCenter knowing that I wanted to do commercials for a while, but that the long-term goal was narrative, specifically feature films. I didn't give it an exact timeline, though, because I didn't know how long it would take to pay off my student loan. My plan was to use commercials to get into narrative. So about five or six years into my commercial career, when I had finally paid off the student loans and was feeling more secure, my wife and I decided to get married. That's when I thought I needed to make some kind of move, because I was getting stuck in these golden handcuffs. So I made a couple of short films and one of them went to Sundance. They both played hundreds of festivals around the world. I used that as a way to get meetings.

Around that time, the commercial production company I was at, Oil Factory, produced Sarah Silverman's concert movie. A while later, Sarah Silverman got a deal to make a TV show called *The Sarah Silverman Show* on Comedy Central. So before there was any official space for them to work, they asked Oil Factory if they could come and use a room. They were at our offices every day for about a month and we slowly became friends. Finally I said, "I would love a shot to direct an episode of your show." They said they would give me a shot, but I still had to meet with the network.

JP: You just talked your way into getting an episode?

ST: Yes. But it took weeks of hanging out and having coffee. You cannot deny the social aspect. Now, in order to get the next meeting with Comedy Central, I used my body of commercial work, and my little shorts. You can't be nobody. And actually Comedy Central was aggressively against me doing the show. It was a very negative energy. They would say things like, "What makes you think you could do this show? As a commercial director, you spend 12 hours doing five-eighths of a page. You know you have to do seven pages in a day for this show. Have you ever done that before?" I said, "You know I haven't done that before. But I can do it." I know that Comedy Central didn't want me because they eventually called me at the last second, right before prep started. So I knew they were looking for someone else all the way to the end. They finally called on a Thursday and said, "Okay. Are you free on Monday? You're hired." Obviously they had been looking for someone else.

That was my break, and it was wonderful. After directing that episode of *The Sarah Silverman Show*, I got a little derailed from pursuing narrative because it was still the height of my commercial career. I was traveling the world, and it was just too interesting. That's why it took me a while, maybe a year, to get my next narrative project, which was *American Body Shop*. Comedy Central just called and said, "Do you want to do this?"

JP: Was there ever a point where you said, "Okay, I'm walking away from commercials to do narrative"?

ST: Yes. I still spent a couple of years making a lot of commercials. Then there was a point about 12 years into my commercial career where I said, "Oh my God. I'm making something that nobody wants." I was almost 40, and I thought, "If I don't walk away from commercials now and try to seriously pursue TV and film, I will be too old. Nobody wants to give a 45-year-old guy a break. Everyone wants to give the 30-something-year-old guy a break." So I just had to go for it. I applied for this NBC diversity program for new directors, and started taking tons of meetings. The people who gave me my break were the Russo brothers.

JP: You came at this whole thing from such a different perspective because you already had this very desirable career in commercials. You were not coming at it from a desperate place at all.

ST: And that's why I could take two or three months to go shadow different shows.

JP: Was there a point where you had to make a choice between commercials and narrative?

ST: No. The thing is, I never left advertising as an art director because I didn't like it. And I didn't leave commercials because I didn't like it. I just wanted something better. I always tell young people that you should never leave a job because you don't like it. You should leave a job because you have a goal. Also, a lot of people tend to give up. I mean, Quentin Tarantino worked for five years in that video store, for God's sake. If you can't learn from the failures, then how will you make it? It's not about falling down; it's about how you get up. I find that it's very difficult for people to have the patience of years of hard work. Not to throw young people under the bus, but it's hard for them to imagine those five, six, seven or eight years of real struggle. They think two years is a long time. It could take ten years.

JP: What got you from the occasional basic cable thing to doing network shows?

ST: I told my agent that since I am not a very good writer, I was interested in meeting non-writing producer-directors. I wanted to meet the Russo brothers, who were doing *Community*, Jason Weiner with *Modern Family*, and Jake Kasdan with *New Girl*. I was fascinated to meet these kinds of guys; if not to work with them, then just to learn how they became what they are. The first meeting I got was with the Russo brothers and that took three months of constant e-mails. After one month of emails, I said, "I'm embarrassed. They're not even emailing me back. I think [their silence] is the answer." My agent was like, "Not true. Until they actually physically email us back and say no, then it's not a no." We kept emailing week after week. It seemed like we were begging. But after three months, I got the meeting. I had a two-hour meeting with the Russo brothers and we just got along. I made my case and said I would love an opportunity to direct on *Community*, and they said okay. And that was my validation, because our business is based on validation. You need someone to give you a brand name network show. *Community* was the big break for me.

Then because of that, I got the meeting with Jake Kasdan. He gave me a spot on *New Girl*. And by then, Jason Weiner had started a new show called *Crazy Ones* with Robin Williams. After the Kasdan interview, I got the Jason Weiner interview. It's all one big thing of, "Oh, that other guy said yes? Let's bring him in." And my agent was playing the diversity card. He would be like, "You guys need a diversity hire." The Russo brothers were the ones who got me started. But it was a strategic effort on my part to meet those kinds of people. I knew I needed that kind of validation to keep on going.

JP: After doing commercials for so long, how did you learn to direct narrative content?

ST: The three episodes I shadowed on *Chuck* and the two episodes I shadowed on *The Defenders* with Jim Belushi were actually very enlightening. I had very good mentors there. Making commercials, or even making short films, is very different than directing a TV show. It was very interesting to watch people shoot that fast with such a giant crew and to have actors that good. There's a vast difference between the actors in commercials and TV. The shadowing really helped. I would encourage young directors to do that.

JP: How would you describe the job of a TV director?

ST: For me, a director certainly needs to be respectful to what the show is. But in some way, you need to be adding your personality to the show or else you will quickly become disposable from a business standpoint. You certainly need to honor the showrunner's vision. You're not coming in there to reinvent the wheel. But you want to make the wheel spin more dynamically than they thought it could. I find that with as much pushback as I get from established actors, I still continue to push them because I want to imagine that they want to be pushed a little bit. And showrunners want to be pushed because they can always say no. It kind of goes back to the advice that was given to me by my creative director in New York. You need to just speak your mind and try to make what you think is the best. Nobody wants a director who's just a yes-man. Well, maybe some showrunners do want a yes-man, but that's not the show for me. If you're not doing something that's coming from within you, you will not be engaged and will therefore be doing a disservice to the show. I try to do a lot of first-year shows and shows that have a unique point of view, propelled by some kind of interesting gender or political or ethnic idea.

JP: Why do you try to do first-year shows?

ST: Because when you do season seven of *Bones*, they'll say, "You saw season six, right? That's what we're doing." If you're doing episode 704, they'll have you watch 703. Different story, but same style. I actually have these kinds of conversations all the time on shows that have been on TV forever. For instance, you say to an actor, "I understand you are the brooding cop, but when you guys are talking about your child at the piano recital, it's a warm moment, so just smile." And the actor says, "I don't smile. I'm the brooding guy. I've brooded for six years. Don't tell me about my character. I've never smiled." Trust me, I get into those conversations all the time where you're just serving what has been done before. And I find that on the network level, it's kind of like that.

On shows that have been going on for too long, the actors are literally saying things like, "Hey, Steven, if I just stand here and don't move from this spot, it will reduce the set-ups and get us out early, right?" It's still going to be a fun job because you're joking around with the crew, but you're kind of losing the artistry a little bit.

Right now, my efforts are mostly with non-network television that pursues fresh perspectives: Amazon, Netflix … all the streamers as well as cable. When I started, I did a lot comedy. One of my other really big breaks was *Inside Amy Schumer*. I was offered almost the entire first season. It was an amazing experience doing all those sketches. Tiny, three-minute films. It was low-budget, but the freedom was unbelievable and the creativity was astounding. I loved that show and it still remains a personal highlight. After the first season, they said, "Amy loves you." They wanted me to come back and do the entire second season. Amy was about to become a big star. I realized that once that happened, I would just become known as a fantastic sketch comedy guy. But I wanted to do a show like *Mad Men*. Shows with greater dramatic depth and a challenging narrative. I thought, who would hire me to direct *Mad Men* when I was solidifying my career as the awesome sketch guy? So I turned the show down. It was a very, very difficult and painful thing to turn down. They were not so happy. But I was trying to get to this different place and push myself creatively. And sometimes you have to leave an amazing job before they become golden handcuffs. It's tough. But that's what I did.

Bill Purple

I met Bill Purple for coffee and pastries at Aroma Café in the Toluca Lake neighborhood of Los Angeles. His signature white beard and thoughtful insights gave me the impression that I was sitting down with a philosopher. Our conversation covered topics that ranged from finding personal happiness to the role of the individual as an agent of social change. Bill is a deep thinker.

A number of the directors interviewed in this book either shadowed Bill or were mentored by him. To a person, they had nothing but glowing words to say about his openness and generosity. I believe such a spirit comes from a desire to be part of the solution in a world with so many problems.

· · · · · · · · · · · · · · · · · · · ·

BILL PURPLE: I grew up in Alexandria, Virginia. We were fairly poor. My parents divorced pretty early, so it was just me and my mom. I had sort of a wealthy grandfather, so I had this dichotomy of a life. I went to a very expensive all-boys private school, but I couldn't afford soccer shoes. I got to play tennis at the country club because my grandfather was a member, but none of my friends could afford to belong there.

JACOB PINGER: Were you an only child?

BP: I have an older sister. When my parents separated she went to live with my dad.

JP: What did your mom do?

BP: She was the office manager in a law firm. My father was a graphic designer. Very early on, I would draw because my dad was drawing. It was my biggest creative outlet as a kid until I got handed a camera.

JP: What was it like to grow up as a sort of underprivileged kid trying to make his way in a privileged world?

BP: You feel like you don't belong anywhere. I mean, in either place. I became a very competitive tennis player, so I felt like I was part of that world because

Along the way to becoming a widely respected director, Bill Purple had to first overcome the unspoken pigeonholing of assistant directors as "uncreative types" (Jacob Pinger).

I would go there all the time to play tennis. A lot of kids in my high school were very wealthy D.C. kids. But I still didn't fit in; I felt like a guest wherever I was. I was the kid who was friends with everybody. I played sports, and so all the so-called popular guys were friends with me. But I was also in the theater and stage crew, so I was friends with the artist types too. I was in every clique, but inside I was more comfortable being a nerd. I would rather be watching movies and playing Dungeons & Dragons.

I was a latchkey kid. After my parents divorced, my mom had to work two jobs. So literally, I was getting myself up, getting myself to school, getting myself home, doing my homework, making my own dinner and putting myself to bed. Basically, I would see my mom on the weekends. I was alone a lot and it made me very comfortable being alone. To this day, I love being alone. I love going to movies and to dinner by myself. It's a real comfort space for me.

In certain situations, like if I was playing sports, I could be very social. If I was working on a play, I could be very social. But if I was at a party with those same people, I was a wallflower. If I'm engaged in an activity, I have no problem interacting. It's funny. I feel like fate pushed me to be a director, because that's something that demands that you communicate well. And I wasn't the greatest communicator. I could be comfortable in my own little world, or whatever I was doing. I also played insular sports, like tennis, golf and running. Very solitary places. Even in the team sports, I was doing my own thing. In soccer, I was a goalie. It's the loneliest position. So there was a bit of a transition for me to becoming a director and learning to get up in front of 300 people and explain to them what we're doing. Being able to speak in public.

JP: Do you think that the skills you learned going to a private school in a privileged, wealthy world may have helped you deal with network executives and people who can often be from that same kind of wealthy, high-end world?

BP: What I understood is that there are different ways to communicate with different people. I learned to gauge it quickly. What do you want from me? I think I'm fairly good in a room. I think it's from having known such ethnically, socially and economically diverse people growing up. I was able to see how everyone is perceived and how others perceive you, and how they expect you to communicate with them. I think it gave me a little edge growing up. I was aware that there are a lot of different perspectives in this world, and it gave me an understanding that people are coming from a lot of different places. I think it built in some empathy for me. By fate, I have a son with special needs. Thank God that I had this immediate, built-in empathy for that. There's a phrase I love: "Don't be too quick to judge anybody because they're fighting a secret battle you're unaware of." That's true for everybody.

JP: It sounds like your experience as kind of an outsider who had access to the high end of society gave you a real sense of identifying with, and having empathy for outsider folks.

BP: It taught me that as different as people can be from you culturally, personally or from a class distinction, they are also so much more the same then you realize. It made me feel comfortable in whatever situation. Maybe that was a good sort of accidental skill set to have as a director, because I've always been observational. I love to watch people. You can drop me in any situation, with any kind of people, and I'll be cool there.

JP: That's a great quality to have, because you don't get intimidated.

BP: I do get insecure about my work. I think that's *all* artists. But not intimidated. I think part of that is also struggle. I think in life you just persevere through all the problems you have. As you get older, you realize that you just get through things. And all that sort of window dressing gets pulled away. You see they are just as flawed and insecure as you are, perhaps more so.

JP: When did you start finding that bug for theater and drama and storytelling?

BP: Early. I remember a very specific memory from 1980 or 1981. Cable was just coming out and we had this set-top box that had levers you click. The cable guy was at the house and he was setting it up. As soon as he plugged the box in, there were helicopters storming a beach in Vietnam. *Apocalypse Now* was on HBO. My dad was immediately like, "We're watching this." I was only seven. It was way over my head. But while we were watching it, my father was pointing out the cinematography. He pulled back the curtain in my brain for the first time and I started thinking, "Oh, there's people behind a camera, and they're taking pictures! How did they get that shot?" And I thought, "I want to do that. That seems cool." I started making these… Not even movies, they were basically Polaroids in succession. Almost like a comic strip telling these little stories. I didn't have any kind of video camera, so me and my friends would make these stories with still images. There was one called *Mister Rogers Nuclear Neighborhood*. It was pictures of us walking around, and there was a nuclear explosion made out of clay. And then we were all melting. We made all these makeup effects. It was super-weird. Then I begged for a video camera. Back then the cameras were those big ones you put VHS tapes in. I think I was ten when I got it. They were like $1800. And we were poor, so I saved a lot of money and we combined a birthday and a Christmas present to be able to afford it. I started shooting horror movies because I think they're more accessible from a storytelling standpoint. So as a kid you get it. There's not much story. It's just a scary thing chasing you. And I was obsessed with the creativity of makeup FX. You can do horror with no budget, but it is a very difficult genre to do well and very easy to do poorly. There was a time when I wanted to be a makeup artist. I was designing my own prosthetics. I was crazy for that all through middle school. We would make horror movies and never complete them. We'd shoot them and then sort of half-edit them and then move on to another project.

Then I got to high school, and went right into theater. I wasn't an actor or performer, though. I don't have the aptitude to remember lines when there's a camera on me. It's a weird mental block. Maybe it's the pressure of the camera. When I'm behind the camera, I'm mouthing everyone's words but in front of the camera I would freeze. I have so much respect for actors!

JP: What was your role in those plays?

BP: In high school, I fell into designing the sets. And I produced a ton of plays. Through theater, I decided that I wanted to go to film school. I hadn't really thought about college until my grandfather, who had gone to Princeton, told me that he wanted me to go there as a legacy. But Princeton didn't have a film program, and I talked him into helping me attend Boston University. At the time, I just wanted to shoot. So I made the decision that I was going to film school. I had never thought about becoming a director before that point. Making little movies was just something I did because I loved it. But I wasn't thinking that it would be my career. For a kid growing up in suburban D.C. with no connections to the film industry, becoming a director felt as likely as becoming an astronaut. I looked at Boston University, and what struck me about their program was that it was very hands-on. You were learning while earning.

I was a good painter, so I went to the College of Fine Arts at B.U. I painted and drew and sculpted. I did that for a year and then transferred to the College of Communications to make movies. I applied to a bunch of internships at Miramax and all these other companies and I didn't get any of them, which was fortunate because then I would have been stuck in an office somewhere. I ended up falling into a production job in New York, which was the thing I really wanted.

JP: How did you get your first production job?

BP: Tom Bernard, president of Sony Pictures Classics, has a younger brother named Paul who was an assistant director. They lived next door to my grandparents at one point. I guess their parents owed our family a little favor. So my grandmother told them, "Here's the favor: Your grandson is going to hire my grandson." My grandmother called me and said, "Call this guy." I called Paul Bernard, who at the time was the second AD on a film called *A Simple Wish*, and he said, "I'll give you three days, and if you're not an idiot, you can keep working." He let me stay on his couch in New York for about a month. I was very fortunate to have an opportunity like that.

JP: That connection got you into the New York production world?

BP: Yeah, which at the time was very small and close-knit, because not a lot of things shot in New York. This was the mid–'90s. They would go to New York and shoot just the exteriors for a week or two, and then go shoot the rest in Toronto or L.A. They had some TV series like *Law and Order* and *New York Undercover* that were shooting there. There was a small group of people, able to eke out a career as an AD. But as a PA, jumping into it, you worked constantly because whatever was shooting in New York needed like 65 PAs. So it was never a question of "Can you get a job?" it was "How much do you want to work?" And so I worked seven days a week. I was fortunate that I fell into that group, because when a big movie came to town, we were usually the ones that got it. So for instance, we did *Godzilla*, *The Siege* and *The Thing*.

I learned a lot. I was just trying to absorb as much as I could. Fortunately, I was working with big directors like Woody Allen, Roland Emmerich, Ed Zwick and David O'Russell. Sometimes I was just the fifty-fifth P.A. stationed ten blocks from the set. On other shows, I was the PA stationed right at the monitors with the director. So I got to talk to them, and I could learn from their successes and their failures. To be honest, some of the best lessons I learned were from watching directors make bad decisions.

JP: How did you progress from PA to director?

BP: I accumulated all my days as a PA and got in the DGA after two and a half years. I went through the assistant director path. All the while, I kept trying to develop stuff. I had some false starts on a few movies and eventually I ended up meeting Jessica Biel when my wife was a producer on a film called *Stealth*, which I was also the AD on. I wrote a feature that Jessica and I took out for a while, but it didn't go anywhere. We ended up doing a short film that I directed and Jessica produced. The short led to an independent feature that I finished earlier this year, *The Book of Love*.

I fell into directing television sort of by accident and by great luck. I had a mentor, Sara Fisher, who I had worked with on some other projects. She was mostly from television and had worked as an AD and producer on *St. Elsewhere* and *Chicago Hope*. Sara was producing a show for Shonda Rhimes in Hawaii called *Off the Map* and she knew I was trying to direct. Sara said to me, "Come to Hawaii and AD this show. Once they get to know you, you'll be directing by the next season." So I went to Hawaii and started on *Off the Map* as a first AD. I ended up directing the second unit and some of the finale. Later Shonda gave me a shot at directing on *Private Practice*. After that, I had another mentor, Jake Kasdan. He was developing *New Girl* and he said, "Come AD the show and we will get you directing." In season three, Jake and the show creator, Liz Meriwether, gave me a shot. I have had so many people like Melvin Mar, Mark Tinker and others give me great opportunities. So I started *New Girl*, and that led to directing on other shows, like *Fresh Off the Boat* and *Speechless*.

JP: What was the connection between you making *The Book of Love*, and finding opportunities to direct television?

BP: There was a running gag with Jake Kasdan about me trying to make *The Book of Love*, which was originally called *The Devil and the Deep Blue Sea*. It was a tough little movie to make, and it took me ten years. During that time, I did about seven projects as an AD for Jake Kasdan. And over that period, I kept potentially having to leave his shows because my movie would be about to go. But then it wouldn't. That occurred when I was on *Bad Teacher*, and then afterwards on the pilot for *Ben and Kate*. I almost had to leave the *New Girl* pilot to go do my movie.

JP: How has your background as an AD affected your transition to directing?

BP: I'm biased, but I think that along with DPs, there is no one on set more prepared to step into the directing chair than ADs. ADs deal with every aspect of production. They direct the actors and they have a great knowledge of every department's needs. But I've always felt that there is a strange prejudice against ADs becoming directors. Having that AD background has helped me in both television and independent films. In television, they hand you a 32- to 40-page script that you have to shoot in five days. And you are going to do that 23 times in a season. More often than not, it should be a six-day script, but you have to figure out how to shoot it in five.

In both television and indie film, you are given a box, and the box does not expand. That's the budget and the schedule. No matter what's in the script, it has to fit in that box. Some scripts fit nicely and some don't. But you still have to figure out how to make it fit, and you don't get extra days or money. I shot *The Book of Love* in 20 days. We had water work, animals, kids and aerials. We were shooting seven to eight pages a day. It was challenging. Having that AD background, knowing how to make your day, how to choose your battles and kill your darlings is critical for me as a director.

The thing I say to aspiring directors who shadow me is that the greatest skill set for directing TV is not so much about directing actors, unless you're on a first season show where they are still building the world. It's more about making your day and knowing it's not worth spending time on a given scene because it's probably going to get cut. I'd rather just move on because I need that time for a more important scene in the afternoon. It's being able to recognize those kinds of things and having the discipline to move on if something is not working. Sometimes you have to just figure it out in post, but make sure you get enough coverage options so that you can build something out of it. You can't afford to gild every lily, but always give yourself options.

I recently did a *Speechless* episode and we had a big stunt where a kid had to go racing down a hill in a wheelchair. We had him on a descender rig and all this stunt stuff. It was only an eighth of a page but it was going to take up half of my shooting day because of all the set-ups I needed. So everything else in the schedule got compacted because now I really only had four and a half days to complete the 32-page script. And they still wanted me to finish at 11 hours every day! You always need extra shots in comedy because so much of it is about timing and building the scene in the cutting room. So I knew that maybe I would have to do fewer takes on things to save time. Having that AD background certainly helps me to schedule it all out and make my day.

Perception is everything. You have to stop AD'ing, or whatever your day job is, and change the perception. People only see you for what you are doing. They want you to stay in your lane. The hardest directing job you ever get is that first episode. Once you do one, and you end up on the studio-approved list, you suddenly start getting hired again and again. It's just about that initial step. And it's sort of arbitrary and strange how you get on those lists.

JP: Could you elaborate on this "approved list" thing, because you're the first person I've heard phrase it in that way. Is it a real list?

BP: I imagine there is certainly a list of people they don't want to work with again.

JP: Even for someone like you who has shown you can direct both comedy and drama, there is still pigeonholing. Can you tell me about that?

BP: You get branded. There's definitely prejudice between comedy and drama. I have directed both, and I've directed a feature that is a dramedy. But I've done mostly comedy lately, and I've been trying to transition back to drama. It's been really challenging because in the last couple years, I've been branded as a comedy guy. Getting branded can be both a positive and a negative.

With my background as an outsider to this industry, I always felt like I had to out-work and out-hustle everyone to get ahead. I had to prove myself. I can't control the breaks but I can control my work ethic and my effort. That's a sort of accidental asset that I have. I want to be the first one on set in the morning, although I don't always succeed. And when I'm at work I literally run from point A to B. I never sit down. Maybe that's from when I was starting out as PA. If you got caught sitting down, you got fired. It's so much looser today, but I still don't sit down. I run. People laugh at it, but I literally run from the monitor to the actors to the cameras. I'm usually by the camera when I direct and I'll run back and forth to the writers at the monitors to get notes. Also, it saves me from going to the gym. I lose weight and my wife gets off my back. But in truth, if I can shave off 15 minutes over the course of a day, that's an extra few takes I can get when I'm fighting the light at the end of the day. It's that little extra effort, that little extra hustle. That's the kind of thing I always tell young directors. Hustle and effort can be the difference between something good and something great. Because if you get that extra little time for a few extra takes, that can make the difference. So never lose that.

JP: Perception and image are so important.

BP: Much of your success in our industry is about perception. You have to think about how you want to be perceived by others. It's something I've personally struggled with because, to be honest, I'm sort of a vanilla guy. My wife taught me it has a lot to do with appearances. It's the old adage: Dress for the job you want, not the job you have. If you dress like an AD, you're going to get hired as an AD. If you dress like a director, people will probably see you as a director. My wife will always yell at me because we will be going to some Emmy party or something and I'll want to put a suit on. She's like, "What the fuck are you doing? You're a director. You don't wear a suit. Agents wear suits."

Creatives are perceived as not giving a fuck. You've got to look the part. You've got to act the part. Even though it's all silly and superficial, that's how it works. So much of it is just convincing people. If you're trying to direct, everybody wants to say no to you. They already have a million reasons to say no. They'll think, "Oh, they're not smart enough. Oh, they're not experienced enough. Oh, they're probably not cool enough." Well, then, how do you define *cool*? Every time you meet with someone, they are already saying no in their head and you have to dismiss every "no" they have. It's hard because so much of it is false. It's play-acting. And I have a hard time with that. I think my biggest struggle as a director is when I'm pretending to be something that I'm not just to convince someone that I can do the things I know I can do.

JP: Was there ever a point in your journey where you thought, "It's not working. I'm going to bail out"?

BP: Yes. Daily. You have to get used to constant rejection and failure and disappointment. I don't know how actors do it. It's so much more constant rejection for them. It's just a grind. I think so much of success in this industry is perseverance. This is an industry of attrition. So much of it is more about persistence than talent. Luck shows up eventually if you just keep at it. You might get lucky when you're 22 and have a hit movie or a hit show. Or you might be 35, or you might be 57. You just keep at it, and you grind and grind and grind. You'll find success. It may not come in the form you expected. It may not come in the timing you wanted or needed. But you stick with your goals and you just don't quit. My wife and I were at a time where she was struggling with her company. It took her 11 or 12 years of development where nothing went. But now in the past year, she just released a movie, and she has the number one show on cable. Suddenly, all that struggle has been justified. We had times, even after all the work and sacrifices, where we thought, "Maybe we should just move to Hawaii and open a coffee shop." I gave up maybe five Christmas vacations to do rewrites on *Book of Love* because we kept getting close to going on the film right around Christmas time. And then, every time, the movie would fall apart. My wife would be so pissed. She would say, "We could have gone on vacation. We lost all that time with the kids. And the movie is not going to go." We started resenting the movie because it was sucking our life away and not paying off. That's hard because you want a balance. You want to be able to enjoy your life and enjoy your family.

This industry is so consuming and you have to give it 120 percent to try and stick it out. It's hard to know when the sacrifices are worth it. But at the end of the day, it's that old adage of, "If you do what you love, you'll never work a day in your life." It's true. I love the process of this industry. I can have exhausting days and be physically and mentally exhausted, but I won't feel like I worked, even with the long hours and all the running I do on set. At the end of the week, I feel exhausted, like after a great workout, but I feel good. It gives you energy. And that sort of energy gives you enough push to keep going to the next thing, and to the next thing. I'm legitimately more tired on Mondays after having spent a weekend with my kids.

JP: Talk about the state of diversity in television.

BP: It's something I believe really strongly in. That may be antithetical to being a straight, white, cisgendered male, but I feel very strongly about promoting diversity. At the end of the day, I just care about the product.

JP: Does a concerned white male have a role to play in fostering diversity in our industry?

BP: Put aside being a director and a person of power in the workplace. I think just as humans, we all have an obligation to fight against injustice. There has been long-standing bias in all industries, including ours, for a long time. I think fostering diversity is imperative and only helps to create better stories. I am the artist I am today because I was influenced by the stories of diverse artists such as Akira Kurosawa, Spike Lee and Jane Campion, to name a few. Unlike corporate culture, however, we have to remember that telling stories is an art and we need to find those voices that have something to say and raise them up and not just tick an HR box. We have to exact change in a smart manner. Otherwise we devalue the legitimacy of the under-represented.

JP: Have you witnessed racism or sexism in the industry?

BP: There was certainly institutional racism and misogyny that created a white man's industry. And there are still elements of racism and sexism in television. I've also seen a lot of horrible misogyny in features.

JP: As a white male on TV sets, I have sometimes overheard insensitive racial and misogynist comments from other white male crew members. I have struggled with how to respond to that in a way that would not create more tension. What are your thoughts on how white males should take that on?

BP: I'm hyper-aware of everyone's conversations. I hear everything, and I have heard insensitive remarks with every "ism" you can name: racism, sexism, ageism, etc. I have heard those comments from every kind of person as well, not just older white men. There is bias across the board. I think, whether you are a white male or African-American female, if you are a leader on set, which is what a director is, then one of the most important things you do is foster a safe and creative environment. You set the tone. You don't grow the plant, but you do create an environment in which the plant can grow. So if I hear something that is offensive or unnecessary, even if it didn't offend anyone, I'm going to call it out.

Comedy is tricky because I believe that comedy should be able to offend equally. That's the writers' and performers' choice, and sometimes those lines can blur. But behind the scenes, it is important to make that distinction, to lead by example as well as by action. I realize that I'm not going to change a crew member who may be later in years or who has a clear bias toward a protected group. So I'm not going to try and lecture or change that person. But I am very clear about what is acceptable and unacceptable on my sets and that they can either get on board or find another job.

How do you change those minds? It's about creating more opportunities so that those minds aren't the only decision-makers. That has been happening slowly over the last couple years. Generally, executives and showrunners trust people they have already worked with.

With openness and diligence, I hope we reach a place of true equity and balanced representation within the industry so we have a fair playing field and everyone can up their game!

Nicole Rubio

I interviewed Nicole Rubio via phone as she was taking a break from shot-listing her latest episode in New York. It was amazing to me that she could jump from her prep to speaking with me about her life for two hours, and then jump right back into prep. As Nicole says in her interview, she is very good at multi-tasking.

As we completed the interview, she left me with this little nugget: "I would say the hardest part about being a director is prepping. But a good prep makes a great show because you're prepared for pretty much anything."

Speaking to Nicole, I was struck by her cheerful demeanor. She is friendly and open, and laughs easily. But reading the printed words of the interview, it's easy to see her no-nonsense core. Nicole embodies the idea that a director can get what she wants and still treat people decently.

· ·

NICOLE RUBIO: I was born in Columbia, South Carolina. I'm the middle child of five. We lived in a small community, with not very many houses. It was not a fast-paced world, just simplistic and beautiful. When I was about three, we moved to Los Angeles. We lived in L.A. until I was maybe nine years old and then my dad got his first overseas job with Northrop Aircraft Company. It was in Tehran, Iran. We lived there for a year and a half. I have lots of memories of living there and going to school. I was fascinated with this giant painting of the shah and empress at the Kings Hotel and I would try to draw it because I had never seen anything like that before. That was stuff you only saw in books, and I wanted to keep that memory. When we came back to the States, we moved to Lancaster, California. I lived there for middle school and part of high school.

JACOB PINGER: What was Lancaster like?

During her career as a script supervisor, Nicole Rubio closely observed dozens of directors before deciding to sit in the chair herself (Lisa Rose).

NR: We went swimming and picked pomegranates off the neighbor's trees during the summer, typical childhood stuff. We would stay out until the streetlights came on. It was a nice upbringing. But then, when I was a junior in high school, my dad got another overseas assignment with Northrop. This time it was in Saudi Arabia. He was going to teach the Royal Saudi Air Force how to maintain their planes. But before we went there, we found out that foreign high school–age kids were not allowed to go to school in the Kingdom of Saudi Arabia. My parents had to send me to an international boarding school in another country. So I got the option of a school in Greece, Switzerland or Alexandria, Egypt. At first I thought I would go to Switzerland, but I ended up at an international boarding school in Alexandria.

It was hard leaving my school in the United States. I had been a cheerleader and a gymnast. It could have been about the worst thing your parents could do—uproot you from your friends and the activities that you loved. But looking back, I see that it was the best upbringing I could have had. I went to school with kids from Nigeria, Egypt, Britain, as well as America. On the weekends, we would go to Cairo to visit the pyramids and spend the night in a houseboat on the Nile. I could go on … it was truly a blessing, living in that country. I feel like nothing has ever stopped me, and I've never felt like I was discriminated against due to my race or anything like that. It's because my life has been so diverse. I think about what my life would have been like if I had never experienced going to an international boarding school and seeing the world at such a young age. It gave me a [chance] to understand the differences and sometimes challenges of living in those countries.

JP: What did you do after high school?

NR: I went to Antelope Valley Junior College. I wanted to be a physical therapist. But that only lasted until I took anatomy and saw an autopsy of a brain. Couldn't handle that. I took drama classes and dance. I got a job at Rockwell International Aircraft Company, tracking parts for the Space Shuttle Program. I eventually transferred to El Camino Junior College. Soon after I got a position to cheer for the Los Angeles Raiders as a side gig.

JP: You're my only cheerleader turned director. I'm really excited about that.

NR: Not a lot of people know that. It's a fun fact and I still keep in touch with my Raiderette sisters.

JP: Was being a cheerleader your first taste of making a living in entertainment?

NR: Yes. Cheerleading opened the doors to show me which part of the entertainment industry I wanted to be in. Some TV shows would hire us to be background. I did a few shows, and then I quickly got a little more serious about things. I let all my day jobs go and started acting.

JP: The life of an L.A. actor is not easy. How was that for you?

NR: It was about having the stamina, drive and ambition to stay in it. When you booked an acting job, it was rewarding, but it was only one job. And then you had to go get the next one. It was about learning to deal with rejection. But I really liked this business and wanted to be able to support myself. So I worked hard, paid my dues, and things started to happen for me. When you find out that you want to be successful at something, you go the extra mile. I was doing plays and hanging out with people who were going for the same goal.

JP: People can look at your IMDb page and see that you were having success as an actor, which is not easy to do. Why did you leave acting?

NR: Work was so inconsistent. I needed to go in a different direction. At that point, I didn't mind not acting any more. I didn't completely stop, but I wanted to learn something that would support my ambitions and keep my feet planted where I was comfortable. I decided that I wanted to stay in the entertainment business. So how would I do that? I loved the filmmaking process. I loved what the directors were doing. I also loved watching the script supervisor. So I paid to take classes from a script supervisor I knew, Dawn Gilliam, and she trained me. It's crazy, but I knew Dawn from when I was a Raiders cheerleader and she was a Rams cheerleader.

JP: Tell me about your training to become a script supervisor.

NR: Dawn trained me on a movie she was doing. It was very hands-on. I remember showing up for my first day on set with her and it was overwhelming. I think they had nine cameras going. I got there and saw all those cameras and I thought, "How does Dawn keep track of all this?" At that point, I knew nothing. I said to myself, "If I get in my car and go home, I can forget all about this script supervisor thing." Then Dawn said, "Don't worry. You'll get used to it." So I sat down, took out my pen and my stopwatch and I watched her. I got through the day and I just kept persisting and learning. I ended up getting in with the producers on that show, and when they made another movie and Dawn wasn't available, they hired me. My advantage was that I was learning things on the job, on the stage floor where it happens in real time.

JP: It seems like coming from a script supervisor background would really help you figure out, as a director, what works for you.

NR: Yes. People from the floor have that advantage. And sitting in my script supervisor position gave me the best advantage I could ask for because I worked closely with so many directors, writers and producers.

JP: A real mistake I've seen some directors make is to turn the script supervisor into an enemy by treating them like the help or thinking of them as an annoyance. Some directors I've seen will be really nice to the male crew members and then turn around and treat the female script supervisor like she's his maid or something. That always puzzled me because it seems backwards. Yes, it's good to be nice to your crew, but the script supervisor is the person who can save your ass. A camera operator can't save the show, but the script supervisor can save a scene if she knows that the director has made a mistake in his or her coverage.

NR: Yes. Because she or he can know what coverage you're missing. And then they can just choose to let it go and not tell you. Our commitment is to the show, though, so I never let that happen. I tried to help and learn what others were thinking.

JP: Did you continue acting when you became a script supervisor?

NR: Yes. I was still getting calls to audition, and I would say, "Oh my gosh. I'm a script supervisor on this job. How do I get off to make this audition?" When you take a movie as a script supervisor, you can't just say, "Hey, I'm leaving to go do this part." I decided to commit to being a script supervisor.

JP: You didn't regret leaving acting?

NR: No, because I didn't completely give it up. It just wasn't my priority. I could always go back to it. But now my focus was being the best script supervisor that I could be.

JP: I think a lot of people would have a hard time with that decision.

NR: Well, you see it was not the end for me.

JP: True. But you didn't know that then.

NR: No, I didn't know that then. But I thought that I should commit to one thing, and script supervising was good. It gave me a career and I was getting work all the time. I was seeing the world and getting to sit right next to the director. I loved it.

JP: For how long were you a scripty?

NR: On *Grey's Anatomy* I left during the eleventh season. I was script supervisor on movies like *Training Day*, *Blade*, *Save the Last Dance* and *Coach Carter*. I got to work next to brilliant directors like Antoine Fuqua. Working with Steven Norrington on *Blade* blew my mind. He told a really interesting, badass story with the first *Blade* film.

JP: A lot of script supervisors probably don't absorb the artistic part of it.

NR: Depends on what you want from the job.

JP: I think a lot of times, being a script supervisor is seen as more of a secretarial role. But I feel like the script supervisor is the unsung hero on set, because a lot of times when everybody is confused. they ask the script supervisor what they should do. What was your experience being a scripty? Did you feel you were getting the respect the position deserved?

NR: I did because I wasn't the kind of script supervisor who would just sit in her chair and take notes. I was always on my feet. I was always up learning what the shots were and listening to what the director was telling the actors and crew. I was hands-on. Being a script supervisor can be overwhelming. You have so many things that you're keeping an eye on. I was good at multi-tasking so that job came naturally to me with all the different elements involved in filmmaking.

JP: I think that in a creative sense, the script supervisor is often more like an assistant director than the actual first AD, whose primary function is running the set. But the script supervisor can play the role of a collaborator and sounding board for the director. Would you agree with that?

NR: Somewhat. The first AD has to worry about getting the day completed on time. The script supervisor can be more of a backup for the director. Directors would often ask me, "Do you think I got all the coverage I need for this scene?" I would advise them, "Yes you did," or "If I were you, I would get this other shot." Sometimes they would say, "Cool," or sometimes they were satisfied with the scene.

JP: How did you go from being script supervisor to director?

NR: With the support of my *Grey's Anatomy* family. They urged me to make the jump. Saying that you wanted to direct and actually doing it are two different things. People were telling me, "You're already there. What's wrong with you? Do it." So I went to my executive producer, Rob Corn, and I said, "Okay, I'm ready." The showrunner Tony Phelan came down and said, "You're going to shadow me." So I shadowed Tony and then he, Rob and Shonda Rhimes gave me a couple episodes. Then Shonda tweeted that she loved one of my episodes and a producer from another show who was following Shonda on Twitter called me to direct on his show.

Grey's Anatomy started to let me go direct other shows and then come back as a script supervisor in between directing jobs. That's very rare, and I'm so grateful for that family. And then I got representation shortly after, but even with representation, you need to do your own networking. The agents are not going to get you a job just because you've done two episodes of *Grey's Anatomy* and one other show. I started to get momentum, but it wasn't overnight. Eventually, I got so busy as a director that the decision to stop script supervising was made for me.

JP: Was it a difficult decision to stop script supervising?

NR: I wanted to make sure I was doing the right thing by making a career change. Leaving the script supervising union was hard. But the more director bookings I got, the more I felt that it was the right move.

JP: Did you have any mentors?

NR: I have a lot of mentors. Rob Corn said, "What are you waiting for, Nicole? Go spend the rest of your life directing." Debbie Allen said, "Rubio, you're ready." Another mentor, Eriq La Salle, hired me to direct my very first episode of *Chicago PD*. He encouraged me to get into an acting class. He said, "Your directing is already there. But once you learn more about talking to actors, the sky is the limit." ⚡

JP: That's interesting advice because you were already an actress. But he still felt it would benefit you to go to acting classes from the perspective of being a director? ⚡

NR: Yes. He told me to get back into acting classes because every personality is different. What you did with one actor is not going to work with somebody else. We need to be learning on every job that we do and take that experience to the next job. We are always learning because there are different styles of directing.

JP: Which one are you?

NR: I'm an all-arounder. I have relationships with the crew that works the floor—camera, sound, hair, makeup, art and the other departments that are vital to producing a show. I care about what the shot looks like with the story I'm telling, and also what kinds of performances I'm getting from actors. I also care about the budget of my episode.

JP: As a former script supervisor, why do you think script supervisors are not promoted more to become directors?

NR: There is a perception that script supervisors are just kind of note-takers. But if you get a script supervisor who wants to direct, they'll show you by coming up with shots and bouncing ideas off of you. They see it from a director's eye and are interested in more than just taking notes.

JP: Did you ever get directors who resented your latent directing talents?

NR: Probably. But I wasn't saying things to imply that they couldn't direct. It's funny because when I was a script supervisor, I used to be judgmental towards some of the directors. Then I found out that there is so much that a director does, and, honestly, people have no idea until they have sat in that seat. There are so many things people don't know about how we do our job. Like how intense the prep can be for a 42-minute TV show. There are things that a director might not have control of, like money, location availability, actor availability, time or tone of the show. Directors are hired guests who come into someone else's house. Sometimes you are given certain things to work with, and that's how it goes. But as a crew member, how would you know those things? I've had to tell camera operators why a certain shot was needed. After I let him in on the tone of the scene, he would understand and get on board. Most people don't intentionally try to get in your way; they just need the knowledge.

JP: Did you ever feel that being a woman of color held you back in the television business?

NR: There could have been some jobs I didn't get because I was an African-American woman. But it wasn't to the point that I could see a racist or chauvinistic thing happening. If I didn't get a job, I never thought it was because I was a woman or because I was a different color. It could have been because I didn't have enough experience. Somebody else might have pointed it out to me. They would say, "When you go in the room, do you see anybody else that looks your color?" Maybe it's my naiveté, but it's not necessarily something I was thinking.

JP: As a female director, have you experienced any pushback from crews?

NR: Every now and then, yes. And it's not the whole crew. I think it would just be maybe a camera operator or an AD who also wants to direct. Or maybe they didn't want to direct but were used to a person of a different gender or color. Who knows? Early on in my directing career, they would look up my IMDb and say, "Oh, it's a script supervisor *slash* director coming in." But now they don't see me as that. They see me as a director.

JP: What kinds of attitudes would you see come up?

NR: I had a male AD on a show call me "honey." I said something like, "You know what, I'm not your honey. And if I *was* your honey, say it like you mean it." The crew fell out laughing. That same AD told me to "stay in my lane" one time. Wrong thing to say to a director.

I think when a director walks onto a set, people are thinking, "How did he or she get the job?" When you do the job right, it shows them that you're not just some person who got hired because somebody felt like you were owed it due to the color of your skin or your gender.

JP: There's a lot of second-guessing on film and TV sets. And there's a lot of assuming the worst. When you're working, do you ever feel that you have to represent your gender or your race?

NR: I don't go into jobs thinking I'm representing my race, but how could I not think that? I don't like putting that pressure on myself and besides, how do I know how many black people have come before me? Other people bring it up. I'll have an actor say, "I'm so excited to work with a black female director. I've never seen that." Or I'll go up to the caterer and be treated a certain way, and when they find out I'm the director, they will say, "Oh, I'm so sorry. I didn't know you were the director." And I'll say, "Don't apologize. Just don't treat people shitty and you won't have to be apologizing."

But yes, in a sense, I am representing other people. Here's a black female director coming in. But I would like to think that every time I walk out of my house, I'm representing something. Just even being a nice human being. I'm representing being a nice woman, you know?

JP: What are your thoughts on the state of our industry today?

NR: I definitely think there are positive changes being made. It's happening slowly. But with time, it will just keep getting better because we are people who are advocating for change and we'll keep the movement going toward a more fair industry. This industry has always been a certain way. So for it to change overnight would be impossible. But it's changing. I see more women and women of color.

JP: I feel like the pool of talent is growing and it's going to get harder to break in because there are just more talented people.

NR: A lot of people with creative talent can't get a break. I'd love to hear their stories. The networks are raising the quality of the shows, so they could be a little cautious about whom they are hiring.

JP: I agree that the expectation of quality is rising. There isn't room any more for people who don't know what they are doing.

NR: These shows are like mini features. And they want you to produce it sometimes in eight or nine days. It's fascinating. It just goes so fast, and I'm amazed that they can turn out such high-quality product, week after week and month after month. As a director, you have to be ready to step onto that moving train.

JP: Is there something that you wished you knew before you became a director?

NR: I didn't sit down with anybody and ask what it's like to be a director. If I had asked that question of a lot of directors and they had said, "Well, I don't like this, and I don't like," I might have thought that maybe I didn't want to be a director. I think there are some things you have to learn on your own because everybody's experiences are different. For instance, traveling a lot is not a big deal for me. I've been traveling since I was three years old. But leaving my family for months at a time to go work on a show … well, if you ask me what that's like, I'll tell you, and you can make your own decisions. I think you should get the job that you want and then make it work in your own way.

JP: What would you tell an 18-year-old Nicole to get her ready to pursue directing?

NR: I would say be ready to work hard. Be ready for long hours. You have to learn how to do the job in a way that you can survive. Build up your stamina because you will definitely need it. Be able to accept feedback and criticism. Have the ability to hear everything as constructive, because everybody is going to have an opinion. Just take it in and think about how can you improve for the next one. You've got to work well with a lot of people on set. So treat them with respect and you'll get that back.

JP: Not all directors care about that, as I'm sure you know.

NR: I don't see why not. You don't have to be an asshole to get a job done. On my last show, the cast gave me a bouquet of flowers to thank me. We had a ball on that show. Why wouldn't you want to have a job where you are respected and have fun?

Glossary

Note: This is not intended to be an exhaustive glossary of filmmaking terms. Rather, it covers much of the lingo used by and around directors on a daily basis. This is what you need to know on set. But be aware that different terms may have slightly different meanings for different people and in different parts of the country. Filmmaking involves a living language and things change.

Abby Singer (n): A term for the second-to-last shot of the day. The first AD will often announce that they are "on the Abby" to alert the crew that their day is nearly over. Abby Singer was a real-life first AD and the mythology is that he would often be wrong when he told the crew that they were on the last shot. The crew began to joke that when Abby Singer said it was the last shot, it was actually the second-to-last shot. Over time, other crews eventually adopted the joke.

Above-the-line: A hiring term that refers to the relative position of an employee in the hierarchy of film and TV. Above-the-line refers to employees who are not considered **crew**: actors, show-runners, producers, writers, executives and members of the production department, such as first ADs, second ADs and UPMs, etc. Aside from the low-ranking members of the production department, such as PAs, individuals who are above the line are often hired on contracts, paid more and are more likely to receive residuals. In addition, above-the-line employees may belong to a guild such as the DGA, WGA, SAG or PGA, but they will not be represented by a union. (See also: **below-the-line**)

AC (n): Assistant Cameraperson. Film and TV productions will generally employ a first AC and a second AC.

Act break (n): In narrative structure, the story is traditionally broken into separate acts. The simplest narrative structure involves three acts. However, in traditional network television, a segment will finish and then start a new act at every commercial break. Those moments are called "act breaks." A one-hour network drama may have up to five or six act breaks.

Action (n): *Multiple meanings*

　　1. The command that the director or first AD will call to alert the actors and camera to start a scene. In some cases, the shot will require for the camera to begin a move before the actors begin to act. In that situation, the director may call "camera action" first, and then call "action." *The director called "action," but the actor couldn't hear her because she was standing next to the wind machine.*

　　2. Any activities that the actors are required to do in a scene. This can involve anything from making a sandwich to fighting a monster. Sometimes the script accurately describes all the action that an actor must do, but very often it is the director's responsibility to explain all the action to the actor. *The script says that the actor is "working on his car," but what is the action you want me to do? Should I be changing the oil or replacing the spark plugs?*

　　3. A term for exciting activity in a script, such as fighting, car chases, battles, etc. *That director wasn't hired for the war movie because she didn't have enough action on her résumé.*

AD (n): Assistant director. Film and TV productions will generally have a first AD, second AD and second-second AD. The first AD is a director's closest ally on any set.

AD (v): To AD is the act of doing the job of an AD on a production. *I am going to AD a pilot next week.*

ADR (n): Additional Dialogue Recording. The post-production process of recording additional lines that the editor needs to complete the final cut. Often times, a production will do ADR for any lines that need to be re-recorded due to poor sound quality on the original recording.

Agency (n): A company of talent **agents**. An agency will employ multiple agents who maintain a roster of clients. Agencies can be large or small. Large agencies will usually have multiple departments that specialize in different areas of the entertainment business, such as features, television and digital media. Large agencies, such as William Morris Endeavor, Creative Artists Agency and United Talent Agency, have tremendous power and influence within the entertainment world.

Agent (n): A person authorized to negotiate deals, contracts and compensation on their clients' behalf in exchange for a percentage of the clients' earnings. An agent may also help to find work opportunities on behalf of their clients. Directors rely on both agents and **managers** to use their industry connections to set up meetings that will get the director jobs. *I had to fire my agent because she wasn't getting me any meetings.* (See also: **manager**)

Apple box (n): A six-sided wooden box that the grip department carries as part of their equipment package. Apple boxes generally come in four widths: full, half, quarter and pancake.

Associate Producer (n): A lower-level producer on a show. Above an assistant, but below a full-fledged producer.

Awards show (n): A one-off television special dedicated to giving away awards. The Oscars, Grammys and Emmys are awards shows.

Back lot (n): The area on a studio **lot** where exterior **sets** have been constructed. The sets are semi-permanent or temporary, and can include a New York street, a European street and a Western street. Traditionally, the sets may have been constructed behind the sound stages and towards the back of the lot. (See also: **lot**)

Back nine (n): The last nine episodes of a traditional 22 or 23-episode season of network television. *The show was such a disaster that the network cancelled the back-nine.*

Background (n): The people who inhabit a scene behind and around the main characters. Literally, they are often in the background. Background performers compose the crowd in a baseball game scene, the dancers in a nightclub scene and the soldiers in a battle scene. Background performers are often treated as an afterthought, but their behavior within a shot can make or break a scene. It is the duty of the second AD to direct the background performers on behalf of the director. (See also: **extra**)

Backstory (n): The story of a character's life that took place before the script begins. The backstory may be alluded to in a script, but is often not spelled out completely. For instance, the audience knows very little of the backstory of Travis Bickle in the Martin Scorsese film *Taxi Driver*.

Back to one: An instruction for the actors and crew to return to their starting marks so that the director can shoot another take of a shot. *After take four, the director told everyone to go back to one for another take.*

Base camp (n): When a show goes on location, this is the collection of trailers and trucks that houses the production staff, the actors' trailers, wardrobe, makeup and hair. On many studio lots, there will also be a base camp collected alongside the sound stage.

Beat sheet (n): A script outline that does not include dialogue. A beat sheet is a common tool for outlining story points as a road map for **improv** comedy and often **reality** shows. A beat sheet will not be written in script format.

Below-the-line: A hiring term that refers to the relative position of an employee in the hierarchy of film and TV. Below-the-line refers to employees who are considered **crew** and crafts people: directors of photography, camera assistants, grips, makeup artists, Teamsters, sound mixers, etc. Below-the-line employees will almost always be paid hourly and are not eligible to receive residuals on a show. Below-the-line employees will usually be members of a local in IATSE. (See also: **above-the-line**)

Block shoot (v): A filming technique whereby a director will choose to shoot pieces of multiple scenes at the same time in order to avoid having excessive *turn-arounds*. Block shooting is often employed when a script has multiple scenes in one location with a large group. A common example of when a director might choose to block-shoot is if the script has two or more scenes that take place in a theater. In this example, the story is about parents in the audience getting into a fight during a school play. In scene one, the play begins and all is well. In scene two, the play starts to fall apart and a few parents in the audience begin to bicker with each other. In scene three, the play goes completely off the rails, and some of the parents get into a fistfight. To shoot more efficiently, the director may choose to shoot all the shots towards the stage for scenes one, two and three first. Then the director will *turn around* and shoot all the shots of the audience for scenes one, two and three. The director has shot multiple scenes as a block, thus the term *block shooting*.

Block (v): The act of creating the *blocking* of a scene. (See "blocking.") *The showrunner loves how this director blocked the scene.*

Blocking (n): The placement, movement and action of the actors in a scene. A director will usually collaborate with the actors and the DP to figure out the most efficient way to *block* a scene. *As part of the director's blocking, she wants all the characters to begin seated and then leave the room one by one.*

Breakdown (v): The process in **prep** whereby a director methodically analyzes a script for story and character to determine the best way to film it. *I just got the script this morning and I'm going to spend the day breaking it down.*

Bump up (v): To promote a crew member to a higher position. *When the first AD quit, I decided to bump up the second AD to take her place.*

Business (n): *Multiple meanings*
　　1. Short for the television and/or film business.
　　2. Small, often unscripted activities that an actor does during a scene. Many actors prefer to be doing something in a scene rather than just standing there. So a director may work with an actor to give them some business, such as making a cup of tea, plugging in a phone or putting the dishes away.

Call sheet (n): The form that the AD department generates and distributes every day to inform the crew, actors and production staff of the exact work scheduled for the following day. The call sheet lists a tremendous amount of information including, but not limited to, the crew **call time**, the schedule of what scenes will be shot, what actors will work, what crew members will work, if there are child actors working, if there are any stunts and if special equipment is needed for the next day.

Call time, Call (n): The time that an actor or crew member must report to set to start their day. *What is the actor's call tomorrow?*

Camera coordinator (n): A term specifically related to traditional **multi-cam sitcoms**. The camera coordinator is responsible for assisting the director with facilitating the elaborate ballet of using four cameras to shoot a proscenium-style show. The camera coordinator uses headsets to call out the sequence of shots as dictated by the director to each of the camera operators during the scene.

Cancel (v): When a network decides not to pick up a series for the next season, it has been cancelled.

Color Correction (n): The process of adjusting the colors and contrast of an episode or movie after the editing process has been finished.

Comedy (n): TV series are usually categorized as comedy or drama. A comedy is generally a half hour, while a drama is generally one hour. On network television, a half-hour comedy usually runs about 22 minutes because of the commercial breaks.

Concept meeting (n): Usually the first important meeting that a TV director will have with the production staff and department heads during her **prep** on an episode. The concept meeting will be run by the first AD, and may not always include the showrunner. The purpose of the concept meeting is for everyone to go through the script together and begin to make both practical and creative decisions about the biggest elements therein. Do we need to build a hospital room set, or can we find an existing one on location? How many extras do we need for the restaurant scene? Are they wearing formal dress or shorts and tank tops? What kind of motorcycle does the lead ride? Is it a Harley or a Yamaha? Is the car work going to be practical or green screen? Can the night scene be finished quickly during magic hour, or is it going to require a full night of shooting?

Continuity (n): The practice of making sure that every detail matches from shot to shot and from scene to scene. Continuity includes, but is not limited to, actors' movements, placement of props, lighting, hair, wardrobe and even the level of theatrical haze or smoke. The **script supervisor** is tasked with maintaining continuity. *The scene was ruined because the continuity was completely off. In one shot, the actor had a cigarette in her left hand, and in the next shot, the cigarette was in her right hand.* (See also: **script supervisor**)

Copy (n): The script written for a host or announcer, usually for when they are speaking directly to camera.

Copy or **Copy that (v):** A walkie talkie term used to indicate that the speaker has understood the previous transmission. "Bring a ladder to set." "Copy that."

Corman, Roger: An iconic producer of ultra low-budget indie horror films. His career has spanned from the '50s to the present and he got a lot of very successful people started, including Francis Ford Coppola, Ron Howard, Martin Scorsese, Jack Nicholson, James Cameron, Robert De Niro, Peter Bogdanovich, Joe Dante and Sandra Bullock. His name is often invoked when talking about doing things on the cheap, but with the extreme creativity that financial restrictions can inspire.

Cover (a scene) (v): To get all the shots needed for the editor to successfully edit a scene or sequence. *The director is getting a lot of different shots to make sure that she has covered the wedding scene.*

Coverage (n): The collection of all the shots that a director has determined necessary to make sure that she has **covered** the scene. *That director did not get asked back because she did not get enough coverage, and now the showrunner has to do pick-ups.*

Craft Services (n): Term for both the department and the personnel tasked with providing snacks and beverages to the crew throughout the shooting day. The table where the refreshments are laid out is the craft services table.

Crafty (n): Shortening of **craft services**. *I just got to set and I'm really hungry. Do you know where they set up crafty?*

Creative(s) (n): A term for a series' writer(s) and creator(s). In essence, the ones who create the storylines and scripts. *The actor has a problem with his lines, so he wants to talk to the creatives and see if they can change the script.*

Creator(s) (n): The person(s) credited with creating a TV series. It is not uncommon for a show's creator to not work on the actual series. *Ricky Gervais created* The Office, *but by the final season, all he was doing was collecting a paycheck.*

Credit (n): The official job description given to a person working on a TV series or movie. *I was a PA on that show, but they gave me a credit as a second-second AD on the final episode.*

Crew (n): A catch-all term for the crafts people on a set. "The crew" is the people who actually make the show or movie. They rig the cameras, turn on the lights, build the sets, put the clothes on the actors, etc. Also known as **below-the-line**. *The crew works harder for that director because she always makes them feel appreciated.*

Cross-board (v): The practice of shooting multiple episodes of a TV series during the same production schedule in order to increase efficiency. Normally a show will shoot one episode at a time. But a production may choose to cross-board if they have multiple episodes with the same actors happening in the same location, especially if that location is difficult to book. For instance, if a show has two episodes that are set on the deck of an aircraft carrier, they may shoot both episodes simultaneously in order to avoid the expense of booking the ship a second time. Cross-boarding can be complicated because it means that the actors, director and all departments have to jump back and forth between episodes.

Crossing the line (v): The act of breaking the 180-degree rule. (See also: **180-degree line/rule**) *The director got into an argument with the DP about if the closeup was crossing the line.*

Cross-shoot (v): The technique of using two or more cameras to shoot in two or more directions simultaneously. Cross-shooting allows for different actors in the scene to be on camera at the same time, thus avoiding having to **turn around** and repeat **takes**. The technique is particularly useful when there is **improv** involved. Today, most comedies cross-shoot as a matter of course, whereas most dramas will shoot one direction at a time. To cross-shoot, you need a minimum of two cameras; some shows will employ three or even four cameras at all times. *Comedians love to cross-shoot because it allows them more freedom to improv lines.*

Cut (v): To stop the camera rolling on a shot. On every shot, it will be the director or the first AD who will call "cut" when the shot has been completed or if a shot has been ruined by an unexpected event. *The first AD called cut because the actor got something in his eye during the shot.*

Cut (n): *Multiple meanings*
  1. The announcement to stop the camera from rolling. *Was that a cut or should we keep rolling?*
  2. In editing, a cut refers to each new version of an episode or scene that the editor generates. In television, the first cut of an episode will usually be the director's cut. After that, depending on time constraints, the editor may create their own editor's cut. Then the showrunner will work with the editor to start creating additional cuts. Each cut will also be shared with the network and studio for notes. Eventually, the editor will create the final locked cut, which is what will eventually be aired and/or streamed. *The showrunner did not like the director's cut, so she threw it out and started from scratch.*

Deck (n): A visual presentation often done in the style of power point. A deck can be part of a director's prep ritual, in which case it will likely include shot diagrams and visual examples to represent themes. This may also be called a **look book**. A deck can also be part of a presentation to pitch an idea for a show or movie, in which case it is also called a **pitch deck**. (See also: **pitch deck** and **look book**.)

Department (n): A film or TV production is organized into departments. There will usually be departments for camera, art, electric, grip, production, sound, hair and makeup, transportation, special effects, post-production, etc.

Department head (n): The person in charge of a given department. The director of photography is the department head of the camera department. The key grip is the department head of the grip department. The production designer is the department head of the art department, etc.

Develop (v): The process of creating and refining an idea for a TV series or film with the intention of selling it to a producer or perhaps producing it oneself. This may also include writing one or more scripts. *I am developing a show about a cop who used to be a racecar driver.*

Development (n): The often lengthy process of creating a TV series or movie. Development often includes securing the legal rights to a story, writing the script(s), attaching actors, attaching a director and associating the project with a production company. A project may be in development for years. *The Wonder Woman movie was in development hell for a long time.*

DGA (n): The Directors Guild of America is the entertainment trade guild that represents the interests of film and TV directors in the United States and abroad.

DGA Training Program (n): A DGA-run program that recruits and trains young people to enter the ranks of production.

Digital (n): Referring to a digital video recording medium as opposed to film. *Quentin Tarantino still prefers to shoot his movies on film rather than digital.*

Digital content (n): Generally, a lower budget production only intended to be presented within the context of an existing website. Digital content can be shorter in length (sometimes only a few minutes long) than a traditional show. Although digital content may be funded by large corporations, it can often pay far lower wages than a traditional show. Projects produced by and for YouTube are considered digital content.

Director jail (n): An informal term that describes a low period in a director's career when he or she has committed some sort of transgression and cannot get work. A TV director might go to director jail by directing a feature film that bombs, or performing poorly on an important episode. Directors will never be told that they are in director jail. It can last anywhere from a few months to a few years. *I finally got hired to do an episode. I think I'm out of director jail now.*

Director's cut (n): In television, a show is generally obligated to give the director the opportunity to deliver an edit of the episode that corresponds to their vision. This is called the director's cut. After the director's cut has been delivered, the showrunner can choose to use some, all or none of what the director has done. It is not uncommon for the director's cut to simply be considered a courtesy to the director, and often times the showrunner will then start from scratch with the editor.

Distribute (v): The act of releasing a film. Generally, a film will need to be picked up by a **distribution** company in order to be distributed. However, some micro-budget filmmakers may attempt to distribute their movies independently.

Distribution (n): The collection of acts that is undertaken to **distribute** a film. They can include marketing, booking a film in theaters, selling it to foreign markets, selling it to a domestic streaming service, etc.

Distributor (n): The company that has agreed to **distribute** a film.

Diversity hire (n): A term used to describe the hiring of a director with the intention of diversifying a show's roster to include more women and people of color.

Diversity program (n): A network-run program intended to diversify the ranks of television directors by bringing more women and people of color into the industry. Every diversity program is different in how it is set up. But generally they all attempt to recruit and/or accept applicants who have a wide range of backgrounds and experience but who have not yet been able to secure a significant directing break. For instance, participants may have experience directing independent features or as executive producers of reality TV. Diversity programs facilitate opportunities for participants to shadow on existing shows, and to meet face to face with showrunners and executives. Once a person is accepted into a diversity program, it can still take a number of years for that opportunity to become an actual job directing an episode of television.

Doc (n): An informal shortening of "documentary."

DP (n): Director of photography.

Drama (n): In television, the term "drama" traditionally refers to a series of one-hour dramatic episodes. In network television, a "one-hour" drama will generally run about 42 minutes because of commercials.

Dramedy (n): A drama that has a lot of comedy elements and straddles the line between a drama and a comedy.

Drive-on (n): The permission given to a guest to temporarily enter, i.e., to drive onto, a studio lot. A drive-on will be given out by a production office or an executive's office for the purpose of a meeting on a studio lot. *I was late for my meeting because they forgot to get me a drive-on. So the guard would not let me into the studio.*

Edit bay (n): The room where the editor works.

Electric/Electrician (n): A rank and file member of the electric department, also known by their IATSE union number, Local 728. An electrician generally operates any item of film equipment that creates illumination, i.e., lights. Never confuse an electrician with a grip! *You better not touch that light or Local 728 will get upset, and you don't want to piss off the electrics.*

Episodic (n): A shortening of "episodic television series." This catch-all phrase refers to any form of scripted television that runs in multiple episodes over multiple seasons. Most TV shows are episodics as opposed to a mini-series or a made-for-TV movie.

Establishing shot (n): Traditionally a wide shot that establishes where the scene is taking place. *The editor was angry because the director didn't shoot any establishing shots and it's hard to tell where things are happening.*

Exec (n): Short for **executive**.

Executive (n): A high-ranking employee of a studio or network, responsible for some degree of management over a TV series or movie. A production will often have multiple executives responsible for such oversight. Depending on the personal dynamics at play, this may create a tense relationship for the showrunner or producers. There are also plenty of examples where the show's producers have wonderful relationships with the executives. *I just got notes from the network executive about the script.*

Executive Producer (n): The highest-level producer on a series or film. Most modern productions seem to credit a lot of executive producers. This does not always mean that they were involved in actually making the show; however, they likely have some claim of ownership, financial and/or creative.

Extra (n): An outdated term for **background**. (See also: **background**)

Feature (n): A shortening of the term "feature film." A feature is a stand-alone movie, long enough to be considered feature-length.

Fight the light (v): Fighting the light happens around sunset when a crew must rush to finish the daylight work before the sun goes down. You can also fight the light on the other end if you are shooting a night scene and the sun begins to come up.

First team (n): A term that refers to all the actors in a given scene. *Once the lighting is ready, the first AD will call for first team to come to set.* (See also: **second team**)

Frame (v): The act of composing a shot. *I love how this director frames things. She is so visually astute.*

Frame (n): The composition of a shot. One of the first things the camera operator does is to work with the director and DP to compose the frame so that the entire crew is aware of exactly what is in the shot. It is then the responsibility of the camera operator to be vigilant that the frame stays clear of any lighting or grip equipment that may make its way into the scene. *The camera operator got angry at the grip department because they left a ladder in his frame.*

Fun-run (n): A term used on a comedy film or TV show that utilizes **improv** to describe a take where the director tells the actors to feel free to go off-script and just have fun with their own improv version of the scene. The fun-run is often employed once the director feels comfortable that he or she has already successfully shot the scene with the scripted dialogue, and now just wants to let the actors do a take in any way they want. A lot of good stuff can come out of a fun-run because the pressure is off at that point.

Gaffer (n): The head of the electric department that oversees lighting. On some productions, the gaffer is called the chief lighting technician.

Gate keeper(s) (n): A colloquial term for the people who can say yes or no to giving a director an episode. The term refers generally to showrunners, executive producers and studio and network executives.

General (n): Short for "general meeting." A general is a meeting that is just intended for the participants to get to know one another. It is not a job interview, and there may not be any particular project discussed. *The director had to take about 20 generals before he got his first episode.*

Good in a room (adj): A broad term used to indicate that a director performs well in important meetings, such as job interviews and **pitches**. Being good in a room implies that a person is skilled at presenting themselves in an appealing way to any decision-makers present. *That director is not very proficient, but she keeps getting hired because she is really good in a room.*

Grace (n): A short period of time that a first AD can delay breaking a crew for lunch in order to finish a shot. When a first AD calls grace, there will still normally be a **meal penalty** incurred. *The AD called grace so that we could finish the scene and be able to move on after lunch.*

Green light (v): The act of giving official approval to moving forward with a production. *After ten years in development, the studio is finally going to green light her movie.*

Green light (n): The badge of official approval to move forward with a production. *I can't hire a cinematographer until we get the green light on the movie.*

Grip (n): A rank and file crew member of the grip department, also known by their IATSE union number, Local 80. The grip department is probably responsible for the widest range of duties on a film set. Grips are responsible for any piece of film equipment that shapes the light, such as flags, silks and nets. The grip department is responsible for most of the equipment that moves the camera, such as dollies, cranes and jib arms. It is also is responsible for most forms of rigging that involves other departments, such as camera, lighting, stunts, transportation and special effects. Also, the grip department is tasked with oversight of safety on the set, such as harnessing a crew member into a construction crane.

Guest director (n): In television, most directors are guest directors. A guest director is not a full-time employee of the show, and is hired one episode at a time. He or she may come in for just one episode in a season.

Half-hour (n): A term that generally refers to a half-hour comedy.

Hip-pocketing (v): An informal practice of television agents where they will associate themselves with a potential client, such as a director or actor, but not formally sign them. The agent will not usually do any work to find jobs for a hip-pocketed director, but if the director gets a job offer on their own, the agent will help negotiate the deal. If the director shows the potential to land more consistent work, the agent may formally sign them as a client.

Honey wagon (n): The trailer on **location** that has the bathrooms. *I really gotta go! Have you seen the honey wagon?*

House director (n): A trusted director who is booked to do a large number of episodes of a show. The house director may or may not do the majority of episodes in a season, but will generally do more than any other director.

IATSE (n): The International Alliance of Theatrical Stage Employees, Moving Picture Technicians, Artists, and Allied Crafts of the United States. An umbrella union for all below-the-line film and television crew members. IATSE is divided into numbered locals, with each local representing one or more departments and crew positions. *IATSE Local 600 represents the camera department and also film and TV publicists.*

IMDb (n): The Internet Movie Database. For nearly every person working in the film and TV industry, there will be an IMDb page that lists their credits. A person's IMDb page will often be checked to get a sense of the sorts of projects that person has worked on. The listed credits on a person's IMDb page are often incomplete and should never be used in place of an actual résumé.

Improv (v): Short for improvise. The acting technique of spontaneously creating dialogue during a scene. Improv is mostly used in comedy. *On some comedies, they will shoot the script and then do a take where the actors are allowed to improv.*

Industry (n): Short for "the film and TV industry."

Invite back (v): To ask a director to return for another episode. *That director insulted the lead, so she was not invited back.*

Lead (n): The main actor in a TV show or movie. Also known as "number one on the call sheet." *Steve Carrell was the lead in* The Office.

Line (n): Multiple meanings

    1. A piece of dialogue in a script. An actor will often say, "Line" when he/she forgets what to say. In that situation, it is the script supervisor's job to call out the actor's line.

    2. The imaginary line that runs through a scene and dictates where the camera should be placed for each shot so as not to confuse the audience about screen direction. Also known as the **180-degree line**.

Line producer (n): The high-ranking member of the production team who deals largely with budgeting and money. The word "line" in the title refers to the line items in a budget. Generally, a line producer is not tasked with creative decisions.

Location (n): Any place a production films that is not on a studio sound stage. A location can be anything from a street corner, to the Pyramids at Giza, to the bottom of the ocean.

Look book (n): A book or presentation that gives visual examples and written descriptions of the stylistic intentions of a director or crew member, such as a production designer, art director, wardrobe person, makeup person or director of photography. A look book can be a stylistic reference that a director creates to give the production designer in order to convey a sense of what the director wants. A look book can also be something that a production designer creates in order to pitch ideas to the director. *The DP made a look book with lots of Renaissance paintings in order to pitch lighting concepts to the director.*

Looping (n): The process whereby an actor's previously recorded dialogue is replaced with new dialogue that fits perfectly into the mouth movements on screen. Looping can be done for an entire scene, or just one word within a scene. In television, looping is often done if a piece of dialogue was ruined by the sound of a passing car on location or a crew member dropping a tool on a sound stage.

Lot (n): Short for studio lot. This is the entire property taken up by a film or television studio. It will often include sound **stages**, a **back lot**, offices, equipment storage facilities, parking, a commissary, power plants, security and maybe even a gym. *I am shooting on the lot today.*

Making your day (v): To finish your shooting day schedule and avoid overtime. "Making your day" is a big deal for a director because it shows that he or she can shoot quickly and not cost the production more money. *That director was not asked back because she could never make her days, and the overtime was enormous.*

Manager (n): A person who gives general career guidance to their clients in exchange for a percentage of the clients' earnings. A manager is also expected to use their industry connections to set up meetings and find work opportunities on behalf of their clients. There is definitely overlap between the activities of **agents** and managers. One key difference is that a manager is not authorized to negotiate contracts, whereas an agent is. (See also: **agent**)

Mark (v): *Multiple meanings:*

    1. The act of placing a piece of tape or line of chalk on the floor to signify where an actor

or camera must start and stop for the shot. Marking is the duty of the second AC. Marks are an extremely important part of the technical process of filmmaking. Once the director has blocked the scene with the actors, the second AC will put down a **mark** at every spot where the actors stopped. The second AC will also put down marks for where the camera starts and stops. Marks are vital for helping an actor remember **blocking** and also for making sure that everything is in focus. *Make sure to mark the actors after the rehearsal or they will forget the blocking.*

2. Part of **slating**, marking is the act of clapping the slate before or after every take in order to create a sound for the editor to sync to. The second AC is responsible for slating and marking. Once the sound and camera have announced **speeding**, the second AC will often call out, "Mark," and then clap the slate.

Mark (n): The spot(s) where an actor and/or camera will start and stop during the shot. If actors miss their mark, they may not be in focus or may even inadvertently leave the shot. *We have to do another take because the actor missed his mark.*

Marking rehearsal (n): The final rehearsal, conducted after the director and actors have worked out all the scene's creative elements. The purpose of the marking rehearsal is simply to lay down the marks for the actors and cameras. Once the director feels confident that he has thoroughly rehearsed the scene, he will ask the first AD to call for a marking rehearsal. The first AD will then announce, "Marking!"

Martini (n): As announced by the first AD, the very last shot of a day of shooting. The first AD will announce the martini shot to the crew so that everyone knows to be ready to start **wrapping** for the day. *The AD just called the martini. We better start putting the extra equipment back in the truck.*

Meal penalty (n): A union-mandated compensation that the production must pay to crew members if/when the lunch break time is exceeded. On a union show or movie, the lunch break must happen no later than six hours after crew **call.** If this norm is violated, the production must pay every crew member a previously negotiated amount depending on how long the meal penalty lasts. *We kept shooting one hour past lunch and I got a huge meal penalty.*

Meeting, General meeting, Series of meetings (n): Meetings are the lifeblood of a director. Sometimes a director will have a general meeting with the studio just to get his or her face out there. When a director has a lot of general meetings in a relatively short amount of time, this may be referred to as a series of meetings. In some cases, an aspiring director may take dozens of meeting before ever being offered an episode. Meetings are also an important part of a director's **prep** on an episode. In fact, the prep period is largely a process where the director goes from one meeting to the next.

Mentor (n): A person who takes an aspiring director under his or her wing to provide vital information, advice and guidance. A mentor may also take on an advocate role and guide an aspiring director towards work opportunities.

Minis, Mini monitors (n): One or more small video monitors mounted on a single stand. Because the full **video village** tends to take up a lot of space, it is common for it to be located away from the set where space is limited. Some directors prefer to be closer to the actors and will ask for minis to be placed as close to camera as possible.

Multi-cam (n): Short for multiple cameras. The term generally refers to a traditional situation comedy that uses four cameras shooting simultaneously, often in front of a live audience. A multi-cam is distinguished from a **single-cam** show. (See also: **sitcom** and **single-cam**)

Narrative (n): A term that refers to fictional story-based content as opposed to commercials, music videos, reality shows, or documentaries. Basically, referring to a TV show or movie with a scripted story vs. everything else.

Network (n): One of the four traditional corporate television entities: ABC, CBS, NBC and FOX. Cable entities such as HBO, TBS and AMC are not referred to as network. Streaming entities such as Netflix, Amazon and Hulu are also not considered network.

NewFronts (n): The digital streaming world's response to the UpFronts. A multi-day entertainment industry gathering taking place in spring in New York during which content producers present their new offerings to potential advertisers and distributors. Just as with the longer-running UpFronts, the NewFronts are where digital content providers will often premiere new shows and pilots to see what generates excitement and, more importantly, advertising commitments. (See also: **UpFronts**)

Notes (n): A catch-all term that refers to any creative notes given during the production of a TV series or movie. Notes are given by different individuals at different stages of every production. The studio executive will give script notes to the showrunner and scriptwriters. The writer(s) will give acting notes to the director on a TV show to deliver to the actors on set. The showrunner will give edit notes to the editor about different cuts of an episode. Notes are a vital part of the process of creating any collaborative effort.

On the bubble (adj): A term that means a show is at risk of being cancelled and/or not picked up for another season. *After we wrapped season two, everyone knew that our show was on the bubble. Fortunately, the network gave us another season.*

One-er (n): A single shot that is intended to cover a large part, or even all, of a scene without any cuts. Many television directors will shy away from relying on one-ers because if there is a problem with the shot, the lack of **coverage** does not allow for any editing of the scene.

OT (n): Overtime. Time is money. When a crew goes into overtime, it can cost the production thousands of dollars in additional wages. In television, directors and first ADs always try to avoid going over schedule in order to avoid overtime.

Overheads (n): Plans that show the dimensions of a set as well the placement of set pieces, such as tables, chairs, kitchen islands, etc. Many directors will request overheads of the sets from the art department in order to create camera plots that show the intended placement of the camera for each shot.

PA (n): Production Assistant.

Page (n): A traditional entry-level network job. Pages will do a variety of tasks, such as giving tours to the public and helping to seat the audience for a live taping of a sitcom.

Pass (v): The act of turning down a show **pitch** or script. *Five executives passed on my script before I finally sold it.*

PGA (n): The Producers Guild of America is a trade association representing television **producers**, film **producers** and New Media **producers** .

Pick-up (n): A partial take of a shot that is done just to get a portion of the shot. For instance, if an actor says five lines during a shot but the director only wants an additional take of the last line, he will do a pick-up of that line. *Does the director need another full take, or is this just a pick-up?*

Pick up (v): The act of approving a pilot to go into full production. Also, the act of approving an existing series to go into production for another season. *My friend's pilot was picked up and will start shooting season one in a few months.*

Pigeonhole (v): The act of putting people into rigid categories and believing that they are not capable of doing jobs outside of their current occupation. In television, pigeonholing means that a comedy director will not be considered for a drama, and a commercial director will not be considered for a scripted series.

Pilot (n): A trial episode of a show. Traditionally, a network will produce a pilot and present it to advertisers at the **UpFronts**. If the pilot is well-received, then the network will **pick up** the pilot for production.

Pitch deck (n): See: **deck**.

Pitch (v): The process of presenting a creative project or even just an idea. You can pitch a show idea to a network and you can also pitch a single joke to a writer. You can even pitch a shot idea to a director. *The actors didn't think the scene was funny so they started pitching jokes to the showrunner.*

Post (n): Short for post-production.

Post-production (n): The process that a show or movie goes through after **production** has wrapped. This includes editing, sound design, composing, special effects, color correction and sound mix.

Post-production supervisor (n): The person in charge of overseeing the often complex process of post-production. One of the complexities of post is that many different companies will often work on the same show or movie at the same time and on a limited time frame. The post-production supervisor will ensure that all parties are communicating and have the elements they need to do their jobs in a timely manner.

Preditor (n): A relatively modern appellation that signifies producer-directors who also edit their own material. A preditor is an unofficial, non-union position that will almost always work on low-budget, non-scripted material.

Prelim (n): Short for "preliminary call sheet." The prelim is a work-in-progress call sheet. Its purpose is to give the first AD and department heads an opportunity to raise any red flags about the next day's work.

Prep (v): Short for "prepare." Prepping is the director's extensive work of preparing to direct an episode or movie. Normally on a single-camera comedy, the director will prep for five days. *The director is busy this week prepping her next episode.*

Prep (n): The period and process of prepping. A prep will include a concept meeting, a tone meeting, department head meetings, location scouts, show-and-tells, script meetings and shot-listing. When a director is booked to direct an episode of a series, he or she will also be booked for a paid prep period. *Sometimes the episode is so big that the director needs a longer prep.*

Private rehearsal (n): A rehearsal for which the director asks the first AD to clear most or all of the crew off the set in order to give the actors some privacy. A director will often ask for a private rehearsal if the scene is intimate, involves nudity, is emotionally intense, or simply if the presence of the crew is a distraction to the rehearsal process.

Proscenium (n): A theatrical term. Short for proscenium arch. In television, proscenium generally refers to the kind of staging that is reminiscent of how an audience views a theatrical production.

Producer (n): A general term for a relatively high-level member of the production staff. A modern show or movie tends to have a lot of credited producers who may have been involved during different parts of the pre-production, production and/or post-production process.

Production (n): *Multiple meanings*
    1. As differentiated from pre-production and post-production, production is the time period during which a show or movie is actually filming. *That movie was only in production for three weeks, but they spent eight months in post-production.*
    2. A general term for the entire organization that comprises the endeavor to create a TV show or movie. *The new* Star Wars *was a gigantic production.*
    3. The department of a film or TV show in charge of producing and running things. *If you don't know what your call time is, you better ask someone from production.*

Prop (n): Any item that the actor interacts with in a scene. Other than an actor, only a prop master should ever handle a prop. Any items that are on the set that the actor does not directly interact with are considered set dressing, not props.

Pull up (v): An editing term that means to edit a scene or shot in order to make it occur faster on screen. Sometimes the editor will need to pull something up by just a few **frames**. A TV director will almost always shoot **coverage** of a scene in order to give the editor the option to pull something up. *In comedy, the editor often goes by the old adage that faster is funnier, so it is common for them to want to pull things up in order to get to the joke quicker.*

Put it on its feet (v): After a **read-through** rehearsal, during which the actors are often just sitting down reading from the script, the director will usually want to have the actors literally walk through the scene in order to begin to figure out the **blocking**. This is called "putting it on its feet." *The director was confident that the actors understood the scene, but she didn't know the blocking yet, so she announced, "Let's put this scene on its feet and see where it goes."*

Read through (n): A rehearsal in which the actors read directly from the script and do not move or do any of the **blocking**. *At the beginning of the day, the director likes to do a quick read through of the first scene before working on blocking.*

Reality show (n): Generally, any show other than a game show, awards show or news program that has a cast composed of non-actors. Also widely referred to as **unscripted**.

Reel (n): A conglomerate presentation of a person's work in the field of film and TV. Reels are used by many different members of the entertainment industry, including directors, actors, DPs, editors, production designers and composers. They are an important part of how a creative person presents their experience in order to get more work. These days, most reels are incorporated into a personal or **agency** website.

Regular (n): Short for "series regular." An actor who has a recurring role in a series over many episodes.

Rehearse (v): The act of practicing a scene with the actors.

Rehearsal (n): The process of practicing a scene with the actors.

Roll (v): The act of recording sound and/or camera. As part of the procedure for initiating every shot, the first AD will instruct the sound and then camera department to roll. Once the sound and camera are rolling, the appropriate crew members will announce that they are **speeding**. *The first AD will almost always tell sound to roll before camera.*

Roll (n): Traditionally, a roll referred to a physical roll of audio tape or film. Each roll on a movie or show received a number starting with one. On a digital production, a roll refers to a memory card that is recorded on, transferred to a separate hard drive, and then recorded on again. As in the old days, every roll still receives a number. *Can you tell me what camera and sound roll we are on?*

SAG (n): The Screen Actors Guild. An entertainment trade guild that represents the interests of film and television actors.

Scout (v): The activity during a director's **prep** of visiting and analyzing the locations being considered for filming. A scout will usually take place with as many **department heads** as possible so that all the departments have the chance to voice concerns. *The director loved the park location when they scouted it, but the sound mixer said it was too close to the airport and that they would have to stop shooting every five minutes due to the planes flying overhead.*

Screen direction (n): Referring to the left or right of the **frame**, screen direction is whatever direction an object or actor's look is meant to go. For instance, if a car starts on the left of frame and travels to the right of frame, the screen direction is said to be going from left to right. Screen direction is important to understand when shooting because a sequence can become confusing for the audience if it suddenly changes without reason. For instance, if you are filming a scene in which a dog chases a cat and the cat runs away with a screen direction of left to right, then the dog also needs to chase the cat with the same screen direction.

Script supervisor (n): The crew member in charge of keeping track of and advising the director on a significant number of script- and editing-related details. As the name implies, the script supervisor is responsible for making sure that the entire script is actually filmed by the director. The script supervisor is also responsible for making sure that actors say all the lines as written. Of equal importance, the script supervisor is the chief guardian of **continuity** on set, including issues of screen direction. Along with the first AD and DP, the script supervisor is one of the most important allies that a director has on any set. In fact, very often a script supervisor can prevent a distracted director from making an unintentional but devastating mistake. Directors are well advised to maintain good working relationships with script supervisors.

Scripted: Any fictional television or **digital** program that employs a script.

Scripty (n): Short for **script supervisor**.

Second team (n): A commonly used alternative term for **stand-ins**. Second team is used to differentiate the stand-ins from **first team**. (See also: **stand-in** and **first team**)

Set up (v): While shooting, the act of getting all the elements in order to execute a shot. *The director needs two hours to set up the shot of the stunt person jumping out of the window.*

Set-up (n): A broadly descriptive term that refers to each camera position employed to **cover** a scene. In other words, every camera position is a new set-up. Because of time constraints in television, a director will often try to use as few set-ups as possible to cover a scene. *How many set-ups will the director need to finish this scene?*

Set (v): To place a scene in a particular location. *The murder scene was set in the hall.*

Set (n): The physical space, either indoors or outdoors, where filming is currently taking place. The set could be a giant convention hall, or it could be a closet. It could a football field or on a raft in the ocean. The set is simply where the crew is currently working on a scene. *The location for the show is a giant abandoned factory, but the set today is a tiny room in the basement.*

Shadow (v): The act of following an established TV director while he or she preps, shoots and edits an episode. The purpose of shadowing is for an aspiring director to learn the specific processes and techniques required of a modern TV director. Shadowing is a privilege because it puts the aspiring director in a mentor-mentee relationship with the established director. In addition, a full shadowing assignment is unpaid and can last over three weeks on a one-hour drama. Despite how difficult it can be to get a shadowing assignment, many aspiring directors have had to shadow ten or more different directors over a period of years before they could hope to get an actual directing offer. *I have been trying to get an opportunity to shadow for years, and it looks like I will finally get the chance next month.*

Shadow (n): The person who is given the opportunity to follow an established director is referred to as the director's shadow. A director may have more than one shadow at a time, and each shadow must do their best to dance the line between staying close in order to absorb as much as possible while also knowing when to keep a respectful distance. Being a good shadow is its own skill. *Sometimes a shadow asks a question at the wrong time.*

Shoot (someone) out (v): To finish all the scenes that an actor has schedule for the day. *I scheduled all of the actor's scenes in the morning so that we could shoot him out before lunch.*

Shot-list (v): The act of figuring out and listing all the shots a director intends to get to cover a given scene. Shot-listing is an important part of a director's prep. When possible, the director will consult with the DP while shot-listing.

Shot list (n): The list of shots that the director created during prep. The director will usually share the shot list with the DP and other crew members so that they will be able to order any special equipment needed beforehand.

Showrunner (n): The primary executive producer in charge of all creative aspects of a show. In television, the showrunner often serves as the head writer and is in charge of the **writing room**.

Sides (n): Script pages distributed by production that are just for the scenes scheduled to be shot that day. Sides are usually printed smaller than a normal script—about half size. Sides are a convenient way for the cast and crew to focus just on the scenes at hand.

Single-cam (n): Traditionally, a show that is shot one angle at a time with just one camera. In truth, however, many so-called single-camera shows are actually shot with two or more cameras. For instance, the HBO series *Veep* was considered a single-camera show even though the production routinely used up to four cameras at a time. So the term "single-camera" is really a reference more to the style of a show than to how many cameras are being used. The style of a single-cam show is basically like a traditional movie rather than a multi-cam, audience-based sitcom such as *Friends*. Pretty much any scripted show that is not a traditional sitcom will be considered single-cam.

Sitcom (n): Short for **situation comedy**.

Situation comedy (n): A long-standing half-hour television comedy format that was originally filmed in front a live audience. Situation comedies treat the performance like a live show and use multiple cameras to capture all the angles in a scene simultaneously. Many situation comedies still film in front of a live audience and will include the sound of the audience's laughter in the soundtrack. Classic situation comedies are shows like *I Love Lucy* and *Cheers*. A modern situation comedy is *The Big Bang Theory*.

Sketch (n): Short for "**sketch comedy**."

Sketch comedy (n): A kind of comedy comprised of short stand-alone scenes. Sketch comedy is often created and performed by a team of comedians that develops the sketches over time. It can be performed as part of a live show or as short video pieces.

Slate (v): The act of shooting a marker board listing vital information about a given shot. The slate will typically list the following information: name of the show or movie, the director, the DP, the date, scene ID, shot ID, take number, if the shot is a different frame rate, if the shot is a **pick-up**, if the shot incorporates visual effects, if the shot is a plate, if the shot is MOS, etc. It is the responsibility of the second AC to slate. It is the responsibility of the **script supervisor** to make sure the second AC has the correct shot information to put on the slate.

Slate (n): The physical marker board that is used to slate. It will typically have a clapper that the second AC hits in order to give the editor a sound to sync to. (See also: **marker**)

Sound mix (n): A post-production process in which all the audio in a show or movie is balanced and smoothed out to make it ready for presentation.

Sound stage (n): A large warehouse-like structure designed to accommodate film and TV production.

Speed (v): The act of rolling the sound recorder and/or camera after the first AD has instructed the crew to **roll**. Once the sound recorder is rolling, the sound mixer will announce, "Sound has speed." Similarly, once the camera is rolling, the camera operator will announce, "Camera speed."

Spotting session (n): Phase of production when a director and composer or music editor view the film together to map out the score, determining where and what the music should be.

Stage (v): The act of working through how and where various aspects of a scene will be executed. Staging involves all physical aspects of the scene—**blocking**, stunts, **business**, camera positions, entrances, exits, and how the set will be utilized as part of the action. *The director staged the big fight scene in the middle of a cornfield.*

Stage (n): Short for **sound stage**. *Do you know if we are on stage tomorrow or on location?*

Staging (n): A description of how a scene has been staged by the director. *This director's staging is really interesting because it incorporates the set in a creative way.*

Stand in (v): The act of repeating an actor's movements and positions in a scene so that the actor can be away from set while the crew sets up a shot. Standing in properly is a vital and vastly under-appreciated job. It is important because it provides the crew with a dedicated person to utilize as an aid in lighting, focusing and overall shot creation while the actor is away from set. *It is important for the person who is standing in to look like the actor and also wear similar wardrobe.*

Stand-in (n): The person who **stands in** for an actor. Good stand-ins are vital to the efficient running of a production. Experienced stand-ins will closely watch actors during rehearsal so that they can repeat the blocking exactly for the crew during shot set-up. Ideally, a stand-in should be the same height, hair color, skin color, gender and even approximate age as the actor. In addition, a stand-in should have a similar hairstyle and wear similar wardrobe as the actor in the scene. *If the scene has five actors, then we will need five stand-ins to set up the shot.* (See also: **second team**)

Streaming (adj): Refers to any series or movie that is produced by a streaming service. This is in contrast to content produced by a network or cable service that is intended to air on television in a traditional manner. *A director with a lot of experience in the network space may have a difficult time getting an episode of a Netflix streaming series.*

Studio (n): *Multiple meanings*

1. A typically large facility that provides production services to multiple shows and movies at the same time. Studios will often have the capacity to provide sound stages, equipment rentals, office space, editing rooms, trucks and electrical power. Some large studios in Los Angeles are Warner Brothers, Universal, Disney and Fox.

2. A term broadly referring to the corporate structure behind the financing, producing and/or distribution of a show or movie. The studio will generally maintain a strong influence over a show or movie through the executive(s) it assigns to oversee the production. The executive producer and/or the showrunner on a series or movie is the main point of contact between the studio and a production. The studio will often be involved at all stages of the development, production and distribution of a series or movie. For instance, on a series, the studio will see drafts of the scripts, give input on casting, approve the hiring of directors and give notes on cuts of the episodes. *The editor will work late tonight because the showrunner just got the studio's notes on the latest cut.*

Table read (n): A meeting that includes the director, the showrunner, the episode script writer, key crew members and all of the main actors in an episode in which the cast reads through the script for the next episode. The table read is often conducted in a conference room as an informal lunchtime meeting during the week before the episode is to be shot. Typically, the cast will sit side by side at a long table that faces the people in attendance that comprise the audience. The table read may also be attended by network and studio executives.

Tail slate (n): A slate that is done at the end, or tail, of a shot rather than at the beginning, or head, of a shot. (See also: **slate** and **mark**)

Take (n): When the director sets up a shot, he will usually film it more than one time. Each instance that the camera rolls and then cuts on a shot is called a "take." *Stanley Kubrick was famous for doing a lot of takes.*

Talent (n): A term that refers to the actors on a set. *We started shooting late because the talent was still in the makeup trailer.*

Teamster (n): A member of the transportation department on a film or TV set. Teamsters have long held the reputation for having the most powerful below-the-line union in the entertainment industry.

Ten-one: Walkie-talkie code for going to the rest room. A film set is a high-pressure environment where breaks are limited and infrequent. When a crew member needs to use the rest room, it is customary to announce the fact to her/his co-workers. There are different set etiquette practices that dictate certain communications. When a crew member goes to the rest room, he will announce over the walkie-talkie that he is ten-one. *I can't find Bob. Is he ten-one?*

Tone meeting (n): Usually, the last important meeting that a TV director will have with the show-runner during her prep on an episode. The tone meeting is where the director and showrunner can talk about the most important story elements in a script. Depending on the show, other people may also be present, such as the producer, editor and first AD. A director may ask about any creative choices that are not clear, such as the intent of a joke, or the specific way the show-runner wants an actor to read a line. The tone meeting is also where a showrunner may convey to the director any specific requests he/she may have about coverage and blocking expectations. Tone meetings generally last from one to three hours, although there is an anecdote of an extreme example where the meeting lasted for eight hours. Yes, it happens.

Trailer (n): A motor home–type vehicle that houses different aspects of a production. There will typically be a trailer for each of the following purposes: hair and makeup, production office, wardrobe, actors' private space, directors' private space. Trailers are almost always utilized on **location** and also on many studio **lots**.

Turn around (v): When shooting a single-cam show, it will often be necessary to shoot one direction at a time. When a director is satisfied that she has finished shooting all the shots in one direction, she will then have the crew **set up** to shoot in the opposite direction. This is called turning around. *The director wants to do one more closeup in this direction, and then we can turn around.*

Unscripted (n): Any television show that does not use a script. Usually, this is a reference to reality shows. The vast majority of reality shows are non-union, which means that per WGA rules the show cannot list a writer in the credits. The strange reality is that many reality shows do in fact have a version of a script, called a **"beat sheet,"** that outlines the story points the show's cast is required to hit upon during the scene. Frequently, the "writers" on an "unscripted" reality show will simply be given a producer credit in order to avoid any legal conflicts with the WGA.

Unscripted (adj): Anything that an actor or director adds to a scene that was not originally in the script. Improvised dialogue is unscripted as is any added action. *The actor wanted to add an unscripted line about his past to justify what he was doing.*

UpFronts (n): A multi-day gathering in New York City where the traditional networks and cable companies present their new offerings to potential corporate sponsors in order to secure commitments from advertisers for the coming season. The UpFronts are where both pilots and existing series will be presented. Oftentimes, based on the response to those presentations, a show will be **picked up** or **cancelled**.

UPM (n): unit production manager

Video village (n): The collection of video monitors and chairs where the director, script supervisor and writer(s) will sit to watch what is being filmed. Depending on the logistics of the location, the video village will often be positioned away from set. Because of this distance, some directors prefer not to be at video village. Rather, they will ask for a pair of **mini monitors** to be set up closer to camera so that they can speak more directly with the actors. When directors do this, they will then have to run back and forth between set and video village in order to get notes from the writer(s). (See also **village**.)

Village (n): A shortening of **"video village."**

WGA (n): The Writers Guild of America. An entertainment trade guild that represents the interests of film and television writers.

Wrap (v): *Multiple meanings*

1. To finish shooting. You can wrap shooting for the day, for the episode, for the season and for the series. You can also wrap an actor, which means that all of their scenes have been **shot out**.

2. At the end of a day's shooting, the act of disassembling the equipment and supplies and storing them away, or, when on location, packing them into the trucks for transport. *After we finished shooting, it took two hours for the crew to wrap all the gear.*

Wrap (n): The completion of shooting. At the end of the day, the first AD will call out, "That's a wrap!"

Writers' room (n): Literally and figuratively, the room where the showrunner and the writers gather to collectively work on the script for an episode of a TV series. The writers' room is a series' war room. It is where the showrunner will lay out the arc of a season and all the story points that the show needs to hit upon throughout the episodes. It is also where individual writers pitch ideas for storylines and jokes.

Index

Numbers in **bold italics** indicate pages with illustrations

production company 44, 59, 69, 80, 90, 150, 151–153
production meeting 17
production report 140
production supervisor 13, 15
Project Kashmir 104, 105
Propaganda Films 150
Pryor, Richard 67
Purple, Bill 88, 95, *157*

race 1, 10, 13, 18, 19, 22, 56, 75, 83, 100, 113, 116, 135, 138, 145, 150, 164, 166, 170
racism 9, 10, 14, 18, 22, 29, 30, 54, 63, 99, 112, 113, 116, 126, 127, 144–147, 150, 151, 164, 169
Raiders of the Lost Ark 78, 86
The Real O'Neals 82
reality show 5, 92
reality TV 70, 78, 79, 80
Redbox 93
Reed, Sean, 97
reel 19, 60, 70, 152
religion 22, 32, 42, 54, 55, 65
Reverend Run 16
Reynolds, Gareth 48, 49
Rhimes, Shonda 30, 62, 160, 168
Richard Pryor Live on the Sunset Strip 67
Rimes, Sydnee, 142
Rita Bell's Prize Movie 11
Rollins, Henry 70
Rooney, Bethany *31*, 39
Rooney, Mickey 32
Rose, Lisa 165
Rosh Hashanah 66, 125
The Rosie O'Donnell Show 15
Roundhouse 15
Rubio, Nicole **165**
Rudd, Paul 70
run-through 17, 119
Russ and Daughters 125
Russo brothers 154, 155
Rutgers University 123, 133

St. Elsewhere 36, 37, 160
Salem, Kario 102
San Francisco, California 75, 77
San Jose State University 44
Sandler, Adam 43, 45, 46
The Sarah Silverman Program 153, 154
Saturday Night Live 13, 18, 42, 43, 46, 70, 111
Save the Last Dance 168
Schmoozing 82
Schumer, Amy 156
Schur, Michael 3, 71
Schutte, Samba 1, *3*
Schwenk, Gregg 45
scout *see* location scout
script 5, 15, 17, 19, 24, 27, 28, 34–36, 46, 47, 48, 58, 59, 62, 63, 72, 73, 81, 88, 90, 91, 93, 94, 100–102, 105, 113, 117, 123, 128–130, 132, 135, 140, 144, 161
script supervisor 51, 63, 142, 143, 165, 167–169

scripted 2, 15, 50, 70, 78–80, 107, 111
Scrubs 115
Searchlight 107; *see also* Fox Searchlight
Seaton, Eric Dean *21*
second AD 24, 140, 160; *see also* assistant director
second-second AD 140; *see also* assistant director
second unit 106, 107, 160
Segal, Peter 108
Seinfeld 41, 119
Sense8 106, 107
Sesame Street 42
sexism 33, 83, 144, 145, 164
Shades of Ray 129–132
shadowing 15, 27, 51, 61, 64, 79, 81, 88, 95, 108, 117, 131–134, 154, 155, 157, 161, 168
short film 5, 41, 45, 53, 58, 59, 70, 79, 88, 90, 91–93, 128, 130, 142, 153, 155, 160
shot-listing 51, 62, 82, 93, 106, 107, 119, 165
showrunner 2, 5, 49, 50, 61, 62, 70–74, 79–81, 84, 93, 100–102, 107, 119, 131, 134, 135, 141, 142, 145, 155, 164, 168
Showtime 15, 96
The Siege 160
Silverman, Sarah 153
A Simple Wish 160
Singer, Abby 34
single-camera 13, 14, 16, 17, 26, 28, 37, 48, 50, 70, 71, 113, 115, 117–119, 131, 134
A Single Rose 59
sitcom 1, 3, 15, 42, 43, 49, 65, 91, 113, 115, 123, 134
Six in the City 59
sketch 2, 13, 15, 27, 41, 45, 47–53, 70, 78, 119, 122, 123, 156; *see also* sketch comedy
sketch comedy 2, 78, 122, 156; *see also* sketch
The Slap Maxwell Story 37
Slayton, Bobby 14
Slumdog Millionaire 130
Smigel, Robert 46
SNL *see Saturday Night Live*
So Random 27
Solomon, John 50
Sonnenshine, Rebecca 59
Sony 46, 47, 95, 160
Sony C-Spot 47
Sony Pictures Classics 160
The Sopranos 126
Sorkin, Aaron 100, 101
South Asian 104, 130
South by Southwest 105, 122
South Carolina 165
Speechless 143, 161
Spielberg, Steven 78, 91
stage manager 113–115, 117
stand-up 43, 44, 111
Star Wars 54
Starkie 129; *see also* Peter Stark Producing Program; University of Southern California

Starz 108
Stealth 160
Strauss-Schulson, Todd 48
studio 1, 12, 14, 17, 18, 39, 46, 47, 50, 51, 57, 61, 63, 70, 72, 80, 83, 84, 91, 94, 95, 102, 103, 110, 114, 115, 118, 119, 129, 131, 132, 135, 142, 150, 151, 162
studio executive 1, 84; *see also* executive
Suburgatory 19
Sullivan, Nicole 18
Sundance Film Festival 45, 57, 58, 104, 105, 123, 153
Sundance Institute 104
Sunny with a Chance 27
Sunnyside 1–3
Sunset Gower Studios 13
Superior Donuts 19
supervising producer 46; *see also* producer
Survivor 78
Survivor's Remorse 107
Swardson, Nick 44, 45
Syria 11

table read 17, 142
Taiwan 75, 76
Tarantino, Quentin 148, 154
Tarses, Jay 37
TBS 28, 70
Teachers 50, 51
Teen Titans 23
Teen Wolf 28
temp agency 105
temping 58, 78, 105
The Temple of I AM 11
Ten Years Younger 92
The Tenderloin 76
Tenth Planet Productions 69, 70
That's So Raven 23–26
The Thing 160
35mm 149
30 Rock 27
Thompson, Hunter S. 118
Thompson, Tessa 60
Tinker, Mark 34, 161
Tisch School of the Arts 122; *see also* NYU
tone meeting 17, 73, 117
The Tonight Show 110
Top Gun 88, 89
Toronto, Canada 105, 106, 132, 160
Training Day 168
Treatment 101
Tribeca Film Festival 104
Troy, Alabama 53
Tsuchida, Steven 146, *147*, 153
Tufts University 127
Turturro, John 44
TV jail 84; *see also* director jail
TV Land 50
20th Century 50
Twin Peaks 150, 151
two-shot 1, 118, 120

UCB (Upright Citizens Brigade) 48, 49
UCB Midnight Show 48, 49